THE RELIGIONS OF TIBET

Statue of the historic Buddha Shâkyamuni

HELMUT HOFFMANN

THE RELIGIONS OF TIBET

TRANSLATED BY EDWARD FITZGERALD

GREENWOOD PRESS, PUBLISHERS
WESTPORT, CONNECTICUT

Library of Congress Cataloging in Publication Data

Hoffmann, Helmut, 1912-
The religions of Tibet.

Translation of Die Religionen Tibets.
Reprint of the ed. published by Macmillan, New York.
Bibliography: p.
Includes index.
1. Lamaism--History. 2. Bon (Tibetan religion)--History. I. Title.
[BQ7576.H6313 1979] 294.3'0951'5 78-11420
ISBN 0-313-21120-5

Reprinted in 1979 by Greenwood Press, Inc.
51 Riverside Avenue, Westport, CT 06880

Printed in the United States of America

10 9 8 7 6 5 4 3 2 1

AUTHOR'S PREFACE

The history and civilization of the Asian peoples is finding growing interest in the eyes of the West, thanks in particular to the great changes which have taken place since the Second World War in the political and ideological situation. In the circumstances, therefore, a book which sets out to describe the religious development of a people which, up to only a few years ago, was cut off from all other peoples and continued to live in mediaeval conditions, hardly requires any further justification.

The general character of this book is historical. Whereas, for example, the well-known books of L. A. Waddell and R. Bleichsteiner seek to provide a more accumulative and encyclopaedic picture of Lamaism, I felt the need to trace the main developments of the historical religious development more graphically. This meant a careful choice amongst the tremendous amount of material available, and a choice restricted to the typical and the absolutely essential, as otherwise all understanding for the real relationships would be lost in a morass of previously unknown happenings and names. An Asian tour and a great variety of friendly contacts with the Lamaists of the Himalaya countries Sikkim and Nepal in 1954 did much to make my studies more fruitful.

My book is primarily intended for those interested in religious investigation, ethnologists, and the growing number of those who are taking a lively interest in the civilizations of the East. However, I also hope that it may prove useful for experts in Tibet too, because quite frequently I have been in a position to make use of previously unavailable sources.

H. HOFFMANN

Munich, April 1956

ADDITIONAL NOTE

Owing to lack of time I was not able to make use of any publication after 1956. This will be remedied in a later edition.

H. H.

CONTENTS

ILLUSTRATIONS

CHAPTER I

THE OLD BON RELIGION

There is hardly another country on earth which has aroused more passionate interest amongst those in the West who long for mysteries and wonders than Tibet, the 'Land of Snows' as its inhabitants call it. There, in the broad upland plateaux, hemmed in by the biggest mountains on earth, the Himalayas and Karakorum, fantastic adventures seem everyday affairs. There, in a veritable jungle of strange religious ideas and practices, even the most astonishing para-psychological phenomenon seems hardly out of the way. And then the hermetic isolation, favoured by such natural geographical conditions, which has been imposed on the country for the past hundred years by its rulers, has contributed its share to intensifying the veil of secrecy.

It is true that in the first half of the last century the courageous and gifted Hungarian investigator, Alexander Csoma de Körös, was able to provide a valuable introduction to the scholarly investigation of the Tibetan language and of Tibetan civilization, but the number of serious investigators who turned their attention to this subject—so difficult to approach in every way!—was not great, particularly as their efforts met with little interest and encouragement from the general public. The result was that a tremendously swollen romantic literature, much of it of very doubtful value, and including the curious dissertations of eccentric followers of mysticism and occultism, represented practically the only source available to the educated European anxious to know something about Tibet and its religion. The combination of these circumstances has made Tibet appear as though it had no real history, as though it had nothing to offer but strange and abstruse curiosities. Only slowly and comparatively recently has there been a gradual change, and the work of the few devoted Western scholars, encouraged by new discoveries, has obtained greater recognition from the general public. In consequence a truer picture of the country and its civilization has slowly emerged; and although many strange and astonishing phenomena have been met with, Tibet can no longer be regarded as without history. The veil of secrecy is gradually being raised, and we shall come to know more and more about this strange world from within, to understand it in accordance with its own laws of development, and be able to find its place in the total history of Asia Major, together with the newly-discovered civilizations along the edge of the Tarim Basin.

The cultural and religious face of Tibet today has been shaped by two main forces: the Indian missionary religion of Buddhism on the one hand, which has dominated the scene outwardly and determined the fate of the Land of Snows for over a thousand years, and the autochthonous Tibetan outlook and way of life, which, though outwardly defeated, has nevertheless filled all the spiritual and psychological channels of the country's national life. Thus the internal situation of Tibet may be said to turn on a polar reaction between a luminous, dynamic, fructifying and historical element on the one hand, and a sombre, static and fundamentally unhistorical element—the ancient Tibetan religion—on the other. The origin of the word 'Bon' to describe it is lost in the past, and it is not readily definable, but it in all probability once referred to the conjuring of the gods by magic formulas. As we shall see, it is not only numerous followers in the north and east of Tibet, who still nominally adhere to this religion, which has been greatly affected in the course of many hundreds of years by Buddhism, who partake in the old original religious force, but also and to no less a degree, its Buddhist opponents. The religious shape of Lamaism, so called on account of its chief upholders, the Lamas, or 'the superior ones', the higher monks, developed from the teachings of Buddha penetrating into the country from India and mixing with original Tibetan religious elements.

Until quite recently we knew very little indeed about this old Bon religion. Today we are in a position to say with some certainty[1] that the original Bon religion was the national Tibetan

[1] I have attempted to explain the phenomenon of this ancient Bon religion in a larger work, 'Quellen zur Geschichte der Tibetischen Bon-Religion', published in the *Proceedings of the Academy of Science and Literature*, Mainz 1950, based on more detailed sources, and in the present book I must confine myself to dealing with the main results of my investigations, and referring the reader to this larger work for more detailed proof.—THE AUTHOR

form of that old animist-shamanist religion which at one time was widespread not only in Siberia but throughout the whole of Inner Asia, East and West Turkestan, Mongolia, Manchuria, the Tibetan plateaux and even China. One profound scholar[1] has even included Iran, at least its eastern districts, and declared the pronouncements of the prophet Zarathustra to have been Shamanist inspired. However, this view has not been generally accepted. Nevertheless, comparative religious historical study of the present-day Shamanist tribes of Siberia, and of the old Turkish, Mongolian and Tungusan peoples of Inner Asia (before the later advent of missionary activities), and also of the Chinese before the general spread of the Confucian State religion, promises to afford us valuable assistance in our efforts to understand the autochthonous beliefs of Ancient Tibet.

Our first task is to try to discover what the original Bon religion was like before it came into contact with Buddhism, but this is made difficult by the great dearth of authentic documentary evidence. In fact, actual documents from those early days are unknown, and they can hardly have existed in any case, because it was not until the first half of the seventh century that, under Buddhist influence, Tibet received a written language and a literature. The literature of the Bon-po, the followers of the national religion, which was created later along Buddhist lines, will no doubt, with careful textual criticism, provide us with some elements for the solution of the problem. However, the first impression this literature creates is somewhat disappointing. The first thing which is obvious is the Buddhist gloss and a profound dependence in the matter of doctrine, and it is only after a detailed analysis that this or that older complex of ideas can be abstracted.

In addition there is the circumstance that we have as yet no very reliable conception of the extent of this literature. The few works which have become known to us are random items, and thus provide us with more or less unrelated information. The first text of this kind was published by Anton Schiefner as early as 1881 under the title *The White Nâga Hundred Thousand*, and an abridged version was published in 1898 by Berthold Laufer. It was possible to obtain one or two indications of the primitive spirit concepts of the old Bon-po from this source, and to an

[1] Cf. H. S. Nyberg, *Die Religionen des alten Iran* (*The Religions of Ancient Iran*), Leipzig, 1938, pp. 67 *et seq.*

even greater extent from a short expiatory poem published by Laufer in 1900. Apart from one or two short notes and extracts, we also have a translation of about a quarter of a longer and really more representative work, the *gZer-myig* published by A. H. Francke. In view of this state of affairs, even allowing for all necessary caution, we have to be grateful for such items as we can cull from the polemical literature of the Lamaist writers. A review such as that provided by Chos-kyi nyi-ma in his book *The Crystal of Doctrinal Systems*[1] has the great advantage that summed up in a few pages we seem to have what we would otherwise have to pick out from mounds of ancient folios. Only gradually, and in the course of further investigations, will it then be possible to compare the evidence of the Buddhists against the evidence of the original Bon literature. We are thus in a somewhat similar situation in this respect as the scholars were who sought to study Manichaeanism. For many years their only source was the polemical writings of Christian and Islamic writers, and yet they met with no small measure of success.[2]

But certain more or less unintentional and casual observations in the historical literature relating to the earliest days of Tibetan history are of even greater value to us in our task. The authors were, it is true, Lamaist monks, but the old Tibetan kingdom which they glorified as the protector of Buddhism, had so many and such intimate relations to the Bon religion that some noticeable reflection of these relations was necessarily visible even in later literary works. In addition, for some years now we have been in the happy position of possessing two extremely important contemporary works from the days of the Tibetan universal monarchy which as yet show no signs of Buddhist adaptation. These valuable documents came to us, together with so many other important writings, from the famous walled library of Tun-huang in North-West China (at that time under Tibetan rule), and they have proved themselves particularly helpful to us in our study of the ancient religious ideas of the Tibetans. However, it will be some time before we shall be able to solve all the linguistic and other problems with which these texts present us. Finally, we must not omit to mention the important information

[1] Translated by Sarat Chandra Das in the *Journal of the Asiatic Society of Bengal*, Vol. 50, 1881, Part I, pp. 187 *et seq.*, and revised by me in my book *Historical Sources of the Tibetan Bon Religion*, pp. 327 *et seq.*

[2] H. H. Schaeder in *Morgenland*, No. 28 (*Oriental Contributions to the Idea of Redemption*), p. 84.

which has been obtained from the works of the Chinese chroniclers, which were based on contemporary reports, and which are available in particular in the two historical works of the T'ang dynasty.

The following is more or less what we can learn of the original Bon religion from these sources: the Tibetans of those days were apparently completely subject to the powerful and formidable nature of their natural surroundings. Their completely nature-rooted and nature-dominated religious ideas revolved reverently and submissively around the powers and forces of their wild highland landscape whose divinities were reflected in the idea of numerous good and evil spirits the Tibetans thought to see all around them. Almost all these many and varied spirits are still alive today in the beliefs of ordinary Tibetan people. They are recognized by Lamaism and accepted into its Pantheon, whereas the old God of Heaven has for a long, long time been a typical Deus otiosus, rarely referred to, seldom revered, and almost entirely forgotten. Valuable material on the age-old ideas of living spirits which are still current amongst the Tibetans today, particularly in the districts of Western Tibet has been collected for us by A. H. Francke; and particularly by Ribbach in his excellent book *Drogpa Namgyal.*

According to ancient Tibetan belief the world is divided into three parts: heaven, air and earth. Occasionally these three spheres are known as heaven, earth, and the underworld.[1] In the lower zone there are the kLu, who bear a certain resemblance to our water sprites, and who can adopt the form of snakes at will, a point which later made them readily identifiable with the Indian Nâgas. The age of these kLu ideas is found happily confirmed by the many theophoric names from the days of the monarchy.[2] The original habitat of these kLu was rivers and lakes, and even certain wells. They have their homes on the bottom where they guard secret treasures. Amongst the trees and the rocks there are the gNyan, and in the earth proper there are the Sa-bdag, or 'masters of the earth', and also the dreaded Sri, vampire-like creatures who go by preference for small children. The particular spheres of the kLu, the gNyan and the Sa-bdag are occasionally confused, and one Bon text reports the kLu as living in strangely

[1] Cf. Hoffmann, *Bon Religion*, p. 139, A. H. Francke, *Tibetische Hochzeitslieder* (Hagen and Darmstadt 1923), pp. 5 *et seq.*

[2] *Journal of the Royal Asiatic Society* 1914, p. 40.

formed heaps, in black rocks whose peaks are pointed like the head of a crow, in burial mounds formed in the shape of a black boar snout, on hills in the shape of lying oxen, in juniper trees, birch trees and spruce trees, in double mountains, double rocks and double glaciers. The expiatory poem already referred to discusses these spirits and their animal following:[1]

The kLu kings are in all streams,
The gNyan kings are in trees and stones,
The Masters of the Earth are in the five kinds of earth:
There, it is said, are the Masters of the Earth, the kLu and the gNyan.
What kind of company is theirs?
Scorpions with long stings,
Ants with notched waists,
Golden frogs,
Turquoise-coloured tadpoles,
Mussel-white butterflies,
These are their company.

The gNyan, who roam around on mountains and in valleys, and make their lairs in slatey rocks, woods and ditches as they please, are easily annoyed by human beings, and then they send sickness and death. The plague, which is known in Tibet as gNyan is a scourge attributed to them in particular. As they also make their haunts on mountains they are closely related to the mountain gods. The god of the powerful Thang-lha mountain chain, who is named after it, is also known as the great gNyan. Like so many other of the mountain gods he is said to have been 'converted' by Padmasambhava, the apostle of tantric Buddhism; in other words Buddhisized and incorporated into the Pantheon of Lamaism. The 'White Goddess of Heaven' (gNam-lha dkar-mo) lives in the neighbourhood of Mount Everest, together with the friendly five 'Sisters of Long Life', each of whom has her special pool, and the waters of the five pools are of different colours.[2] Near the frontier of Bhutan lies the domain of Yar-lha sham-po, who is the god of the mountain chain of the same name.

[1] Text from B. Laufer, *An Expiatory Poem of the Bonpo*, p. 32 *et seq.*

[2] Ribbach, *Four Pictures of the Padmasambhava*, p. 32; and also L. A. Waddell, *Buddhism of Tibet*, p. 370.

He appears in the shape of a white man, or of a white Yak bull.

In the royal annals rGyal-rabs there[1] is a saga according to which the widow of a Tibetan king, who had been driven away, conceived of a son in a dream in which the mountain god appeared to her in the shape of a white man. This son was destined to restore the fortunes of the dynasty. As the widowed queen awoke she saw a white Yak rise from her resting place and go away. And finally there is the mountain god Kangchenjunga (Gangs-chen mdzod-lnga), whose feast as that of the highest god of the Himalaya State of Sikkim is celebrated with elaborate mask and sword dances in the Temple of Gangtok and in other monasteries throughout the country.[2]

The air is the domain of the bTsan, a group of demons who still live on in the minds of Tibetans today. Ribbach writes that they are supposed to appear as 'savage huntsmen, red in colour, wearing helmets and armour, who ride on light-red horses over the mountains under the leadership of their king'. Whoever is unfortunate enough to fall in with them in the loneliness of the mountains is pierced by their arrows and falls victim to a deadly sickness.[3]

All the information in our possession indicates that Heaven was held in high honour by the old Bon-po, not only as a natural, impersonal reality, but also as the personified god of Heaven, who, however, as a Deus otiosus, hardly seems to have played any role in men's lives, i.e. its role was the same as amongst the old Turkish and old Mongolian Shamanists. The rare sources suggest that 'the King of Heaven' lives there surrounded by a host of supernatural spirits, some of whom were gods (Lha), and the others spirits (dMu, Theu-rang, and bDud). In the old days the bDud were heavenly spirits, but under Lamaism they were degraded to devils, and their leader, the bDud himself, was identified with Mâra, the tempter of Buddha. Heaven itself was regarded—as amongst the present-day Siberian Shamanists—as consisting of various strata; incidentally, so was the underworld. According to the very earliest reports Heaven consisted of nine strata or degrees, with special reference to the heavenly degree, the cloud degree and the rain degree. Later on even thirteen different degrees were mentioned. The fact that these degrees

[1] Hoffmann, *Bon Religion*, p. 139; cf. also L. A. Waddell, *Buddhism of Tibet*, p. 383.

[2] Ribbach, *Four Pictures of the Padmasambhava*, p. 32, and also E. Schaeffer, *Geheimnis Tibet*, Munich 1943, pp. 31 *et seq.*

[3] Ribbach, *Drogpa Namgyal*, pp. 21, 25, 62, 221, 237.

were quite realistically regarded as stages of the universe can be seen clearly from the fact that in order to go from one degree to the next a spirits rope (dmu-thag) or a spirits ladder was necessary for climbing up and down.

The first King of Tibet, according to ancient reports—as in the sagas of many other countries—came to his people as the son of the gods of Heaven, making his way down this heavenly ladder. After having fulfilled their earthly tasks, he and his six successors returned to Heaven by the same means. However, the eighth of these kings, Gri-grum, who fell a victim to a black magic attack carried out by his minister, cut the ladder, so the saga relates, and in this way made any return impossible. This ruler was therefore the first to leave his body behind when he died, and since then, according to the etiological saga, men began to concern themselves with burial rites.

One particular group of these spirits, including the 'Field God', the 'Tent God', the 'House God' and the 'Hearth God', is more closely connected with man's everyday life. The Hearth God is similar to the Fire God and the 'Hearth Mother' of the Mongolians, and to the Chinese 'Hearth God' Tsao-shên. The Tibetan Hearth God (Thab-lha) is very easily annoyed. Any neglect of his fire he punishes remorselessly with sickness and other misfortunes. If butter is sacrificed to him it gives him pleasure, but woe betide the offender if a hair, an old rag, or dog's dirt finds its way into the fire, or if a pot boils over and dirties the hearth! The offender can look out for danger. In order to ward off the threatening misfortunes when some such accident has happened the owner of the hearth must call in an experienced Bon priest to perform the appropriate cleansing rites. The soiled hearth is dug out, the priest goes into a trance and takes a lump of the earth, which is then examined. If some living larva or grub is found in it then the ceremony of cleansing and propitiation is regarded as successful. The larva or grub which is now the incorporation of the demon of pollution is immediately destroyed. If no trace of any living thing is found in the lump of earth then the demon has obviously made good his escape. The priest is then no longer in a position to help, and the unfortunate owner of the soiled hearth must prepare himself for the advent of misfortune.[1]

The obviously very ancient idea of the 'Man-God' (pho-lha),

[1] Cf. Sarat Chandras Das, *ibid.*, p. 196.

probably an ancestral spirit, and of the 'Foe-God' (dGra-lha), is of particular interest for the study of Bon animism. Two such spirits take up their habitation in every human being, and are to be regarded as a sort of guardian angel to ward off demonaical influences. The 'Foe-God' is thus not to be regarded as the embodiment of evil in man, but, on the contrary, as an effective helping spirit. Like the related Mongolian Sülde, these dGra-lha appear as armed warriors. Should they for any reason have to leave the body of the human being in question in order to go to heaven, then that person is in great danger from the attacks of evilly-inclined demons. In consequence he can fall victim to sicknesses and other misfortunes, and unless some experienced priest is called in to conjure the missing spirits back into their human habitat, the person concerned must surely die in the end.

Very interesting in this connection is the ancient story of the mythical King Gri-gum btsan-po, which is recorded in the rGyal-rab annals. The king allowed himself to be inveigled into a duel with his chief minister, and unknowingly he laid himself open to the black-magic arts of his opponent by placing a dead fox on his right shoulder and a dead mouse on his left, whereupon the Foe-God left his body through the dead fox, whilst the Man God left by the dead mouse, with the result that the now unprotected king was easily killed by his enemy. From a number of indications it would appear that these two gods, and occasionally other spirits too, are regarded as appearing—as in the myths of other animist peoples—in the form of winged insects.[1] In order to ward off the attentions of such winged insects when they are of an evil character, the Tibetans have from time immemorial devised spirit traps in which the demons are caught as in a spider's web. These devices are known as mDos; they consist of two or more crossed sticks on which are spun numerous threads, usually of different coloured materials. Such mDos are to be met with throughout Tibet in all shapes and sizes from small ones perhaps an inch or two across to huge nets set up on tall masts. When in the opinion of the priests evil spirits have been caught in these mDos the latter are burnt.

A further important characteristic of the old Bon religion is the offering up of animal sacrifices. In the time of the Tibetan universal monarchy, which represents the oldest historical epoch of the country, such animal sacrifices played an important part

[1] Cf. F. F. Lessing, *Yung Ho Kung*, *I*, Stockholm 1943, p. 148.

in the official State ceremonies. Chinese records have preserved valuable information in this respect. The annals of the T'ang Dynasty mention that when Tibetans made the oath of fealty this was accompanied by the offering up of sheep, dogs and monkeys. And during a specially solemn ceremony which was held every three years, horses, oxen, donkeys, and even human beings were sacrificed in order to propitiate the gods of Heaven and Earth.[1] Such sacrifices were also offered up in connection with the repeatedly concluded State treaties between Tibet and China. Such rites were, of course, anathema to Buddhism, which held all forms of life inviolate—Ahimsâ. And when Buddhism gained the upper hand and obtained State recognition the defeated Bon-po were forbidden to indulge further in such practices. But even down to the present day Buddhism has not entirely succeeded in eradicating this form of sacrifice, which is deeply rooted in the beliefs of the Tibetan people. Substitutes for living animals were sacrificed instead, representations of yaks and sheep, and wooden carvings of deer heads. From the Mi-la ras-pa chants we learn that when an important Bon-po fell ill in the eleventh century the evil demons were propitiated by a veritable hecatomb of hundreds of yaks, goats and sheep. In more recent times travellers in Eastern Tibet have reported that followers of the Bon religion are still using the blood of cocks to conjure peace.[2] The Bon text *gZer-myig*[3] provides us with a cruelly realistic description of a human sacrifice. In order to bring about the recovery of a sick prince one of his subjects had to be sacrificed to propitiate the demon. The text reads: 'The soothsayer seized the man by the feet whilst the Bon-po took his hands. The black Han-dha then cut open the life orifice and tore out the heart. The two, the soothsayer and the Bon-po, then scattered the blood and flesh of the victim to the four corners of the heaven.'

According to information from all sources, another characteristic of the old Bon religion was a deep concern with death rites. As we have already seen, the ancient sagas connect the introduction of such rites with the death of King Gri-gum btsan-po, who was the first king not to clamber back into heaven up the

[1] Cf. *Journal of the Royal Asiatic Society* 1880, p. 441.

[2] Cf. Albert Tafel, *Meine Tibetreise*, Vol. II, pp. 153 and 198; Notes 2, 232 and 236.

[3] Cf. *Bon Religion*, p. 181.

heavenly ladder. His body was therefore buried by his sons under a pointed tent-shaped tumulus of stamped earth.[1] The *Crystal of Doctrinal Systems* makes the interesting observation[2] that the Tibetan Bon-po were not sufficiently acquainted with the appropriate rites and therefore had to bring in three Bon priests from the West, from Kashmir, Gilgit and Guge, one of whom was possessed of the necessary knowledge. This man carried out an operation known as the 'Taming of the Dead'—apparently with a magic knife. The rites in question are probably connected with the idea of preventing the dead from returning and harming the living, i.e. they are obviously related to similar ceremonies such as can be met with amongst most primitive peoples. Even in present-day Lamaism the spirits of the dead are exorcized by burning the representation of the dead person at the end of the forty-nine days the burial ceremonies last. At a later period the Bon-po codified all the chief rites and laid down '360 ways of Death', 'four ways of preparing graves', and 'eighty-one ways of taming evil spirits'. Unfortunately only the names of these texts have come down to us.[3]

For Lamaism the disposal of the dead body is also regarded at the same time as a sort of sacrifice. The corpse of the deceased is dismembered and left to the vultures, the wolves, the fishes or the worms; or offered, when it is burnt, to those spirits which nourish themselves on effluvia.[4] This idea was completely foreign to the ancient Tibetan religious beliefs. Consider, for example, the following instructions for the funeral of a Bon priest:[5] 'When a casket of stone slabs has been prepared in a spirit shrine on an appropriate rocky mountain for the corpse of a Shaman Bon-po, the dead man should be clothed in blue silk and placed on a seat in the form of a swastika. Two drums should be put into his hands, and before him should be placed the white feathered divine arrow with silk strings of five different kinds; and also excellent wine. Amidst the smell of scents and the smoke of various kinds of wood, bind the forehead of the dead man with adornments of white wool and then place his body between grains of corn and wood.' The similarity of this form of burial with that of the Siberian Shamans is immediately

[1] Cf. Bacot, *Documents de Touen-houang relatif à l'histoire du Tibet*, p. 127.

[2] *Bon Religion*, p. 330.

[3] *Journal of the Asiatic Society of Bengal*, Vol. 50, 1881, Part One, p. 204.

[4] Cf. Alexandra David-Neel, *Heilige und Hexer*, p. 40.

[5] *Bon Religion*, p. 190.

obvious.[1] There is the setting out of the body on a mountain, the addition of the typical Shaman burial furnishings, and a kind of viaticum in the shape of corn and wine.

We are particularly well informed concerning the burial customs at the funerals of the great kings of the once powerful and united country.[2] From a number of indications in the ancient Tun-huang annals it is evident that the bodies of the dead kings were preserved for months, and sometimes even for a year, in a mortuary, in the same way as is done, according to A. David-Neel,[3] in present-day Tibet with the bodies of prominent religious personages. They are embalmed by immersion in brine or by boiling in butter. The actual interment takes place only after this preliminary period. The ancient kings were, as we have already mentioned, interred under a simple pointed tumulus of stamped earth, but from the death of the great Srong-btsan sgam-po (649 AD) on, extensive underground burial works filled with precious things were customary. One year after the actual interment a memorial service and lamentation was held. This information reminds us irresistibly of what we know of the burial customs of the Shamanist Turks of Inner Asia at about the same period.[4]

Whilst the ancient Bon religion had a highly complicated ritualistic system, its religious architecture seems to have been very modest and restricted. There are no reports from the earliest times concerning actual temples or perhaps monasteries, such as were built by the hundred by the Lamaists in later centuries. The only references are to spiritual shrines of a quite modest nature such as are mentioned frequently in the *History of Kings according to Bon Tradition*.[5] A great host of priests and sorcerers were devoted to the Bon service, though what all their functions were we can only vaguely guess nowadays. There are references to heavenly Bon-po and earthly Bon-po, Bon-rje (High Priests) and Lha-Bon-po (God Bon-po), who obviously concerned themselves with divine ritual, whilst, according to the rGyal-rabs, the sGrung and lDeu seem to have concerned themselves with

[1] Cf. Harva, *Die religiösen Vorstellungen der altaiischen Völker*, p. 295 *et seq.*; and also Nioradze, *Der Schamanismus bei den Sibirischen Völker*, p. 103.

[2] Cf. my own work 'Die Gräber der tibetischen Könige im Distrikt " 'P'yons-rgyas" , published in *Nachrichten der Göttinger Akademie der Wissenschaften*, 1950.

[3] *Heilige und Hexer*, p. 40.

[4] Cf. the *Zeitschrift der Deutschen Morgenlandische Gesellschaft*, Vol. 78, p. 132.

[5] T'oung Pao 1901, pp. 24 *et seq.*

funeral rites and occult and oracular matters. However, the gShen were the most important and the most frequently referred to of the Bon priests. The word gShen, which also appears in the name of the mythical founder of the later systematized Bon religion (gShen-rab means the 'pre-eminent gShen' and is thus not a proper name) originally referred to the Shamans[1] but was later also used for Bon priests who were not Shamans.

The old Tibetan Shamans seem to have been in many respects very similar to their colleagues of north and central Asia. Like them, they used fantastic head-dresses whilst carrying out their religious observances, wearing a blue robe, or a blue fur garment as a Shaman robe, and, in particular, making use of small drums, which were essential to their ritual. When we are now told that one of those priests who were summoned from the West to perform the funeral rites at the interment of King Gri-gum was able to move through the air on his drum, we recognize the story as a reference to a typical Shamanist performance of those ancient days—the ability to fly through the air. It is reported that in the eleventh century Mi-la ras-pa engaged in a trial of magic with a Bon priest; it being agreed that whoever was first on the summit of the holy mountain Kailāsa at dawn should win the prize, namely the command of the holy mountain itself. The Bon-po sought to gain the victory by 'sitting on a drum, striking a tambourin and flying through the air'.[2] Such reports are valuable to us as proof of the close typological relationship between the ancient Tibetan religion and the Shamanism of our own day. It is also reported of an Altai Shaman that 'beating his drum he flew over the mountains like a bird'. Similarly, the Yakutian Shamans believe that during their ecstatic dances, when their familiar spirit has entered into them, they are capable of 'flying into the realm of the spirits on or behind their drums'. In this way the wise Yakutian Shaman Nurullan-Ko is reported to have been carried on her flying drum through the seven degrees of Heaven to her fathers. And, according to a Buryat legend, a Shaman, also sitting on his drum,[3] is said to have penetrated into the realm of the highest Divinity who had carried off a soul.

[1] Cf. *Zeitschrift der Deutschen Morgenlandische Gesellschaft* 1944, p. 340 *et seq.*, and also F. W. Thomas, *Tibetan Literary Texts and Documents* III, London 1955, p.102.

[2] Cf. H. Hoffmann, *Mi-la Ras-pa. Sieben Legenden*, pp. 73-4.

[3] Cf. Ohlmarks, *Studien zum Problem des Schamanismus*, pp. 77, 139 and 166: Harva, *Die religiösen Vorstellungen der altaiischen Völker*, p. 543; and Friedrich Budruss, *Schamanen Geschichten aus Siberien*, Munich 1955, pp. 70 81 and 294.

The central experience of the Shaman is 'the flight of the soul', the penetration into the upper or nether regions whilst in a state of trance; generally speaking, as we have seen in one of the examples quoted, in order to bring back a soul which has fled or been carried off. This trance experience, during which the body of the Shaman is in a state of cataleptic rigidity, usually occurs spontaneously amongst the Shamans of the Arctic North, whereas amongst the peoples of more southern climes resort is had to some sort of narcotic; the desired frenzy is induced by alcohol or by some herb infusion; and sometimes the supernatural experience is just symbolically imitated. Amongst the Altai tribes it has been observed that a pretended flight is carried out on a representation of a goose,[1] or by climbing up a tree in which footholds have been notched to represent the degrees of heaven.[2]

There is evidence that these old Shamanist practices still live on today even amongst the followers of Lamaism. In his book 'Drogpa Namgyal', Ribbach describes a good example of a typical shamanist healing of the sick in present-day West Tibet.[3] A caster-out of demons (Lha-pa) is summoned from Lhasa to call back the departed soul of a woman. He uses all sorts of magic Lama devices, but, in addition, he also resorts to the fumes of juniper berries and juniper twigs burnt on a coal brazier as a narcotic. 'The Lha-pa now called on his protective demon to enter into his body, and went into an ecstasy, becoming very agitated, his eyes staring fixedly and his lips foaming; and then leaping to his feet, uttering shrill cries and dancing around wildly. Now the conjured spirit demanded through the lips of the medium (the Lha-pa): "Who has called me?" Someone answered: "The Lha-pa. Who caused the sickness of Parlapang Rolma?" The spirit answered "The Naskorpas". Someone then asked: "What can we do against the sickness? How can we bring back the departed life of this woman?" The Lha (the spirit which has entered the Lha-pa) now announced that a sku-rim or sacrificial ceremony must be arranged and sacrificial gifts should be scattered.' This is an authentic Shamanist performance characterized by a high degree of trance and by the significant co-operation of a familiar spirit.

[1] Ohlmarks, *Studien*, p. 124.
[2] Harva, p. 49.
[3] Ribbach p. 187.

Finally it should be pointed out that an official place is reserved for Shamanism even within the framework of the present-day Lamaist State religion, namely in the shape of the oracular Lama whose opinion is canvassed in important political matters. His habitat is the small shrine gNas-chung in the neighbourhood of the great State monastery 'Bras-spungs to the west of Lhasa. The familiar spirit which takes possession of him is called Pe-har. This Lama ejaculates his oracular utterances in a state of wild ecstacy, writhing on the ground in convulsions.[1]

[1] Cf. L. A. Waddell, *The Buddhism of Tibet*, p. 480; R. Nebesky-Wojkovitz, in the *Archiv für Völkerkunde* 1948, p. 136 *et seq.*; E. Schäfer, *Fest der weissen Schleier*, Braunschweig 1952, pp. 153-65, 190 *et seq.*

CHAPTER II

THE DEVELOPMENT OF BUDDHISM IN INDIA AND ITS PENETRATION INTO TIBET

In the previous chapter we have sought to sketch the essentials of the old autochthonous religion of Tibet as far as the known sources allow. We must now turn our attention to Buddhism, the foreign religion which penetrated into the narrowly limited sphere of the old Shamanist-animist beliefs, and by its amalgamation with native religious elements produced that special religion which we know today as Lamaism. It will be necessary for us to give a brief sketch of the history of the Buddhist teachings in their country of origin, because from the death of its founder up to the time of its penetration into Tibet, over a thousand years had passed, and in that time its own face had fundamentally changed.

Siddhârtha Gautama, whose followers call him 'the Enlightened One', the Buddha, came from the small dynasty of the Shâkya, who ruled a small principality at the foot of the Himalayas. After a youth spent in the pleasures of the world, Siddhârtha left the house of his fathers to learn from the teachers of Yoga and to satisfy his urge for salvation. But neither Arâda Kalâpa, who led his disciples along the meditative path to the stage of nothingness, nor Rudraka Râmaputra, who went even further and guided his followers to a sphere beyond both the conscious and the unconscious,[1] nor the harshest asceticism and self-mortifications were able to satisfy him. After this he separated himself from all other seekers, and under the holy Bo tree in the neighbourhood of present-day Bodh Gayâ he at last found enlightenment. After a certain amount of hesitation he decided to make known his inspiration, and he revealed it for the first time to five of his former companions in meditation in the now famous sermon at Banaras. After a life which lasted eighty years, and which was spent after his enlightenment in spreading abroad the truth

[1] Cf. Beckh, *Buddhismus*, I, p. 48.

he had discovered, he died near Kushinagara in the year 480.[1]

The teachings (dharma) laid down by Buddha and preserved by a growing community of monks (sangha) did not represent the traditional popular brand of religion with a rich pantheon of gods and an impressive and colourful ritual. Instead it was a strictly philosophical theory of salvation for the elect. It is characterized primarily by the Arhat ideal, the ideal of the religious individual who recognizes in a manly struggle the afflictions of this life, and overcomes it by reaching a state in which the power of the life-force (trishnâ) is broken, a state which is known as Nirvâna, or the effacement of all desires. Very soon after the death of its founder, Buddhism began to change and develop, but despite this development it is still quite clear that the teaching of the four noble truths belongs to its original stock: the truth of suffering, of the origin of suffering, of the effacement of suffering, and of the noble eight-fold path which leads to the effacement of suffering. Similarly, we know that the original fund of Buddha's teachings included the doctrine of 'origin in dependence' (pratîyasamutpâda), which seeks to describe the development of a living being by a series of twelve factors, which represent less a strict causal series in the occidental sense than a mutually dependent series, whose final basis is described as the ignorance of the holy truths (avidyâ).[2] Early Buddhism did not reject the popular Indian gods and their heavens, but they too were regarded as subject to the laws of development and decline, the circle of birth and death (Samsâra), whose individual, more of less happy, stages were regulated by the law of retaliation (Karma). It is important to bear in mind that as Buddha recognized gods but no God, so he also recognized no immortal soul. The ego (Âtman) is only a conglomeration of life factors, the so-called Dharmas, and after death their bond is released. However, if Nirvâna is not reached in life then they release impulses which result in the origin of new life. Thus it is not the ego which is immortal, but only the sorrowful process of development and decline, and the

[1] A comprehensive study of the last days of Buddha according to the various traditional indications in the Mahâparinirvânasûtra is given by E. Waldschmidt in 'Die Überlieferungen vom Lebensende des Buddha' published in the *Proceedings of the Göttingen Academy of Sciences* 1944 and 1948.

[2] For the teachings of early Buddhism cf. H. Oldenberg *Buddha*, Stuttgart 1923; H. Beckh, *Buddhismus*, II, Berlin and Leipzig 1928; H. von Glasenapp, *Der Buddhismus in Indien und im fernen Osten*, Berlin and Zurich; and E. Conze, *Der Buddhismus*, Stuttgart 1953.

aim of the Buddhist is to avoid precisely this. What Buddha set out to provide is a practical doctrine of salvation. He always rejected that preoccupation with metaphysical speculation to which the spirits of his age were so devoted.[1]

Buddha did not claim to be the only enlightened one. In his view there had been Buddhas in the world in earlier ages too. Speculation began to attach itself to this idea very early on and to provide a basis for that mythology which is peculiar to Indian religious thought. The series of six predecessors of Buddha—Vipashyin, Shikhin, Vishvabhû, Krakucchanda, Kanakamuni and Kâshyapa—probably belonged to a quite early period of development. Further, differences of opinion about the teachings and the regulations of the Order led early on to splits and the formation of sects, as can clearly be seen from the reports on the early Buddhist rehearsals. However, up to the time of the Emperor Ashoka (the third century BC) the teachings of Buddha seem to have been preserved in a relatively unadulterated state and on a high ethical level, a situation indicated by the famous edicts of this ruler.[2] However, the sculptures decorating the Stûpas built over the Buddha relics at Sânchi and Bharhut suggest that Buddhism was now well on the way to becoming a mythology, with the idolization of its founder, a fate which hardly any religion can escape. But so far the Enlightened One himself was not graphically, but only symbolically represented; for example, by the wheel of his teachings. A noteworthy fact was the accretion of popular divinities, and in particular those of the lower orders, such as the Yaksha and the Nâgas.

At about the beginning of the Christian time reckoning, Buddhism reached a decisive phase of its development. At this time, or perhaps somewhat later, that version of the teachings must have been perfected, whose followers described themselves as adepts of Mahâyâna, or 'the Great Vehicle', as distinct from the followers of the older Buddhism with its Arhat ideal, which was now referred to with less respect than formerly as 'the Small Vehicle'. The new ideal, which had taken the place of the old Arhat ideal to be arrived at by a stern struggle for personal perfection, was the Bodhisattva, or 'Being of Enlightenment'. The Bodhisattva is a future, a designated Buddha, who, out of pity for the suffering world, has taken an oath not to enter into Nirvâna

[1] Cf. Oldenburg, *Buddha*, pp. 313 *et seq.*
[2] Cf. W. Schumacher, *Die Edikte des Kaisers Asoka*, Constance 1948.

before the last living thing has been saved. The deliberate, cool and aristocratic simplicity of the older Buddhism now gave way to a more emotional epoch in which an increasing number of Buddha and Bodhisattva figures developed, offering a more tangible object to the faithful devotion and the desire for salvation of the Indian Buddhist; like, at a later stage, the Bhakti piety of the Hindu centred on Vishnu. Before long the mythical Buddhas in their mythical paradises, far away but still effective; figures like Vairocana and Amitâbha; and Bodhisattvas like Avalokiteshvara, the great god of mercy, and Maitreya, the saviour of the coming world period, began to overlay the importance and significance of the historic Buddha.

Even down to the present day the experts have not succeeded in clearly separating the various stages of this development which led to the Mahâyâna, and the reason for this failure is to be found in the strange lack of historicity in the spiritual life of India. No doubt we must reckon with a revival of the old popular religious beliefs of India; for example, and in particular, the gradual taking over of the Hinduist pantheon by Buddhism, which we see reflected in the graphic arts. In the end even Mahâkâla-Shiva was adopted and came to be acknowledged, and with him an ever increasing number of terrible gods. However, it would also appear, particularly in its later stages, that non-Indian and in particular Western cultural influences played a role in the development of Mahâyâna. It can hardly be regarded as fortuitous that the period of Mahâyâna development ran more or less parallel to the development in North India and Eastern Iran (at that time a country strongly under Buddhist influences) of that strange Indo-Greek art known after the Gandhâra region, but flourishing also in the neighbouring regions of Udyâna (Nüristân), Gilgit and in the area of old Taxila, and whose ramifications were spreading not only in India proper but also in East Turkestan. The Gandhâra artists presented the faithful with portrait representations of Buddha in beautifully stylized robes flowing in the Greek manner. It must therefore be regarded as highly probable that these districts of North-West India and Eastern Iran, which in later centuries were the classic birthplace of numerous syncretic innovations, mostly on the basis of Buddhism (a phenomenon with which we shall have to deal later on) were also the gateway through which Hellenic art and culture and western Asiatic eligious ideas found their way into India.

Parallel with this more popular and exoteric development of Buddhism went a philosophic-esoteric development. Nâgârjuna, who seems to have lived in the second century, may be regarded as the father of philosophical Mahâyâna. We know little or nothing about the circumstances of his life, and the legendary reports to be found in the works of Târanâtha and other Tibetan historians[1] obviously refer chiefly to a later Nâgârjuna, a Tantric and sorcerer, whose figure has become merged into that of the earlier philosophical Nâgârjuna in the consciousness of later times. The 'middle' teachings of Nâgârjuna and the Mâdhyamika school to which he gave rise, deny the reality of all phenomena and of all life elements, and describe them latterly as 'empty' (shûnya). This Shûnyatâ (emptiness) is elevated to the highest philosophical concept, object (grâhya) and subject (grahaka) of understanding; Nirvâna and Samsâra are no longer materially separated, but are regarded more or less as different aspects of an intangible, purely negative 'emptiness' or 'voidness'. Apart from Nâgârjuna, there are the two brothers Asanga and Vasubandhu, who can be regarded as, so to speak, important fathers of the church for the Mahâyâna in the fourth or fifth centuries. Unlike Nâgârjuna, Asanga, the founder of the Yogâcâra or Vijnânavâda school, recognized a so-called 'treasure-house consciousness' (âlayavijnâna), thanks to which the continuity between a being and his successor resulting from the post-mortal surviving forces is maintained at least in consciousness. As H. von Glasenapp puts it very succinctly: this 'treasure-house consciousness' is not a persisting soul monad, but rather like a river which changes as a result of constantly receiving and giving up water'.[2] Vasubandhu was at first one of the most renowned of the Hînayâna teachers of his day, but was then converted by his brother to the Mahâyâna. The author of the Hînayâna compendium Abhidharmakosha, who bears the same name is not, as the recent investigations of E. Frauwallner have shown, identical with Asanga's brother, but belongs to the fifth century.[3] The last of this influential series of Mahâyâna masters was Dharmakîrti, who lived in the first half

[1] Cf. the description of the Nâgârjuna legend given by Grünwedel in his book *Mythologie des Buddhismus*, p. 29 *et seq.*

[2] *Buddhistische Mysterien*, p. 15. With reference to the Âlaya-vijnâna, see also the note on the subject in L. de la Vallée Poussin's book *Mélanges chinois et bouddhiques III*, Brussels 1935, p. 145.

[3] Cf. E. Frauwallner, *On the Date of the Buddhist Master of the Law Vasubandhu*, Rome 1951, p. 55.

of the seventh century and was a contemporary of King Srong-btsan sgam-po, in whose reign Buddhism first succeeded in penetrating into Tibet.

The spiritual conditions for the development of the third stage of Buddhism, the Vajrayâna, or Diamond Vehicle, must have been present several centuries before Dharmakîrti's time.[1] Pursuant to the teaching of this new vehicle Buddhism now often followed the relativist teachings of the Mahâyâna to the point of paradox; by persistently seeking a *modus vivendi* with Hinduism (for the sake of greater and more widespread effect) and assimilating its ritual (in the so-called Tantras or doctrinal systems) on the one hand, and taking an increasing number of strange gods into its pantheon, or creating new ones in their likeness, on the other. A belief in the infallible power of properly enunciated magic formulas placed the religion in danger of a grave alienation. Salvation, the Nirvâna, for which in Buddha's time 'the sons of noble families abandoned their homes and went on pilgrimage', devoting their whole lives to the search, was now, under certain circumstances, obtainable in a flash by the mere uttering of the appropriate magic formula. The long path of onerous self-discipline and self-purification was now left to the spiritually untalented, whilst the real initiates took 'the direct path', the Vajrayâna.

Typical of the state of mind behind many of the texts of the so-called Diamond Vehicle is that they are by no means confined to a consideration of the highest perfection, or Siddhi, but deal also and at great length with the lower Siddhis—the transmutation of base metal into gold, the discovery of hidden treasures, the phenomenon of the seven-league boots, the possibility of physically changing shape, and other vulgar sorceries—thus showing a strange relationship with similar hokus-pokus popular in Europe in the Middle Ages. But apart from these alienated sorcerers, there were also serious mystics whose esoteric teachings sought a oneness with the absolute, which began to appear more and more in the shape of an Urbuddha or Âdibuddha. The idea of the Âdibuddha, which is already adumbrated in a text such as the Guhyasamâja, found its highest peak of development in the Kâlacakra system, which obtained a good deal of influence in India in the tenth century, and which probably arose under the

[1] A valuable summary of our certain knowledge concerning this form of Buddhism is provided in H. von Glasenapp's book *Buddhistische Mysterien.*

influence of the increasingly strong Hindu reaction to Buddhism (Vishnu belief and Shivaism), and also in all probability as a result of contact with Western ideas. The investigation of this latter question must be regarded as one of the most burning problems of future research into Buddhism. It was from approximately the time of Dharmakîrti on that the erotic element began to enter into the Vajrayâna, and since then female gods have been created on a large and growing scale, attached to definite Buddhas and Bodhisattvas, in the way that Kâlî-Durgâ is attached to Shiva. The polar antithesis of the world is supposed to find its resolution in the sacred and profane love of such a divine pair; and the initiated mystic copied that unification on earth when he had intercourse, in exactly the way laid down, with a consecrated woman, known as a Shakti, Mudrâ, or even Vidyâ (literally wisdom), though the last-mentioned expression is very reminiscent of the Sophia of numerous gnostic systems.

We have very little information about the masters of the Vajrayâna and their relation to each other in time, but we are entitled to hope that the investigation of the Tantric commentaries and of the records of the Tibetan historians—of which so far only Târanâtha's work has been made available and examined—will help us in this respect, and allow us to draw up at least some sort of relative chronology.[1] The figure of Saraha, or Râhulabhadra, seems to begin the history of the eroticized Vajrayâna. This was the teacher of the above-mentioned sorcerer Nâgârjuna, who, as we have seen, should not be confused with the second century philosopher of the same name. This man came from a Brahmin family of Orissa, but he lost caste because he was very partial to the consumption of intoxicating liquor (something which is also laid to the account of most of the other Vajrayâna masters of Siddhas) and also because he lived together with a low-caste woman, who served him as his Vidyâ. 'In the land of Marhata,' says Târanâtha,[2] 'he saw the Yoginî of his sphere of labour, which was to resolve the essence of his ego, in the shape of the daughter of an arrow maker. When through the straight-

[1] Cf. A. Schiefner, *Târanâthas Geschichte des Buddhismus in Indien*, Petersburg 1869; A. Grünwedel, *Târanâthas Edelsteinmine*, published in the Bibliotheca Buddica XVIII, Petrograd 1914; and by the same author, *Die Geschichten der vierundachtzig Zauberer*, published in the Baessler-Archiv V, Leipzig and Berlin 1916.

[2] Cf. the *Edelsteinmine*, p. 7. The original text is not at present at my disposal.—THE AUTHOR.

ening of the arrows and other manipulations on her part, and by means which revealed the purpose of the object, a weapon was produced, she became of guidance to him in respect of the nature of things; he recognized the Dharmatâ completely, conferred the mudrâ on the daughter of the arrow-maker at once, and henceforth, wandering with her through many lands, pursued the trade of arrow-making. As his wisdom grew steadily he received the name of Saraha, or "he who hits with the arrow".'

We may regard this report as typical, and it may serve us to characterize the spiritual climate of the time. The followers of the later Vajrayâna have a dangerously meretricious philosophical and moral relativism in common. Incidentally, the paradoxical mystical verses of Saraha have come down to us.[1] One or two other leading mystics, such as Lûi-pâ, Jâlandhari, Krishnacârin, Kambala, Indrabhûti and Padmasambhava (of whom the three last-named come significantly from North-West India, the land of Udyâna) belong to a later period. They all devoted themselves primarily to a cult of mystic Buddhas and strange newly-arisen Tantric gods, such as Yamântaka, Samvara, Hevajra, and Heruka (the last-named three being to some extent deified hypostases of the active antitherical elements, i.e. the conjuring Yogin itself) which were conjured in meticulously executed magic circles, or Mandalas.[2] Each of the chief divinities had its own definite and exclusive Mandala in which a display of the physical and spiritual universe with all its divine hierarchies was symbolically represented. Characteristic of this epoch is also the importance attached to the 'sky-goers', the Dâkas and the Dâkinîs, both male and female, in whom we may see a reflection of perfected and departed mystics, also of either sex, who transmit mystic doctrines to their pupils who are still in this world, sometimes directly, sometimes indirectly, occasionally making it possible for them by means of special instructions to 'discover' hidden documents, so-called 'treasures'.

We must take account of all these briefly indicated teachings if we are to obtain any real picture of the spiritual powers which animist-shamanist Tibet faced when it came into contact with Buddhism in the seventh and eighth centuries. Although it was

[1] Cf. M. Shadidullah, *Les chants mystiques de Kanha et de Saraha*, Paris 1928; and D. Snellgrove in E. Conze, *Buddhist Texts throughout the Ages*, Oxford 1954, pp. 224 *et seq.*

[2] With regard to these Mandalas see G. Tucci, *Teoria e Pratica del Mandala*, Rome 1949.

certainly the innovations of the Vajrayâna which particularly occupied men's minds in those days, we should create a false picture of the spiritual atmosphere of the time if we failed to note in particular that older tendencies, such as the philosophic Mahâyâna of Nâgârjuna and Asanga, were still fully effective. In fact there was even a sect of the old Hînayâna, that of the Sarvâstivâdins, which seems to have been of some importance at the time, to judge at least by the quite considerable number of the doctrinal texts of this school which were translated when Buddhism began to be taken over in Tibet.

The light of history dawned over Tibet, previously a completely wild and cultureless land, in the region of the great King Srong-btsan sgam-po, who reigned from approximately 620 to 649. His father gNam-ri srong-btsan had already united the country at the time of the Chinese Sui dynasty, making it into a feared military power, and opening it up to the cultural and religious influences of the surrounding highly civilized countries of China, India and East Turkestan, the last-named country having adopted the Indian Buddhist culture. The Tibetans have, it is true, preserved a legend according to which, as early as the reign of the fifth predecessor of the king mentioned above, Lha-tho-tho-ri, member of a small dynasty reigning in neighbourhood of the Yar-klung Valley, not far from the Bhutan frontier, men came into possession in a mysterious fashion—they are alleged to have fallen from Heaven[1]—of two Buddhist writings and a miniature representation of a Stûpa, or Caitya. However, there seems to be no historical basis to this legend, and it is far more likely to be a subsequent adaptation of an old Bon legend, for, as we have seen, in Bon tradition Heaven, and everything coming from it, is regarded with great veneration. It was not until the reign of Srong-btsan that the Tibetans were assisted to a higher level of culture, and provided with other blessings, including their first contact with Buddhist teachings.

Whereas in all the material things of Western life such as the drawing up of State treaties, the introduction of paper and ink, and civilized social behaviour, the Tibetans turned to the Chinese as their teachers,[2] in spiritual and religious matters they turned,

[1] Bu-ston, *History of Buddhism II*, S.183; Deb-ther sngon-po 120a 1ff; rGyal-rabs B66b; Pad-ma dkar-po 97b 3.

[2] Cf. O. Franke, *Geschichte des chinesischen Reiches II*, Berlin and Leipzig 1936, p. 376.

though not exclusively, to India, which was the home of Buddhist beliefs, Buddhism having by that time spread to almost the whole of Asia Major: Eastern Iran, Turkestan, China, Japan, Indochina and Indonesia. The King of Tibet recognized that without a written language any higher culture and civilization was impossible. According to Chinese reports,[1] the Tibetans of those days had only a very primitive method of recording their thoughts namely by means of knotted strings. The king therefore sent his chief minister, Thon-mi Sambhota, to the neighbouring State of Kashmir in order that under the tutelage of Buddhist monks he should learn the Indian written characters which were in use there. The Tibetan historian Pad-ma dkar-po, who is in agreement on the point with the older historian Bu-ston, describes the incident as follows:[2] 'As at that time there was no written language in Tibet, the king sent Thon-mi, son of A-nu, an embodiment of the Bodhisattva Manjushrî, named Sambhota, to Kashmir to learn the letters there. He studied industriously under the master Devavidyâsimha, learning the written language, and, he then returned to Tibet where he reduced what he had learnt to thirty consonants and four vowels to meet the requirements of the Tibetan tongue. Working in the Ma-ru Palace in Lhasa he created an alphabet from the Kashmir letters and drew up eight grammatical text-books.' In a later description contained in the chronicle of the fifth Dalai Lama, the Brahmin Li-byin is mentioned as another teacher of Thon-mi. Whether this was so or not, this report of the introduction of a written language into Tibet from neighbouring Kashmir is quite in accordance with what we know about the relationship between Tibet and India at this period and later: the path taken by culture and religion did not lead directly over the Himalayas to Magadha (Bihâr) but through the western lands Nepal, Kashmir, Ladakh (which was not Tibetanized at that time), Gilgit and Udyâna. Paleography is also in complete agreement with this version, and the Dutch scholar J. Ph. Vogel has traced the Tibetan written characters from the usual form of the Gupta script which were in common use in North-West India at the time.[3]

According to the unanimous testimony of the chroniclers, the new written language was now used as a medium for the trans-

[1] *Journal of the Royal Asiatic Society* 1880, p. 440.

[2] Cf. Bu-ston, *History of Buddhism II*, p.183; Pad-ma dkar-po, 98a, 1 *et seq.*; Deb-ther sngon-po (I 20a, 5).

[3] Cf. *Epigraphindica* XI, p. 266.

lation of Buddhist texts. Mentioned as translators are the Indian master Kusara, a Brahmin named Shankara, the Nepalese Shîlamanju, and a Chinese monk (Hva-shang) named Mahâdeva. They were assisted by Tibetan pupils under the king's minister Thon-mi. It is interesting to note that amongst the foreign monks invited to take part in the work of translation was also a Chinese. The events which will be described later suggest that the Tibetans did not obtain either their sacred texts or their helpful monks exclusively from India, but also from China, a country in which Buddhism was already flourishing under the great T'ang dynasty.

This double relationship of Tibet with both India and China at the time was also reflected in the fact that the king, apart from a number of Tibetan wives, also wedded a Nepalese and a Chinese princess. Both these marriages were quite certainly of a political nature, but the fact that both these princesses were zealous followers of Buddhism no doubt greatly contributed to the increase of Buddhist influence in the Land of Snows. Both the Nepalese princess, Bhrikutî, the daughter of Amshuvarman, King of Nepal, and the Chinese princess Wên-ch'êng, brought numerous religious statues and other religious objects with them from their homes, and, in addition, the zealous desire to civilize the Tibetan barbarians and convert them to Buddhism. Both these women succeeded in capturing a place for themselves in the memory of the Tibetan people, and they continue to exist as incarnations of the white and the green goddess Târâ respectively. Even down to the present day the romantically embellished story of the marriages of Srong-btsan sgam-po, as they have been handed down to us in the *Ma-ni bka-'bum* (the *Hundred Thousand Precious Words*[1]), is very popular in Tibet. Under the influence and with the active participation of his wives, the king proceeded to found numerous Buddhist centres, including four temples in Central Tibet, namely the Temple in the Four Horns (Military districts[2]), four temples for the Conversion of the Frontiers, four 'Temples for the Conversion of the Districts still beyond the Frontiers', and in particular, two important edifices

[1] Cf. J. Bacot, 'Le mariage chinois de roi tibétan Sron bcan sgan po' in *Mélanges chinois et bouddhiques* III, pp. 1 *et seq.*

[2] With regard to the old distribution of the Tibetan province, Ü and Tsang, cf. F. W. Thomas, *Tibetan Literary Texts and Documents*, I, p. 276 *et seq.*, and with regard to the foundation of the temples by the king cf. rGyal-po bka'i thang-yig 40b, 2 *et seq.*; Lo-pan bka'i thang-yig, 65b, 4 *et seq.*; Bu-ston, *History I*, p. 184; and chaps. XIV and XV of the *rGyal-rabs*.

in Lhasa itself, Ra-mo-che; or 'the great enclosure', erected at the instance of the Chinese wife and Jo-khang, or 'the House of the Lord'. The great fifth Dalai Lama himself has provided us with a description of these temples, which are still held in high honour down to this day, and of the cult objects preserved in them[1]. One detail mentioned by the rGyal-rabs chronicle in its description of the building of Ra-mo-che strikes me as particularly interesting; namely that in choosing the symbols of this Buddhist temple the wishes of the Bon priests were taken into consideration. This circumstance, and the fact that at that time there was no open conflict between Buddhism and the native religion of Tibet, indicates very clearly that as far as the reign of King Srong-btsan sgam-po is concerned we can hardly speak of any actual 'imposition' of a new and foreign religion, because for a century after this the whole Tibetan people remained attached exclusively to the religion of their forbears. Despite all the laudatory legends, the interest of the king was obviously political: he made use of the new religion which had come into his purview because it facilitated the desired advance of culture. It is also significant that the king founded only temples, and no monasteries with living accommodation for monks. The Chinese Buddhist traveller Huei-ch'ao, who went to India and returned to China in 727 via Eastern Turkestan has nothing to say about Buddhism in Tibet. 'As far as the country of Tibet in the East is concerned,' he writes in his report of his travels,[2] 'there are no monasteries there, and the teachings of Buddha are unknown.'

During the reigns of the first two successors of the great Srong-btsan sgam-po, Indian Buddhist beliefs do not seem to have made much progress in Tibet, though—even in the absence of direct proof—we may assume that the dynasty itself and a minority amongst the influential aristocratic families showed a certain interest in the cultural significance of Buddhism. However, this particular period is most strongly marked by the foreign-political activity of the Government under the leadership of the powerful ministers or Majors Domo of the palace, who all came from the mGar family, who followed the policy already laid down by Srong-btsan of making Tibet into a decisive factor in

[1] Cf. A. Grünwedel, 'Die Tempel von Lhasa' published in the *Proceedings of the Heidelberg Academy*, Philosophical and Historical Class 1919.

[2] Cf. Walter Fuchs, 'Huei-ch'ao's Pilgerreise durch Nordwestindien und Zentralasien um 726', published in *SPAW* 1938, Berlin 1939, p. 443.

Asian politics. Tibet already had an important word to say in the affairs of West China, East Turkestan, and also Ferghâna, Gilgit and other more western countries. It also maintained important political contacts with the ten tribes of West Turks. But it was not until the reign of Mes-ag-tshoms (704–55)[1] that there was anything of importance to note in the history of religion. This king is reported to have founded a great number of new temples, and under his regime a number of further Buddhist texts, including the legends of Karmashataka and the famous 'Gold Lustre' Sûtra (Suvarnaprabhâsa), were added to the translated store of early Tibetan literature. The translations were made by the Tibetans Mûlakosha of Bran-ka and Jnânakumâra of gNyags. On the other hand, the messengers sent by the king to the Kailâsa district to invite the two Indian masters Buddhaguhya and Buddhashânti, who were engaged in meditation and conjuration there, returned without success.[2] All they brought back with them was five Mahâyâna-Sûtras, which they were taught on the spot and learned by heart so that they could be recorded when they arrived back.

For the moment therefore the attempt to establish a direct connection with Indian Buddhism had failed. As against this, the spiritual influence of other Buddhist countries became all the more marked. Like his forbear Srong-btsan, King Mes-ag-tshoms also brought home a Chinese princess of the house of T'ang, named Chin-ch'êng, whom he married in the year 710. The princess now introduced the habits and customs of Chinese civilization into the Land of Snows, and, in particular, she did a great deal for the cause of Buddhism. It was no doubt due to her influence that representatives of Chinese Buddhism, the Hva-shang (called Ho-shang in China) again began to play a role at the Tibetan court. Their co-operation was decisive in a certain incident which brought the Tibetans into contact with the Buddhism of East Turkestan, in which country the Indian religion could already look back on a history of several hundred years. Two Buddhist writings of the *ex eventu* type, *The Prophecies of Arhat Samghavardhana* and *Prophecies from the Land*

[1] Cf. the reports of the Tibetan chroniclers Bu-ston II, p. 185; Deb-ther sngon-po I, 20b, 6 *et seq.*; *Chronicle of the Fifth Dalai Lama* 30b, 4 *et seq.*; and Dpag-bsam ljong-bsang, p. 170.

[2] A description of these two masters is contained in Târanâtha's book *Geschichte des Buddhismus*, p. 222 *et seq*. However, obviously in error, this historian puts the incident of the rejected invitation to Tibet under the reign of the king's successor,

of Li (*Khotan*), provide interesting light on religious history, though, of course, they are not historical documents as such, but texts written in order to edify.[1] We learn from them that the Buddhism of inner Asia was subjected to a good deal of buffeting in those uneasy times; for instance, the monks of Khotan had to flee from their own country. They went first of all to Tshal-byi in the east, a southern border area of eastern Sinkiang, which was at that time already under Tibetan administration. The local Tibetan authorities did not dare to receive such a large number of foreign monks on their own initiative and they therefore asked for instructions from the central government. The princess Ching-ch'êng now interceded with the king on behalf of the fugitive monks, and she succeeded in obtaining food and clothing for them and even an invitation for them to come into Tibet proper. It is reported that no less than seven monasteries were built to house them and allow them to continue their religious life.

These fugitive monks from Khotan were later joined by other fugitive monks from such central Asian regions as Kashgar, Ferghâna, Bukhâra, Samarkand and Tokhâristân, who had at first sought safety in Gilgit (bru-sha). We may assume that the arrival of this mass of foreign monks greatly furthered the cause of Buddhism, though at the same time there is reason to believe that this mass influx led for the first time to a certain amount of Tibetan national resentment. The obviously growing influence of these monks on the royal counsels filled the powerful Tibetan noble families, and the ministers and Major Domo who came from their ranks, with mistrust and fear. They therefore looked for an opportunity of getting rid of the interlopers. About three years after the arrival of these unwanted strangers there was an epidemic of smallpox, (740-1) and one of its many victims was the Chinese princess. The Tibetan ministers now publicly interpreted the epidemic as a sign of the anger of the ancient gods, whose wrath, they said, must have been aroused by the incursion of the Buddhist monks. On this pretext they succeeded in securing the expulsion of the hated strangers, who had once again to take to the road. Their first asylum in this new pilgrimage was Gandhâra. The statement of the two 'Prophecies' that as a protest Tibetan monks voluntarily followed their foreign col-

[1] Both translated by F. W. Thomas in his book *Tibetan Literary Texts and Documents concerning Chinese Turkestan*, I, pp. 53 *et seq.* and pp. 77 *et seq.*

leagues into exile does not agree with the established historical fact that it was not until the reign of King Khri-srong lde-btsan that the first Tibetans, seven of them, were ordained as Buddhist monks.

The Deb-ther sngon-po and the chronicle of the Fifth Dalai Lama declare expressly that at that time no Tibetan had renounced the world and gone into a monastery. However, the happening itself is of great interest to us as affording information concerning the two-hundred-year struggle between Buddhism and the Royal House on the one hand, and the powerful noble families, and the Bon religion which they encouraged and developed as a counterweight to Buddhism, on the other. During the last years of the reign of Mes-ag-tshoms, and probably at the insistence of the Royal House, four Tibetans were sent to China under the leadership of Sang-shi in order to collect and bring back Buddhist writings. They succeeded in obtaining the support of some Chinese Ho-shang, and were thus given an honoured reception at the court of the Chinese Emperor. They also obtained permission to examine Chinese translations of the 'Gold Lustre', parts of the Vinaya (the collection of Regulations of the Order), and certain medical texts. When they arrived back—accompanied by a Chinese monk—they found that the king, their patron, was no longer in the land of the living, and that the general situation in Lhasa was very much less favourable to Buddhism than before they left.

After the death of King Mes-ag-tshoms, who—owing to the popular interpretation of the great epidemic of smallpox—had latterly been unable to do a great deal for the practical furtherance of Buddhism, but who had at least to some extent been able to protect the Buddhists, the ministers who belonged to the party of the Tibetan nobles took advantage of the minority of the late king's son, Khi-srong lde-btsan, to prepare for the final overthrow of Buddhism which was anathema to them not for religious but political reasons.[1] Such Chinese and Nepalese monks as still remained in the monastery of Ra-mo-che were now also sent away, and an enactment was issued suppressing Buddhism throughout the country. An attempt is reported to have been made to remove the famous Buddha image, first exhibited in Ra-mo-che and afterwards in the main temple, the Jo-khang of

[1] My version here follows generally the versions of Bu-ston (112b, 7 *et seq.*; cf. Obermiller II, p. 186 *et seq.*) and Pad-ma dkar-po (99a, 2 *et seq.*) which conform.

Srong-btsan sgam-po, and send it back to China, whence Wên-ch'êng, the incarnation of the White Târâ, had originally brought it. The pious legend has it that the men sent to remove it from the spot were unable to do so, and that they therefore contented themselves with burying it in the sand. However, soon after this failure two Tibetan ministers died unexpectedly, and their demise was put down to the evil effect of the buried image, which was now dug up and 'banished' to the town of sKyid-grong (Kyirong) not far from the Nepalese frontier. Two of the holy places built by King Mes-ag-tshoms were destroyed.

The two chief leaders of the anti-Buddhist reaction were sTag-ra klu-gong and Ma-zhang Khrom-pa-skyabs, of whom the latter seems to have been all-powerful during the minority of the young king. His motives in opposing Buddhism were not religious, but political; and this was true in general of the anti-Buddhism of the old Tibetan aristocracy. It should not be forgotten that the King of Tibet was only primus inter pares, and that the noble families were very jealous of their privileges. The alliance between the royal house and Buddhism threatened these privileges—hence their opposition. When the king had grown up he thoroughly justified the fears of the Tibetan aristocracy, and as the great Khri-srong lde-btsan he used Buddhism as they used the Bon-po—as a tool with which to establish his own absolutist regime. It is obvious that a weak ruler would himself have fallen under the influence of the new religion; and the most striking example of this danger was offered by the later King Ral-pa-can. Seen from this angle, the efforts of the aristocracy to limit the power of the new religion are not without a certain historical tragedy. In the end their efforts failed, for although the kingship was destroyed in the bitter struggles of the following centuries, the hated religion rose again from the ruins, and down to the present time it has maintained its influence and preserved its mark on the whole spiritual and political life of Tibet.

Those days which saw the beginning of the struggle of the Tibetan nobility and its ministers against Buddhism, no doubt also saw the development of the old native Bon religion from the primitive, barbaric people's belief whose acquaintance we made in the previous chapter, into a more sophisticated religion with higher claims based on a written literature. We learn from sTag-ra klu-gong, one of the two chief enemies of Buddhism, that he himself adopted 'the five golden stems of the Bon doctrine' and took care to see that they were appropriately disseminated.[1] It was natural that the Tibetan nobility should regard the old native religion as a suitable ally in their struggle against the new religion, but their ministers were shrewd enough to recognize the tremendous cultural dynamic of Buddhism, and to realize that the Bon religion in its then primitive state was no match for the spiritual and cultural powers of the foreign interloper which already illuminated and controlled enormous areas of Asia. They therefore decided that Buddhism must be defeated with its own weapons, and that the rival Bon religion must be given a literature and a philosophic-religious doctrinal edifice on Buddhist lines. This particular service was rendered to the Tibetan ministers by the Bon priests of Zhang-zhung, the country lying to the west of the Kailâsa area. Today Zhang-zhung is Tibetanized, but in those days it had its own language and its own political character. These were the men who were behind the mythical gShen-rab, the supposed founder of the systematized Bon religion. We shall deal with the later systematized Bon religion in a forthcoming chapter, but for the moment let it be said the Zhang-zhung, in common with the Western Himalaya countries in general, originally belonged to the same primitive religious substratum as old aminist-shamanist Tibet; but these countries were subject to infiltrations of various religions, such as Buddhism, Hinduism, and a number of beliefs from Western Asia, much earlier than was the case with their eastern neighbour; and, together with the already mentioned districts of Gandhâra and Udyâna, they became a positively classic basis for syncretism. There are, in fact, indications that an early and independent start was made in Zhang-zhung, and the neighbouring Bru-sha, with the systemization of the Bon religion with the assistance of Buddhist and Western Asiatic teachings,[2] and we can only hope that when the historical Bon-po literature becomes more readily available we shall obtain important information on this point. But at least it seems fairly certain that the tradition according to which the translation of the first Tibetan Bon texts was made from the language of Zhang-zhung is not without a sound basis. Although Zhang-zhung was not formally incorporated in the Tibetan Empire until the reign of Khri-srong lde-btsang, very close cultural and political relationships had been in existence for at least a hundred

[1] bLon-po bka'i thang-yig, 42a, 5.

[2] Cf. G. Tucci, *Il libro tibetano dei morti*, Milan 1949, p. 45.

years, and Srong-btsang sgam-po actually married a princess from this land.[1] There are also documentary sources such, as the biography of Padmasambhava, which tell us very clearly that the Tibetan ministers obtained their assistants from Zhang-zhung.

From the beginning the young king showed definite leanings towards Buddhism, but for a long time he was not in a position to further its development. For the time being—out of fear for his powerful Tibetan ministers—the texts that Sang-shi and his companions had brought back from China were kept secret, and even the king himself dared not study them except in private. An attempt was however made by Me-mgo and Pandit Ananta, with the assistance of the Chinese monk who had come to Tibet with the party, to translate the texts[2] but this proved impossible owing to the strict prohibition issued by the Tibetan minister Ma-zhang. In the meantime, Sang-shi, the leader of the party, and a certain young Tibetan named gSal-snang, who was an enthusiastic Buddhist, had compromised themselves so openly in the matter that the king thought it wise to send them away from the court for a while, and gSal-snang was appointed governor of the province of Mang-yul, bordering on Nepal.

Taking advantage of the opportunities afforded by his new post gSal-snang now made journeys to India, where he visited Mahâbodi, the place where Buddha had once found Enlightenment, and also the monastery of Nâlandâ, which was one of the chief centres of Buddhist scholarship at the time. In Nepal he met Shântirakshita, one of the most famous Indian teachers of the day, and a man who holds a considerable place in the history of Buddhist philosophy. His work *Tattvasamgraha* is still extant. Shântirakshita seems to have regarded the young Tibetan Governor as the ideal instrument for the definitive introduction of Buddhism into Tibet, and he expressed this opinion in a secret audience with the king, who was, however, very much afraid that the minister Ma-zhang might get wind of the affair, and therefore instructed his emissary to remain under cover for a while. In the meantime he called a meeting of those ministers who were his supporters. At this meeting one of the most prominent of them declared that the introduction of Buddhism into Tibet would be impossible so long as the power of Ma-zhang

[1] *Chronicle of the Fifth Dalai Lama*, 28a, 1.

[2] Obermiller (II, p. 187) has misunderstood this passage from Bu-ston.

remained; whereupon another 'the Old Man of 'Gos' ('Gos-rgan) offered to put Buddhism's main enemy in Tibet out of the way. This offer being accepted, he arranged for the official soothsayers to provide him with an oracle according to which the interests of the kingdom required that two prominent ministers should stay for a while in an underground burial place. When this was made known he volunteered to be one of the ministers if Ma-zhang would be the other. By means of a trick 'Gos escaped from the underground burial place, but the minister Ma-zhang was bricked in by his relentless enemies and perished.

Once the king had been freed from the leading strings of his Chief Minister in this very unBuddhist fashion, he was in possession of full political power and there was nothing more to prevent him from furthering the cause of Buddhism. The image of Buddha which had been banished from sKyid-grong was brought back in triumph to Lhasa, and an invitation was extended to Shântirakshita to visit Tibet. It is interesting to note that the opposition, which still existed in the State Council, insisted that the Indian master should first be approached to see whether he would accept such an invitation. With the co-operation of Kashmiri Ananda as interpreter it was discovered that the proposed guest had nothing to do with the disreputable magical practices of Nepal or with the obscene indulgences of the Vayrayâna, and that he was, in fact, a thoroughly virtuous man. This is the first indication we have of opposition to the eroticized Vajrayâna Buddhism by nationally conscious Tibetans, but it was an attitude which was to persist. Shântirakshita now came to Tibet and spent four months in one of the royal palaces teaching the doctrines of Buddhism, and his choice of subjects throws some light on his mentality. It is reported that he preached on the ten moral injunctions (dashashîla), the eighteen component parts of the individual (ashtâdasha dhâtvha), and the twelve parts of the Pratîtyasamutpâda, the genesis in dependence; in other words, on matters of moral discipline and on fundamental philosophical questions.

However, this is said to have disturbed the demons of Tibet, and they announced their displeasure through evil omens. In other words, the anti-Buddhist party adopted the same tactics as it had done in the days of Mes-ag-tshoms, and it actually succeeded in securing the temporary departure of Shântirakshita to Nepal. The king waited until grass had grown over the affair, but in the meantime he sent gSal-snang to China to fetch more Buddhist texts. When he deemed the moment favourable he invited the master again, but the latter had been somewhat intimidated by what had happened and he replied that as a learned philosopher he did not feel himself capable of wrestling with the Tibetan demons. According to Padma-dkar-po, the king's messenger was told by him: 'The spirits of Tibet are evil and will not allow the Buddhist way of life. In order to tame them invite the greatest sorcerer in Jambudvîpa (the whole Indian continent) master Padmasambhava instead.'

This suggestion was adopted and a delegation was sent to Padmasambhava. This strange holy man and sorcerer, who was to place his own particular stamp on a certain aspect of Lamaism, and with whom we shall deal in greater detail later, was obviously far more capable of dealing with the demons of Tibet than was the gentle scholar Shântirakshita. According to legend on his journey from the frontier district of Gung-thang, where he met the reception party sent by the king, to that spot on the northern bank of the Brahmaputra where he proposed to found a temple and a large monastery Padmasambhava subjugated all the evil spirits he met with. He was also obviously the right man to pick the most favourable astrological hour for the beginning of the building operations, to examine the site from the standpoint of its occult qualities, and to break the resistance of all the local hostile spirits. However, the laying of the foundation stone, and the whole building plan, is said by Bu-ston and Padma-dkar-po to have been the work of Shântirakshita. It was he who decided to copy the most famous of the Buddhist holy places of the time, the Buddhist temple of Otantapurî built by the King of Bengal, Gopâla, in Magadha. The result was the famous first monastery of Tibet, the 'incomparable, unchangeable holy place arisen through miraculous means', named bSam-yas for short. According to the most likely calculations it was probably completed in the year 787 after a building period of several years.[1]

An extremely valuable and undoubtedly contemporary description of the pile and of the opening ceremonies is provided in chapter eleven of the *Report on Kings*, a work of Padmasambhavan literature. It is this description which forms the basis for the account given in the royal annals *rGyal-rabs*.[2] It was obviously

[1] L. Petech, *A study on the Chronicles of Ladakh*, p. 70.
[2] B. Taufer, *T'oung Pao* (1908), pp. 19 *et seq.*

also Shântirakshita's idea to make the layout a symbolical representation of the universe according to Buddhist cosmography. The three-storied main temple with the Avalokiteshvara sanctuary was erected in the centre to represent the world mountain Sumeru; and as according to Buddhist ideas four different world continents (Dvîpa) surround the world mountain, one at each compass point, each with two small sub-continents, the main temple had another large and one small temple at each point of the compass. Then there was a temple for the sun and another for the moon, three holy places erected by the various queens, a number of auxiliary buildings, living accommodation for the priests, four Stûpas in white, red, black and blue respectively, and a special temple for the patron god of the whole, the god Pe-har. The whole layout was enclosed by a great wall. The artistic and symbolic details of the buildings and their decorations, and in particular the mural paintings, are of the greatest ethnographical and religious historical interest. On each of the three stories of the main temple the representations of the gods were uniformly carried out in Indian, Chinese and Tibetan style. The three doors of this main temple symbolized the three doors of salvation, whilst its six flights of steps symbolized the six 'perfections of wisdom' (prajnâpâramitâ). The story of the statue of the patron god Pe-har is also interesting. It was brought back as booty, together with a great deal of other temple loot, by the victorious troops of King Khri-srong from a sacked Meditational School of a subjugated Turkish people in the North, and thus it represents a further proof of the cultural influence exercised on Tibet by the peoples of the Turkish North.[1] When the building operations were at an end a great popular festival was organized at which both Shântirakshita and Padmasambhava jointly consecrated the temple. The priests present, the king, the members of his family and all the high officials sang specially composed festival songs, whose themes have come down to us through previously mentioned sources.

This monastery, the first and oldest in Tibet, still exists today, but in 1808 it was almost completely destroyed (apart from one or two buildings on the periphery) by fire, but was then rebuilt largely in the old style. But today even the buildings erected then are in a dilapidated condition, and the whole place is

[1] F. W. Thomas, *Tibetan Literary Text*, pp. 295 and 300; G. Tucci, *Tibetan Painted Scrolls*, pp. 734 *et seq.*; R. A. Stein, *BEFEO XLIV* (1951), p. 249.

threatened by the shifting sands which have turned this part of the Brahmaputra Valley into a Gobi in miniature. The well-known Tibet explorer Alexandra David-Neel gives us an account of a visit paid to bSam-yas.[1] 'The oasis Samye, already half-condemned to destruction, lies there and waits as the terrible sea of sand rises higher and higher around it, threatening to engulf it. Who knows whether it still dreams of its flourishing past, or has already reached the culmination of renunciation, and has abandoned all hope of a future? Sand has already laid its cerements almost to the peak of the hills which surround the monastery, and the sand dunes have already reached its entrances. All that still juts out above the sand is the pitiful tops of a one-time line of growing trees.'

After the foundation of bSam-yas twelve Indian monks of the Hînayâna sect of the Sarvâstivâdin were invited to come to the new Tibetan centre of Buddhism; the idea no doubt being to create a counterweight to the magical tendencies of Padmasambhava. It was now time to reinforce the many foreign monks at the new monastery with a contingent of monks of Tibetan nationality in order to fill up the new and magnificent quarters. As, however, it was not quite certain that the inhabitants of the Land of Snows had any talent at all for the spiritual life, the first seven volunteers who took it on themselves to make the experiment were known as sad mi mi bdun, or trial candidates. All seven stood the test with flying colours, and prominent amongst them was Vairocanarakshita of Pa-gor, usually known briefly as Vairocana, who was to make a particular name for himself in the translation of Buddhist texts into the Tibetan language. The seven Tibetan candidates for the Buddhist priesthood were all ordained by Shântirakshita, and, according to Buddhist custom, this was reflected in the spiritual names they now adopted, all of which had 'rakshita' as the second part of their names to record their relationship with the revered Indian philosopher. The foundation of bSam-yas and the ordination of the first seven native monks must be regarded as an event of far-reaching importance for the religious history of Tibet. Since then, in fact, the teachings from India have represented a factor not to be abstracted from the life of Tibet.

[1] *Heilige und Hexer*, p. 149.

CHAPTER III

PADMASAMBHAVA AND PADMAISM

It is advisable that we should now interrupt our examination of the religious historical development of Tibet at the time of the universal monarchy, when the basis for all later epochs was laid, and pause to take a closer look at the personality of Padmasambhava and the school inaugurated by him in Indian, and, above all, Tibetan Buddhism. There can be no doubt about the historical importance of this strange Indian master, though those investigators who call him 'the father of Lamaism' and leave it at that are probably going rather too far, because, as we have seen, at the time in question, other schools of Indian (Shântirakshita) and of Chinese Buddhism were also active in the formation of Tibetan religious life. However, Padmasambhava undoubtedly exercised a very powerful influence on this development and he founded a special religious tradition which has remained alive down to the present day, and has, despite the interacting relationships with other Lamaist sects, maintained its own specific features.

Padmasambhava received his own spiritual formation in that centre of syncretism in North-West India to which we have already referred, and whose great importance must again be stressed at this point. The Indian North-West Frontier has always been the gateway into India for foreign peoples and foreign spiritual influences. In the ancient days the Arian Indians themselves penetrated into what was to become their five-streamed homeland through the lands of the North-West. And later on the influx of peoples which so disturbed the peaceful life of the Ganges continent both politically and spiritually flowed in through the same way. Alexander the Great and his successors the Greek kings of Eastern Iran marched along the same roads, and were followed by inner-asiatic peoples like the Saka, the Kushan and the Hephthalites. And finally came the Mohammedan conquerors to whom the Buddhism of India, already internally decayed, now succumbed.

But even more important than these political upheavals was the constant influx of outside spiritual and religious ideas, which turned Eastern Iran, Udyâna, Gandhâra, Bru-sha (Gilgit), Zhang-zhung, which is Tibetanized today, and Kashmir into a real cockpit of divergent religious beliefs, a circumstance which naturally had its effect on what was at the time the most influential and widespread Indian religion, Buddhism, and which we have already noted when referring to the Graeco-Indian art of Gandhâra. Research into these questions is still going on, and by no means all possibilities have as yet been exhausted in order to interpret the puzzling features of these areas satisfactorily. The big spiritual and religious influences operating in the eighth century in the days of Padmasambhava were Helenism in the widest sense, the influence of Greek scientific theories and of the gnostic systems, the antique mystery religions, and then the national Iranian religion both in its orthodox and in its heretical zurvanist forms, and, of course, Islam too, and those primitive beliefs of the Western Himalaya districts, whose Tibetan sister beliefs we have already met as the Bon religion.

In addition, Manichaeanism was a particularly important factor; that world religion founded by the Babylonian Mani in the third century from the christianized gnosis, which swept in an extraordinarily short space of time to North Africa in the one direction and over Iran, West and East Turkestan to China.[1] We are interested here only in the history of Eastern Manichaeanism. Although its basic teachings did not change, yet in its lower and more popular reaches it was open to the influence of those ideas held by the converted Eastern peoples. The procedure adopted by Mani of using the religious and mythological language of whatever people he was trying to convert; that is to say, addressing the Christians as a Christian, the Persians as a Persian, and thus the Indian and inner-asiatic Buddhists as a Buddhist,

[1] It is impossible to list all the enormously voluminous literature concerning Manichaeanism here. There are, however, two works by H. H. Schaeder which are excellent as general introductions to the study of Manichaeanism, 'Urform und Fortbildungen des manichäischen Systems', *Lectures of the Warburg Library* 1924–5, Leipzig 1927, and 'Der Manichäismus nach neuen Funden und Forschungen' in *Morgenland*, Vol. 28, (Oriental Contributions to the Idea of Salvation). The most important summary of recent times is Henri-Charles Puech, *Le Manichéisme*, Paris 1949.

facilitated the penetration of Manichaeanism everywhere and favoured the spread of syncretism. An exact analysis of the influence exerted on later Buddhism by Mani and his teachings, and by his successors in the East has not as yet been made, and detailed practical correspondences have still to be proved. But the assumption that there were connections is, in view of the general spiritual and historical situation in the world at the time, highly likely. It only needs to be recalled that Mani himself, prior to his decisive appearance at the court of the Sasanid King Shapur I, had carried out a highly successful missionary tour to India; in other words, especially into the Iranian-Indian frontier districts and the Punjab.[1] G. Tucci, a cautious and far-seeing investigator, regards the teachings of Âdibuddha and the five Tathâgatas which developed from it (the so-called Dhyâni-Buddhas): Akshobhya, Vairocana, Ratnasambhava, Amitâbha and Amoghasiddhi, as quite comparable with the Manichaean Father of Light and its five light eons.[2] Quite generally, the great significance of the role of light and of rays of light in Mahâyâna and Vajrayâna should not be overlooked in this connection. In particular the figure of Buddha, 'immeasurable light', Amitâbha, with his paradise Sukhâvatî, regarded as being in the West, strongly suggests the influence of Iranian religious ideas. Originally conceived in the spirit of Zoroastrianism, Amitâbha's character could readily be incorporated by Manichaeanism in its mythological identifications. In addition there is a luxuriant symbolism of numbers and a special preference for dogmatic rows of five, which are both specifically typical of Manichaeanism, and which proved of significance in the Kâlacakra system (Wheel of Time) which arose after Padmasambhava's time in India and Tibet. For example, I do not believe that the division of the Kâlacakratantra of this doctrine as we know it in five books is a mere coincidence. In view of the great importance of this whole question it can only be regretted that so far there has been no detailed treatment of the spread of Manichaeanism to the East.

The possibility of influence from such spiritual forces as we have just briefly described must not be left out of consideration when dealing with such figures as Padmasambhava. The documentary reports about the famous Magi himself, as preserved in

[1] H. H. Schaeder in *Gnomon* 1933, pp. 348 *et seq.*

[2] *Mélanges chinois et bouddhiques*, III, pp. 345 *et seq.*; Tucci, *Il libro tibetano dei morti*, pp. 45 *et seq.*

Tibetan literature in the writings of the sect rNying-ma-pa, or 'the ancients', which claims him, and as provided in resumés of church history, reveal an almost inextricable mingling of legendary and historical happenings, and contain many contradictory accounts. It would seem, for example, that particularly in the glorification of Padmasambhava by the rNying-ma-pa sect, legends attaching to other Tantrist Magis have crept in, and it would take a good deal of careful research before the various threads could be disentangled.

First of all we propose to give a general sketch of the life of the master according to the historian Pad-ma dkar-po,[1] supplemented in individual cases by material from the rNying-ma texts, the biography of Padmasambhava, which is available in numerous versions, and, finally, the *Collection of Five Reports* (consisting of the reports concerning the demons, kings, queens, translators, panditas and ministers).

The very birth of the Holy Man is said to have been miraculous, and the sources describe how a lotus bud grew up in the estuary of the Indus, and how when the bud unfolded the future Holy Man was sitting there in the form of an eight-year-old boy. Let us recall at this point that this form of miraculous birth is the same as that through which the followers of Amitâbha appear in the paradise of the West, and Amitâbha is, of course, the spiritual father of Padmasambhava. King Indrabhûti of Udyâna, himself a great Tantrist, heard of this marvel and adopted the lad as his own son. Incidentally, this king is the one the sources refer to as the 'Great' or Indrabhûti the Elder. Later this king withdrew completely from public life in order to devote himself to his mystic tendencies, leaving his adopted son to rule in his place. Just like Gautama Buddha, Padmasambhava now married, and then left his family and abandoned his kingdom in order to become a monk and to study first of all the teachings of 'the Small Vehicle', and then the magic lessons of the Tantras. Like many other Buddhist holy men, he wandered restlessly throughout India and the adjacent Buddhist countries, and he is reported to have come into contact with followers of the Bon religion, a suggestion which is interesting from our point of view. He also studied numerous sciences and particularly secret teachings from numerous masters.

A favourite spot for obtaining transcendent knowledge was the

[1] Fol. 62b, 4 *et seq.*

places of interment, and he began by visiting Shîtavana, or 'the cold grove', where he meditated and devoted himself to necromancy. The teachings were transmitted, as with other Tantrics, by initiation goddesses known as Dâkinîs, and there were a very great number of them haunting the burial places, turning them into a real Witches' Sabbath, and affording an excellent example of the psychological horrors of this sort of initiation. The biography tells us that 'rays of light like sunshine came from the eyes of some, others rode on buffaloes with a noise of thunder, others held knives, stared with eyes like grains, held piles of skulls, rode on tigers, carried human corpses, rode on the backs of lions, ate entrails and rode on the backs of garuda birds, some with fiery lances rode on jackals, several with five heads conjured up a sea of blood, some had innumerable hands and carried many different kinds of creatures, some of them held their own decapitated heads in their hands, others held their torn-out hearts in their hands . . .' And so on. As a result of all these horrifying experiences the Magi learnt the doctrines of the eight Dâkinîs known as Kairima. After each secret initiation he was given a new initiatory name, a custom which makes it very difficult to gain a clear picture of the personal relationship in this whole literature.

After this came conjurations at the eight interment places of the four winds and the places between them, where he succeeded in looking into the faces of Dâkinîs of unearthly wisdom with the leading goddess of the initiation, Vajravarâhî, at their head, whereupon all the great planets became subject to him; in other words, he made himself master of the cosmic knowledge of heaven. Then he studied the 'triple yoga' in India, and also philosophy, logic and the secret sciences once again. In the end he obtained the immortal Vajra body. In the Indian kingdom of Za-hor he now performed miracles and won one of the five (earthly) chief Dâkinîs reserved for him. This was Mandâravâ, the daughter of the king of that country, and henceforth she accompanied him wherever he went.[1] The rNying-ma-pa literature gives us a description of this woman. When he returned to Udyâna, the life he and his Shakti led aroused the ire of King Indrabhûti, who had them both burnt at the stake. But the fire turned miraculously into a lake from which a lotus bud grew up, and inside the blossom were seated Padmasambhava and Mandâravâ unharmed. In India

[1] Cf. Grünwedel, 'Padmasambhava and Mândâravâ' in the *Zeitschrift der Deutschen Morgenländische Gesellschaft*, 1898, pp. 447 *et seq.*

he once again defeated heretical teachings, i.e. Brahmanical teachings, in magic contests. In Nepal he meditated in the rocky grotto of Yang-le-shod, a holy place which is still held in high honour today; and when demonic forces tried to overthrow him he defeated them with his magic dagger (vajrakîla) and won the highest perfection, named Mahâmudrâ, or the Great Symbol.

It was then that the invitation of the King of Tibet, Khri-srong lde-btsan, to come and overthrow the demons of that land reached him, demons which were, as we have seen, opposing the introduction of Buddhism. He accepted the invitation, went to Tibet and overthrew the demons one by one, obtaining an oath from them that henceforth they would serve only the cause of Buddha. As one example which will do for all the others, let us quote the overthrow of the Bon mountain god Yar-lha sham-po, as recorded in the biography:[1] 'When he thereupon journeyed to the valley Sham-po, the god Sham-po took on the form of a white Yak standing on the side of a hill. From mouth and nose whirled snow storms. But the master seized him by the muzzle with the Mudrâ of the iron hook, bound him with a noose, and placed the holy iron shackles on him. And when he had defeated him by means of the Mudrâ bell and subjugated both body and soul, the god gave his heart's blood and was bound by an oath and was given a treasure (holy writings) to guard.'

This was the often repeated method used by the Buddhist Magi to overthrow the old gods of the native religion and subdue them to his own purpose, taking them as 'protectors of religion' into the enormously enlarged syncretic pantheon of Lamaism. As we have already seen, the demons of the site on which the bSam-yas was to be built were subdued in the same way; in other words, Padmasambhava succeeded in breaking the resistance of the resentful and suspicious Tibetan nobles. But despite all the triumphant boasting of the old reports, we see this opposition making itself clearly felt again and again. Particular disapproval was aroused amongst the Tibetan nobles by the fact that the master persuaded the king to give him one of his wives. This woman was Ye-shes 'tsho-rgyal, who counts as the fifth of the special Dâkinîs of Padmasambhava. In addition to Mandâravâ there were two Nepalese, Kâlasiddhi and Shâkyadevî, and a woman from the Himalaya district (Mon) named bKra-shis khye 'dren. Mandâravâ and the Tibetan are often portrayed to

[1] 223a, 5 *et seq.*

the left and right of the master in the religious pictures of the rNying-ma-pa sect.

The legendary biography naturally gives Padmasambhava the chief credit for the conversion of the king and his people, and makes most of the Indian monks and the newly ordained Tibetan monks subject to him and his teachings. Naturally, there is no shortage of miracles in Tibet. Padmasambhava turned barren land into fruitful land and diverted the river Brahmaputra into an underground cavern. Water conjured in a magic fashion from the land of the gods for the king to refresh himself was not unnaturally regarded with some suspicion by his ministers. For future times and future generations, who would have sufficient understanding, Padmasambhava hid mystic texts, so-called 'treasures' (gter-ma) in all parts of the country. Finally after long and beneficial activity on behalf of Tibet he took his departure, let himself be accompanied by the king and his court as far as Gungthang on the Nepalese frontier, and then flew from there into the south-west country of the Râkshasa demons in order to convert them. According to the Lepcha version, he flew through the air on the back of the magic winged horse Valâha.[1]

It is extremely difficult, as we have already pointed out, to extract those things which are indisputably confirmed as historical fact from the morass of legend, including mutually contradictory versions. The first authentic date we can accept is that of the arrival of Padmasambhava in Tibet and his co-operation in the founding of the bSam-yas monastery. We may also assume with safety that he belonged, at least spiritually, to the previously mentioned circle of syncretic Buddhists in Udyâna, the land of the Dâkinîs. The appearance of the older and the younger Indrabhûti in the legend must be regarded as typical in this connection, and it suggests relationships between Padmasambhava and the group of Udyânist Siddhas, including apart from Indrabhûti—from whom incidentally a Vajrayânist work has been preserved[2]—his sister Lakshmîmkarâ in particular and her teacher Kambala, whose biographies are preserved in the work concerning the eighty-four Mahâsiddhas.

It is particularly difficult to decide just what is the spiritual property of Padmasambhava because of the circumstances already

[1] Grünwedel, *Mythologie*, p. 55.

[2] Jnânasiddhi, issued by B. Bhattacharya in *Two Vajrayâna Works*, Gaekwad Oriental Series No. 74, Baroda 1929,

mentioned that after the initiation into each new teaching a different name is adopted, with the result that not only in legend but also in church history he appears under various names. For example, in the historic works of Târanâtha, he is called Padmavajra, Padmâkara and also Saroruha. In other words he bears names to which the story of his miraculous birth in a lotus bud is etiologically attached. Another important circumstance is that the *Report of the Translators and Panditas* belonging to his sect was translated, according to the transcript, from the language of Udyâna,[1] whilst other texts of his successors were translated from the idiom of the neighbouring Bru-sha. Obviously, in the syncretic religion which it was clearly his intention to found, and which we call 'Padmaism', the languages of Udyâna and Brusha were intended to fill the same role as sacred church languages as Sanscrit played for Buddhism in general, and as—as we shall see later—the languages of Zhang-zhung played in the literature of the later and systematized Bon religion.

In the chronological list of masters and teachers in Târanâtha's *Mine of Diamonds* Padmasambhava is recorded as the pupil of Buddhajnânapâda;[2] that is to say as pupil of the same master whose other pupils Buddhaguhya and Buddhashânti, the Tibetan King Mes-ag-tshom tried in vain to invite from the Kailâsa district to Tibet. This information may be regarded as chronologically probable. On the other hand, according to the information given in the same book,[3] he was a pupil of Anangavajra, who is also known to us as an author; and Anangavajra is said in his turn to have been ordained by Mahâpadmavajra. Padmasambhava, described here as the smaller or younger Padmavajra, handed the appropriate mystical teachings on to the middle Indrabhûti, i.e. the same king who, according to the legendary tradition, at first tried to burn Padmasambhava and his Shakti at the stake, but then let himself be converted. Indrabhûti handed it to Jâlandhari, and that teacher to Krishnacârin. This list of teachers also has an inner probability in so far as Krishnacârin already had contact with the Kâlacakra system, which came to India only in the second half of the tenth century.

The evidence concerning the length of Padmasambhava's stay in Tibet differs. Whereas the biography makes it clear that the rNying-ma-pa regard the master's stay in Tibet as extending into the reign of King Khri-srong's son and second successor Mu-tig

[1] Laufer, *Roman einer tibetanischen Königin*, p. 3. [2] P. 99. [3] P. 43.

btsan-po Sad-ma-legs (798-817), the historian Sum-pa mkhan-po, basing his statement on the valuable work 'Yig-tshang rnying-pa' or archive records, declares that Padmasambhava remained in Tibet for eighteen months, though the followers of the sect which goes back to him believe that he stayed in Tibet for fifty years, a belief which is however hardly credible.[1]

We have already pointed out that Padmasambhava obviously made an attempt to found a religion of his own, and this attempt was to some extent successful, because 'Padmaism', the doctrine of the sect rNying-ma-pa which honours him, or U-rgyan-pa (U-rgyan is the Tibetan form of the name Udyâna), has always held its own specific and rather independent place in Lamaism despite internal relations with other trends. But the aims of Padmasambhava, or 'the Second Buddha' as his followers called him—to the great displeasure of the other Lamaist sects—could not be carried out in their entirety. Even the transference of parts of the Buddha legend to the story of Padmasambhava, as we have previously seen done, was not entirely effective, though this action was an indication of the universalist claim of Padmaism, just as it was evidence of the universalist claim of the later Bon-po when they equally unscrupulously annexed the legendary career of Buddha for the founder of the systematized Bon religion, gShen-rab. The method which the Magi adopted in order to convert Udyâna and the surrounding eight countries may also be quoted as indicating the syncretic universalism of Padmasambhava.

Grünwedel translated the reports according to the version of the biography in his possession, and we quote here as typical the story of the conversion of the land lying in the south, west and south-west.[2] 'To the south side, in the land of Parvatadvîpa, were sixteen million towns. The people living there ate meat, so their aim was constantly to kill game. Power was in the hands of Yama, whilst the tribe of the Tinashrî ruled as king. As these people had a liking for the Dharma of the black Manjushrî, when Padma came into their land as Guru he turned the doctrinal wheel of the good and angry Manjushrî, and met with success in this way. After that he went to the west, into the land of Nâgapotadvîpa (just previously called Kapita). There were ten million big towns there. There was also a wood with many

[1] dPag bsam ljon bzang, pp. 125, 383.

[2] *Mythologie des Buddhism*, p. 51.

flowers, like lotus blossom. The power was in the hands of the Nâga, whilst the tribe of the Dharmalakosha ruled as king. They had a liking for the teachings of the good and angry Padma (pâni). When the Guru Padmasambhava came into this country he turned the doctrinal wheel of the good and evil Avalokiteshvara, and met with great success in this way. Then he went to the south-west, into the land of the Râkshasas. The people there lived from three kinds of flesh: human flesh, horse flesh and dog flesh. Their god was Satyaghna; their king Dashakantha of Lankâ. They honoured Vishnu as god. For them he turned the "Wheel of Time" (Kâlacakra) of the conversion of Vishnu, and met with great success thereby.'

The jungle of cults and systems conjured up here—to which Kâlacakra has been anachronistically added—is as characteristic for Padmaism as the method used to convert various peoples by exploiting their own current beliefs. This method is strikingly reminiscent of that adopted by Manichaeanism, which, without changing the core of its own teachings, nevertheless took the local religious concepts and the names of local gods to present its own great mythos as from the doctrines and the mythology of the peoples and of the religious communities which it desired to win over.

As far as the actual doctrinal content of the Padmaist religion is concerned, it is likely to take a great deal of time and effort before it is possible to separate the doctrines of Padmasambhava himself from those which subsequently sprang up within the framework of the sects he founded. It must be pointed out though that this development, which took place over the centuries, continued in a logical form congenial to the original, if one can use such a term with regard to a doctrine which, despite one or two undeniably profound ideas, is psychologically more interesting than sympathetic. Since the days of Padmasambhava himself, who boasted that he was a greater necromancer than Buddha, blatant magic, and usually black-magic, rites take far too important a position, whilst at the same time the eroticized Vajrayâna was also very prominent. In this connection we must remember the great role played by the Dâkinîs, who were not merely spirits of mystical inspiration, but who actively assisted in the discovery of the texts, often in secret writings and secret languages, which had been hidden in various places such as holes in and under rocks, and in religious buildings by Padmasambhava, and even by the original Buddha, in order to facilitate the salvation of later generations. The discoverers of such treasures (gter-ma) were, in the course of time, to play an ever increasing role not only in the rNying-ma-pa, but also elsewhere.

A passage in the *Report on Kings*, which I would like to quote here,[1] gives a very instructive picture of the magic arts as practised under Padmasambhava in newly converted Tibet:

> 'When under the government of the religious King Khri-srong lde-btsan,
> The Master Padmasambhava was invited,
> He blessed the whole Tibetan earth.
> When he had shed the heart's blood of the evil demons,
> He transmitted mystic initiations to eight spiritual sons,
> And to the King and his people.
> Showing them actually the face of the host of gods.
> And giving them certain incantations for the gods, and secret lessons.
> In mChims-phu and many other settlements
> He let them devote themselves individually three years to conjuration.
> And when signs of perfection became clear,
> Âkashagarbha could ride on rays of sunshine,
> Buddhajnâna could bury his magic dagger in the rocks.
> The neighing of the horses of rGyal-ba mchog-dbyangs echoed through the ten world parts.
> (The Queen) mKhar-chen mtsho-rgyal called the corpses of dead men to life;
> Shrîjnâna subjugated the Ma-mo female demons;
> Shrîsimha made slaves of gods and spirits;
> Vairocana was blessed with the eye of wisdom;
> The ruler, King (Khri-srong) obtained the gift of perfect meditation;
> gYu-sgra snying-po was blessed with the highest understanding;
> Jnânakumâra wielded the highest magic power;
> rDo-rje bdud-'joms found like the wind no obstacle;
> Ye-shes-dbyangs went to the place of the Dâkinîs;
> Sog-po lha-dpal seized wild animals by the neck;

[1] Chapter 10, Fol. 30a, 5 *et seq.*

dPal-gyi dbang-phyug killed with certainty with a magic dagger
lDar-ma rtse-mang obtained the magic words of eternal memorability;
Shrîkûta of sKa-ba knew the thoughts of all others;
dPal-seng of Shud-pu caused a stream to flow upwards;
rGyal-ba'i blo-gros turned an enchanted corpse into gold;
Khye'u-chung-lo caught the birds of the heavens;
Dran-pa nam-mkha brought wild yaks from the North;
O-bran dbang-phyug moved like a fish in water;
rMa-thog rin-chen took the rocks as food;
dPal-gyi rdo-rje was not hampered by the rocks of the mountains;
Langs-'gro dkon-mchog hurled great lightnings like arrows;
And rGyal-ba byang-chub remained in the air with legs crossed under him.'

We have here a really typical list of magical properties and parapsychological phenomena, and although none of the Tibetan sects can be said to be completely free of such things, they are particularly familiar to the rNying-ma-pa. There is the phenomenon of levitation and that of de-materialization (of a rock, for example), and, of course, the restoring of the dead to life, and various necromantic practices of a nature horrible enough to satisfy the most robust appetite. The 'Rite of the rising corpse' (ro-langs) does not belong to the original stock of the Bon-shamanists, but made its way into the Land of Snows with the Tantric magicians of India. The followers of other sects also adopt such practices, as we know from the biography of Nâ-ro-pa, the spiritual father of the bKa-rgyud-pa sect, with which we shall deal in a later chapter.[1] Alexandra David-Neel who has dealt in her book *Heilige und Hexer* with many parapsychological phenomena which have come to her notice, as well as others taken from Tibetan literature, also gives a description of the Ro-langs rite:[2] 'The magician is locked in a dark room with the corpse. In order to raise the dead the magician must lie on the corpse mouth to mouth, constantly repeating the same magic formula, without ever once allowing his thoughts to stray. After a few moments the corpse moves, rises up and attempts to flee.

[1] Padma dkar-po, Fol. 80a.
[2] *Heilige und Hexer*, pp. 161 *et seq.*

The magician must then hold him very tight in his arms. The dead man struggles more and more violently, and whilst he follows these movements the magician must not take his mouth from the mouth of the corpse. Ultimately the tongue of the corpse hangs out, and this is the decisive moment. The magician must seize it and tear it out, and when this is done the corpse falls back motionless once again. The magician now carefully dries and preserves the tongue of the corpse and it becomes a powerful magic weapon.' To supplement this account it must be added that should the magician fail in this rite he himself falls victim to the demon-possessed corpse and is killed by it.

No less horrible, but unlike Ro-langs (which is a black-magic rite undertaken for selfish reasons) not without profounder psychological significance is the ceremony of gCod—the 'cutting off', namely of human egoism. The ritual text of this was drawn up by the rNying-ma-Lama kLong-chen rab-'byams-pa (1308-63) and made known to us by Evans-Wentz from the translation of the Tibetan Kazi Davasamdup (Zla-ba bsam-'grub).[1] Its practical execution is once again described to us by Alexandra David-Neel in her book. The gCod has been very appropriately called a mystic drama with one actor, the conjuring mystic himself; and only during the course of the proceedings is he joined by unearthly beings and demons as created by his imagination. The ceremony is invariably performed in a lonely and eerie place, and this for a good reason; perhaps on the south side of the Himalayas, in a jungle, or—as Padmasambhava records—at interment places, and, in general, in any place the imagination of the Tibetan peoples with evil spirits. Certain magic equipment is necessary for the ceremony as laid down in the ritual: a small double drum (damaru), a horn made from a human skull (rkang-gling), a bell, and a symbolic tent which has to be erected in a certain prescribed fashion. First thing in the morning the adept celebrates the so-called 'white sacrificial repast'; in the day the 'mixed', in the evening the 'black', and during the night the terrible 'red'. Whilst the mystic is engaged with the black repast he collects all evil Karma, all spiritual pollution, sickness, evil, sin and suffering everywhere in the world; and during the red repast he offers his body as a compensation for a selfish life and actions over the aeons to the voracious demons he has conjured up. Similar to the process of 'awakening' of a Mandala or a magic

[1] Evans-Wentz, *Yoga und Geheimlehren Tibets*, pp. 201 *et seq.*

circle, a goddess, creature of his imagination, now rises from his head and then cuts it off. The body is then cut into pieces and offered as a sacrifice to the accompaniment of the following words: 'The day has come on which my debt must be paid; and therefore I offer up as a sacrifice this so beloved and so cossetted body of mine for destruction. I give my body to the hungry, my blood to the thirsty, my skin to the naked, and my bones as fuel to those who suffer cold. I give my good fortune for the unfortunate ones, and may the breath of my life restore the dying. Shame on me if I draw back from this sacrifice! Shame on all who hesitate to accept it!' The object which the aspirant must attain—without even a hint from his Guru—through the constant repetition of this ceremony (during which some all too imaginative adepts are said to have lost their reason) is the not-thought but experienced recognition that all the gods and demons are merely products of his own spirit; that under certain circumstances they can be as 'real' in their effects as a tree or a stone, but that they are also, just as these, only of a relative reality and in the last resort, empty or void, (shûnya). We can therefore regard the ritual of gCod as a practical demonstration of the old philosophical Mahâyâna teachings of the Indian father of the church Nâgârjuna.

Similar ideas and intentions are at the bottom of the texts which a Lama whispers into the ear of a dying man in order to prepare him for his wandering (which is generally regarded as lasting for forty-nine days) in the between state (Antarabhâva, Tibetan Bar-do), and if possible to bring him to recognize the highest enlightenment, which is symbolized by a radiant light; or, at least, if this is not possible, to help him to obtain a favourable rebirth and to prevent his re-entering the world through bad 'womb gateways'. In this case too, the person concerned is to recognize that all the gods, both mild and terrible, with which he comes in contact, and the whole death judgment with the death god Yama and the two spirits who examine the respective weights of the good and bad deeds represented in the shape of white and black gravel, are no more than pictures projected from within him, and of merely relative reality, mere symbols which provide the adept with information concerning the direction of his path after death.

The concept of Bar-do is common to all Tibetan sects, but each sect has its own special doctrines concerning the experiences after death. Those teachings so far known to us are taken from the Bar-do thos-grol (salvation from Bar-do even when a mere recital of the text is listened to),[1] and a gTer-ma, or 'treasure', a work of the rNying-ma school.

Obviously, there is often a good deal of deceit practised in the finding of the 'treasures' containing rNying-ma doctrinal writings hidden here, there and everywhere by Padmasambhava, or even by the Âdibuddha himself—a procedure quite familiar in India, and even earlier in Udyâna. The monkish orders hostile to the Padmasambhava sect, constantly accused the 'treasure finders' of having slipped in texts of their own containing highly doubtful teachings. According to the *Crystal of Doctrinal Opinions*, after the master had left Udyâna a deceitful Brahman posed as a second Padmasambhava, wearing the typical robes of the U-rgyan Za-hor-ma, which the authentic master can be seen wearing in all religious pictures, and spreading false rNying-ma teachings.[2] The author himself, Chos-kyi nyi-ma, repudiates this report, saying that it was put into the world merely in order to discredit the rNying-ma sect. But Sum-pa mkhan-po[3] also knows of such a swindler, who, after the departure of the real Padmasambhava, and on the assumption that he was dead, adopted corrupt teachings, hid them in bSam-yas and other places, thus ensuring their dissemination.

As far as we can see today, apart from the 'discoverer' of Padmasambhava's biography, O-rgyan gling-pa (born in 1323), the Lama Gu-ru Chos-dbang (1212-73) played an important role in these treasure hunts and in the subsequent development of the rNying-ma teachings. In the year 1232 and again in 1256 he discovered important texts; and, according to Chos-kyi nyi-ma, there are even Lamaist authors who regard him as the real organizer of the sect, and credit him with the introduction of the U-rgyan Za-hor-ma robes. Writers belonging to the orthodox church of the later Dalai Lamas can, generally speaking, find little good in him. Sum-pa mkhan-po declares that during the day he would sit in black monkish habit and hood drinking intoxicating liquor, and that at night he would disport himself with females, describing this behaviour as 'the ten-day sacrifice'. Sum-pa mkhan-po also charges him with other impure practices,

[1] Evans-Wentz, *Das tibetanische Totenbuch*, 5th ed., Zurich 1935. The new translation by G. Tucci is scientifically preferable: *Il libro tibetano dei morti*, with a valuable introduction.

[2] *Journal of the Asiatic Society of Bengal*, 1882, p. 9; *Zeitschrift der Deutschen Morgenlandische Gesellschaft*, 1898, p. 448.

[3] P. 392.

2 Stone offerings to the Tree Spirits

3 Assembly of a Lama Procession before the main temple of Lhasa

finally quoting from a work of the school of the great Bu-ston refusing heresy, which says:

> 'The representative of the Devil known as Chos-dbang
> Discovered evil writings which he claimed to have come from Him (Padmasambhava)
> And invented many corrupt teachings.'[1]

According to the rNying-ma version, Buddhist doctrine comprises nine sections, or 'Vehicles', of which the first three are regarded as from 'the Body of Change' and were proclaimed by the historic Buddha. They are: 1. the Vehicle of the Disciples (Shrâvaka), who follow the preachings of Buddha and attain the state of an Arhat; 2. the Vehicle of Pratyeka-buddha, those who recognize the teachings for themselves but are not in a position to preach them to the world; and 3. the Vehicle of the Bodhisattvas, who follow the teachings of moral perfection (pâramitâ). The next three are ascribed to 'the Body of Pleasures in Heavenly Paradises' (sambhoga-kâya), to the Buddha Vajrasattva, and contain in the Kriyâ- (4), Upâya- (5) and Yoga Vehicles (6) the lessons of the subordinate tantras with their ritualism and their not as yet eroticized doctrines. Then come the three highest Vehicles, revelations of 'the Body of Doctrine' (dharma-kâya), of Âdibuddha Samantabhadra, whose three sections Mahâyoga- (7), Anuyoga- (8), and Atiyoga (9) Vehicles, comprise the teachings of the highest, the so-called Anuttarayoga Tantras. The followers of the important sub-sect of the rDsogs-chen-pa, so called after their monastic centre rDsogs-chen, which lies in the north of Tibet on the edge of the grass waste, and is the most important centre of occult study for the Padmasambhava sect, are devoted in particular to the ninth Vehicle. Further important and still existing centres of rNying-ma teachings are rDo-rje-brag and sMin-grol-gling, to the south of Lhasa on the right bank of the River Brahmaputra.

[1] P. 394. Concerning the gTer-ma in general see in particular Tucci, *Tibetan Painted Scrolls*, pp. 109 *et seq.*, and p. 258.

CHAPTER IV

RELIGIOUS STRUGGLES OF THE EIGHTH AND NINTH CENTURIES

Having dealt with the special form of Lamaism founded as Padmaism in the eighth century we can now return to the main line of development, which we followed as far as the founding of the great monastery bSam-yas and the ordination of the first Tibetan monks by Shântirakshita. Thereafter the aim of the new religion and its followers was to give Buddhism, which had been introduced from outside with pomp and ceremony, deep and lasting roots amongst the Tibetan people. For this it was necessary to invite further Indian masters of religion to Tibet, and also to arrange for the translation of the holy writings of Buddhism into Tibetan on a really big scale. But, above all, it was necessary to choose the most suitable amongst Tibetan young men of lively minds and keen intelligence to assist the foreign monks in their work, as otherwise its success would be problematical. The leading personality amongst the Tibetan translators, the so-called Lo-tsâ-ba, was Vairocanarakshita, a man of linguistic genius and religious zeal who has been extolled by texts such as the biography of Padmasambhava. The writings of the rNying-ma-pa contain a biography of Vairocanarakshita. Together with him the linguists dPal-brtsgs of sKa-ba, and kLu'i rgyal-mtshan of Cog-ro were also active. These first translators recruited others as the years went by, and before long there was a whole army of translator-monks. Vairocana and another young Tibetan, Legs-grub, were given the task of making personal contact with further Indian masters in the various centres of Indian Buddhism. These two young men were the first of a long line of zealous Tibetans who thirsted for knowledge and so left their high tablelands to go down into the burning plains of India to seek for a Guru or Gurus. Some of these pilgrims never returned to Tibet at all, but fell victim to a climate to which they were unaccustomed. Vairocana visited the Temple of Vajrâs-ana at the spot where Buddha found enlightenment, and he succeeded in establishing contact as arranged with men of the highest spiritual eminence. But Legs-grub became so homesick that he returned before he had carried out his task; however, he died on the return journey; and ever since his demise has been regarded by Buddhists as a punishment for his sin of disobedience.

Vairocana, on the other hand, carried out his instructions dutifully and then returned to bSam-yas, where, however, he did not receive the expected appreciation. Instead he met with a good deal of opposition; on the one hand from the Indian pandits who were there, and on the other from the Tibetan ministers, who were supporting the old Bon religion.[1] The nobles at the head of this latter movement after the death of Ma-zhang were mDo-bzher rdo-rje spre-chung, Li-stag chen-po and Li-thi khra-mi. It was they who were primarily responsible for introducing the modernized form of the Bon religion from the land of Zhang-zhung, and they did their utmost to spread it amongst the people. Both the supporters of the Bon religion, and the hostile Buddhists, used the same arguments. They declared that Vairocana was not representing the true teachings of Buddha as explained in the texts which he had brought with him, but was propagating instead a kind of black magic and necromancy which could only bring evil to the country.

The reception met with by Vairocana is a further documentation of the resistance which arose in Tibet to the Tantric teachings of later Buddhism. Vairocana was, in fact, a conscious representative of the Vajrayâna and a supporter of the Magi Padmasambhava, so that, learned translator though he was, we too must regard him as representing the things objected to. In the end the clamour against Vairocana became so violent that the opposition roundly demanded that he should be put to death. King Khri-srong, though still favourably inclined towards his protégé, had to bow to the storm—at least outwardly. The solution he found to his dilemma is typical of those thoroughly unsentimental times, whose general outlook was very far removed from the spirit of Buddha, with its law that no living thing should be harmed. The king removed Vairocana from the public view

[1] See the description in the biography of Padmasambhava, 276b, 1, and Toussaint, *Le dict de Padma.*, pp. 293 *et seq.*

and kept him in a secret apartment where he could continue his translation of the Tantric literature he had brought with him. As a sign of his continued favour he personally brought the honoured prisoner's food every day. But those powerful elements clamouring for Vairocana's life had to be satisfied, so the king caused a beggar to be seized and bundled into monk's clothing. This man was then presented to the people, but at a distance sufficient to prevent recognition. The unfortunate beggar who was involuntarily playing the role of Vairocana was now placed inside two inverted bowls and cast into the river. However, neither the people nor the Tibetan nobles were altogether convinced by this performance and in order to lull their suspicions the king had to swear an oath to the bTsan demons that the hated Vairocana no longer lived. But here too the wily king chose an ambiguous formulation and thus avoided doing violence to his conscience.

Despite all the trouble he had gone to, however, the king's deceit was soon discovered; and the one who revealed it was none other than his chief wife Tshe-spong-bza, also known as dMar-rgyan, or 'Red Ornament', the mother of the heir apparent and two other princes. This woman is described, not only in the literature of the Padmasambhava sect but also in that of the Bon-po, as an irreconcilable opponent of the Indian teachings and a follower of the Bon religion. According to the *Report of the Queens* she came out openly in favour of the Bon religion, and explained the reason for her views very significantly: 'I fear that the throne may be lost if we make common cause with the new religion'.[1] In view of the activity of Padmasambhava such fears were well founded, and history has since confirmed them and those of the Tibetan aristocracy whose representative she was. As a result of the protracted internal struggles the political kingdom of Tibet finally collapsed and the country became a priest-dominated State.

However, it is also necessary to record the contention of her enemies that her fierce hatred of Padmasambhava's pupil, Vairocana, had its roots in despised love. The *Report of the Queens* has a highly-coloured version of the affair, during which the Queen is said to have conducted herself much like the Lady Potiphar. But whatever the truth may be it is an undoubted fact according to the Padmasambhava biography that it was she who

[1] Laufer, *Der Roman einer tibetischen Königin*, Chap. XV; Laufer's translation, see p. 179.

discovered the king's secret in connection with Vairocana, and then brought her discovery to the notice of his ministers. The only way the king could save the life of his favourite monk after this was by banishing him to Eastern Tibet and thus extricating him from the clutches of his enemies, and this was done. Whilst in banishment Vairocana is reported to have continued working for the cause of Buddhism.

But the king was persistent, and despite all opposition he went on working for his cherished plans. As Vairocana was now too compromised, he sent a new delegation of five young Tibetan scholars to India. It is noteworthy that these men also chose a Vajrayâna master, the Tantric Hûmkâra, as their teacher, and he initiated them into the magic secrets of necromancy. However, in the meantime the Tibetan ministers were not idle, and somehow they got wind of what was happening, for they compelled the king to send a message to the five, couched in terms obviously hostile to Tantrism. When the five consulted Hûmkâra he declared that for the time being they must remain with him, since if they returned to Tibet at the moment their lives would clearly be in danger. Four of the Tibetan pupils obeyed the voice of their Tantric master and continued with the magic conjurations they were engaged in. Only one of them, dPal-gyi seng-ge, was of a different view, declaring that the main task was now to return to Tibet and spread the doctrines they had learned.

Not unexpectedly, punishment was hard on his heels for his disobedience, and on the way back he was killed in Nepal by a nâga demon (kLu)—at least, according to Padmaist tradition this is what happened. The four who had remained behind were ultimately recalled, and they undertook the journey under the leadership of Nam-mkha snying-po. On their arrival the latter was able to cure the king of a dangerous sickness, at which the king was so grateful that, together with some of his followers, he took part in Tantric rites. Once again it was his Queen Tshe-spong-bza who led the opposition and informed the suspicious ministers of what was going on. Her contemptuous remarks about the ritual are worthy of reproduction:[1]

'What is called Kapâla is a human head laid on a stand;
What is called Basuta is entrails spread out;
What is called bone trumpets is made of human leg bones;

[1] Biography of Padmasambhava, Fol. 284b, 1.

What is called "the Holy Spot of the Great Field" is human skin spread out;
What is called Rakta is blood scattered on sacrificial pyramids (bali);
What is called Mandala consists of iridescent colours
What are called dancers are people carrying wreaths of bones!
This is not religion; it is the evil that comes from India to Tibet!'

Here we find the whole Tantric ritual summed up, complete with all its accessories, precisely the things the Tibetans hated so much. The Tibetan ministers now lodged a formal protest with the king and demanded that he should make an end of such hocus-pocus, declaring that if such things were allowed to spread, everyone would go in danger of his life. Obviously, this was a reference to the mysterious death of dPal-gyi seng-ge on his way home to Tibet. The ministers seem to have doubted the story of the Nâga demon, and to have suspected that he had fallen victim to some more mundane evil. Even the king now seemed rather suspicious of the whole business, and he banished the four monks to various areas.

These events seem to have strengthened the Bon party, because for some time thereafter, and despite his abiding sympathy for Buddhism, the king continued to allow both religions to exist side by side, favouring first one side and then the other. For example, a prominent priest of Zhang-zhung, the home of the systemized Bon religion, was invited to Tibet. This man was Shang-ri'i dbu-can, and he was now entrusted with the translation of the four books of the *Naga Hundred-thousand*, a well-known Bon text. An indication—almost farcical—that the two religions were more or less abreast of each other is given in an order of the king, who wanted to build himself a monument, and therefore instructed the Buddhists to provide a Stûpa, and the counter-party to provide a bang-so, according to old Tibetan custom, both to be erected on the Mu-ri, the traditional interment place of kings in the 'Phying-yul Valley.[1]

The creation of a Tibetan religious literature in translation was now vigorously encouraged, and the interests of the two rival religions were both taken into consideration. The big advance of

[1] See my essay, 'Die Gräber der tibetischen Könige', p. 9.

Buddhist scholarship in this respect seems to have been due to the arrival by invitation of a further famous Indian teacher, Vimalamitra. This man, apparently a spiritual brother of Padmasambhava, also met with a good deal of opposition at first, and was denounced as 'a heretical magician'. In consequence the king could not publicly receive him, but in the end the opposition was overcome, and Vimalamitra even secured the recall of Vairocana from his banishment in Eastern Tibet. But at the same time there was a counter-stream of priests of the systematized Bon religion from Zhang-zhung, and together with the High Priest Shang-ri'i dbu-can and his Tibetan translator Thang-nag bon-po, they laid the basis for a future Bon canon in Tibet by translations from the language of Zhang-zhung. The work was carried out in the Avalokiteshvara temple in bSam-yas, because at that time the Bon po had no temples or monasteries of its own. It is noteworthy but not I think altogether astonishing, that according to report the Buddhist Vairocana actually took part in the translation of the Bon texts.[1]

In the meantime the army of foreign monks had tremendously increased, as also had the native Lo-tsâ-ba. As the transcripts of the two great Buddhist encyclopaedias of Tibet show, the reign of King Khri-srong saw the addition of a tremendous number of texts to the body of Tibetan literature. It was an impressive and altogether admirable performance; and, indeed, science owes the zealous monks a good deal, because most of the Indian originals from which they made their translations have since been lost. Apart from the great lights of contemporary Buddhism such as Shântirakshita, Padmasambhava and Vimalamitra, there was also Buddhaguhya, whom King Mes-ag-tshoms had once invited in vain, Shântigarbha, Vishuddhasimha, the three Kashmiris Jinamitra, Dânashîla, and Ananta, and the Tantric Dharmakîrti, who should not be confused with the great philosopher of the same name who lived in the reign of Srong-btsan sgam-po.

Some idea of the great number of foreign monks who were now in the country is given by a list entitled 'Report on the Translators and Panditas', though it also mentions the masters of the next century.[2] Notable is the fact that amongst them were several Chinese monks under the leadership of their most important representative, Hva-shang Mahâyâna. These Chinese

[1] Hoffmann, *Bon Religion*, p. 264.
[2] Fol. 66a, 3 *et seq.*

monks were quartered in one of the three westerly temples of bSam-yas, the Acaladhyâna, where they devoted themselves in particular to meditation on the Chinese form of Buddhism.[1] It is also interesting to note that according to report work was also going forward on grammatical and lexicographical works, whilst lists of all the translations were drawn up with information concerning their contents, giving the number of chapters and verses.

Even at a time like this when the two religions existed side by side, it is not difficult to imagine that there was friction between the Bon-po religion and Buddhism. In particular, the bloody animal sacrifices carried out by the Bon-po aroused the ire of the Buddhist monks. When on one occasion Bon priests carried out the ceremony of 'the Stag with the spreading Antlers', the Buddhist monks protested eloquently to the king, pointing out that the toleration of such practices was impossible for Buddhism. Just as there could be only one king, they pointed out, so it was impossible for two religions to continue to exist side by side. They then informed the king that if he continued to tolerate such crimes in his jurisdiction they, the Buddhist scholars from India, would return to their own homeland.

From all the reports available there can be very little doubt that the king himself favoured Buddhism, but he was obviously not sufficiently strong to have his own way completely, and was compelled to take the opposition of the Tibetan nobility and the Bon-po into consideration. In his reply, therefore, he counselled continued patience, and made the noteworthy observation that the Bon-po was very powerful amongst the people, whereas Buddhism was not. However, a day did come when the king was able to follow his own desires and show clearly whose side he favoured. We are not in a position to reconstruct the political situation which now allowed the king to put the tiller of the ship of state hard over in favour of Buddhism. Traditional accounts[2] connect the successful repression which now opened up against the Bon-po with a great disputation organized by the king at Don-mkhar in the centre of that district from which the Tibetan dynasty originally took its rise ('Phying-yul). The representatives of the Bon-po and of Buddhism were opposed to each other in appropriate pairs. Shântirakshita disputed with Shang-ri'i dbu-can, Padmasambhava disputed with Thang-nag bon-po, and

[1] Bu-ston 114b, 6, Obermiller, p. 191.

[2] *Biography of Padmasambhava*, Fol. 293a *et seq.*, Toussaint, pp. 318 *et seq.*

Vimalamitra with Li-shi stag-rings. As a result of this disputation the king now publicly declared that he was convinced by the arguments of the Buddhists, and that the Bon-po had been defeated.

According to another report, the Kashmiri scholar Ananta called the Tibetan inhabitants together on the market place and publicly defeated the heretics in dispute. However it came about, the fact is that henceforth the king was no longer prepared to tolerate the existence of the Bon-po side by side with Buddhism. According to the evidence of the *Annals oj the Kings—according to Bon tradition*[1] the king called the Bon priests together and placed before each one the choice of becoming a Buddhist monk or a tax-paying citizen. If he wished to do neither the one thing nor the other he would be allowed to leave the country. The king is then reported to have upbraided the Bon priests in the following words, clearly directed towards the party of the Tibetan nobles: 'As the Bon-po is so strong I suspect that you are trying to win my subjects away from me'. Many heretics now publicly went over to Buddhism, but their consent was only formal. The greater number preferred to go into banishment. This incident, which was of great consequence for the future history of Tibet, is described very graphically in the biography of Padmasambhava:

> 'A fox cap was set upon his head, and half-drums were handed to him;
> Cotton garments were given to him for clothing, and impure food was given him to eat.
> And all the Bon-po customs involving sin were abolished.
> For such Bon rites as were concerned with the warding off of immediately threatening worldly danger
> Wooden stag heads with spreading antlers were made;
> And effigies of yaks and sheep of porridge.'

It is clear from their characteristics and their clothing that the Bon-po were typical Shamanists. Henceforth animal sacrifices were forbidden to them, and they had to use substitutes in place of animal victims. But, as we have already seen in our first chapter, it was not possible to extirpate animal sacrifices altogether. The Bon-po—riding on oxen and donkeys—were banished to barren lands along the frontiers of Tibet, and this

[1] *T'oung Pao*, 1901, p. 38.

was important as having a great influence on subsequent religious history, because even down to the present day the Bon religion has maintained itself in the northern and eastern frontier districts, where it still has self-sufficient communities with numerous monasteries. For centuries conditions were very similar along the western frontier areas, as numerous abandoned holy places of the heretics in the neighbourhood of Kailâsa and farther westward indicate. The disappearance of the Bon religion in these districts must have been of fairly recent origin. In the central districts proper the heretics were confined to a very few districts, and today in Tibet proper there is, relatively speaking, small trace of the 'Black Belief'. The *Crystal of Doctrinal Systems* tells us that the king threatened to put to death those who turned Buddhist texts into Bon texts by subtle alterations. Many of the smaller shrines (gsas-khang) are reported to have been destroyed, and others taken over by the Buddhists. Under the pressure of this religious persecution, whose causes were primarily political, the Bon-po now began to conceal their holy writings at remote places, on mountains, in ravines, and even in the monasteries of unsuspecting Buddhist monks, so that they should be saved for future generations. As with the Padmasambhava sect, in later centuries the discovery of literary treasures (gter-ma) played an important role, and in the case of the Bon texts too, doctrinal authenticity was claimed for a mass of later interpolations.

King Khri-srong did not succeed in destroying the Bon religion altogether, but his intervention did put an end once and for all to any claims on its behalf as the universal State religion of Tibet. The later Bon-po led an isolated existence apart from the main stream of spiritual development as a discarded heretical sect, as a provincial tendency in religious belief whose main tendency was and still is a purely negative one, namely anti-Buddhism.

A second religious dispute of decisive historical importance, but one which has received far too little attention in the text-books, must also have taken place in the reign of King Khri-srong lde-btsan. In this case it was a question of disagreement within the body of Buddhism itself. We have already mentioned the differences between the Tantrics gathered around Padmasambhava, and the philosophical Buddhists around the scholarly figure of Shântirakshita, who wished to uphold the moral laws of the older Buddhism. But there was also a third school which could look back on a long tradition, and which increased considerably in numbers and influence during the latter years of the reign of King Khri-srong. This was the special form of Buddhism introduced from China and propogated by numerous Chinese monks (ho-shang) under the leadership of Hva-shang Mahâyâna. This school called itself sTon-mun-pa, whilst the followers of Shântirakshita were known as Tsen-min-pa. Both these names are of foreign, i.e. Chinese, origin.[1]

The death of the master Shântirakshita had a very unfavourable effect on the cause of Indian Buddhism. The great philosopher is said to have been killed by the kick of a horse. His successor, the Tibetan dPal-dbyangs, who was made Âcârya, had not the same authority. In consequence the very effectively propagated teachings of the Chinese steadily gained ground. The supporters and followers of Shântirakshita, and in particular dPal-dbyangs and gSal-snang (whose Indian religious name was Jnânendra), fought against this tendency, and there was friction—to such an extent, in fact, that even the authority of the king was not sufficient to suppress the disputes. According to Bu-ston the supporters of the Chinese party threatened their rivals with knives, so that in thc end Jnânendra fled and withdrew himself for meditation in the province of Lho-brag. He even ignored two orders of the king to return, for the king was obviously anxious to end the disagreeable doctrinal struggle. It was only when on the third occasion the order was backed up by a threat to put him to death unless he obeyed, that Jnânendra actually did return. During an audience with the king, he urgently reminded that monarch of the teachings of Shântirakshita, and persuaded him to invite Shântirakshita's pupil Kamalashîla to Tibet. Like his great teacher, this Kamalashîla was one of the most outstanding and illustrous philosophers of his age, and, in addition, he was famous as a commentator on the main work of Shântirakshita.

In order to bring some clarity into the confused situation the king once more organized a disputation, as he had done between the Bon-po and the Buddhists, and it took place at court in his

[1] For the dispute between these two tendencies see Bu-ston 115a, 2 *et seq.;* Obermiller II, p. 191; dPag-bsam ljon-bazng, p. 173, and the more detailed account in *Report of the Ministers*, Fol. 18b, 1 *et seq.* In addition of late there have been important publications from Chinese sources by P. Demiéville, *Le concile de Lhasa* in the Bibliothéque de l'Institut des Hautes Etudes Chinoises, VII, Paris 1952. For the Chinese names of the two parties see also the same source, p. 184. See also G. Tucci, *Minor Buddhist Texts*, Vol. II, Serie Orientale Roma, Introduction.

presence. Both representatives, Hva-shang Mahâyâna at the head of the sTon-mun-pa, and Kamalashîla at the head of the Tsen-min-pa, were provided with a garland of flowers, such as the defeated contender presented to the victor before leaving the country.

Hva-shang Mahâyâna was obviously a typical representative of the Chinese Buddhism of the T'ang period, which combined the Indian teachings with national Chinese Taoist elements in intuitive contemplation. Only recently, thanks to a valuable study published by W. Liebenthal,[1] we have made the acquaintance of an earlier representative of this school in the person of Chao, the pupil of the famous translator Kumârajîva of Kutcha. The most important matters of doctrine in which Hva-shang differed from his Indian rival were (1) the attainment of Buddhaship does not take place slowly as the result of a protracted and onerous moral struggle for understanding, but suddenly and intuitively—an idea which is characteristic of the Chinese Ch'an and of the Japanese Zen sect which derives from it; (2) meritorious actions whether of word or deed, and, indeed, any spiritual striving, is evil; on the contrary one must relieve one's mind of all deliberate thought and abandon oneself to complete inactivity. At this point we can clearly see the influence of the Taoist philosophy, which sets up Wu-wei, non-activity, as the ideal to be aimed at. One should not disturb the harmonious flow of the cosmos by any individual activity of one's own, but instead allow the immanent sacred law, the Tao, to operate both in oneself and throughout the outside world; as a result of this inactivity absolute harmony and paradisal perfection will develop on their own.

The following are, according to the version of Bu-ston, a few typical observations from the arguments of the Chinese representative: 'If you perform virtuous or commit sinful deeds then you will go either to heaven or hell, but, one way or the other, you will not emerge from the Samsâra, and obstacles will arise in the way of attaining to Buddhaship. But the man who thinks of nothing and turns his attention to nothing, will free himself completely from the Samsâra. By means of a complete abstention from all thought, consideration and action man will attain the state of "taking notice of nothing" (anupalambha), and thereafter he

[1] Walter Liebenthal, *The Book of Chao*, Monumenta Serica, Monograph XIII, Peiping 1948.

will suddenly enter the stage of enlightenment and become akin to a Bodhisattva who has reached the tenth stage (bhûmi).'

Kamalashîla, on the other hand, argued that a complete renunciation of all spiritual activity was calculated precisely to make the way of the yogi to the recognition of the instability of the Dharma and of voidness (shûnya) impossible. If a man were to say to himself 'I will not think of any Dharma', then this too was activity. If the complete emptying of mind from thoughts and intentions were the aim, then someone who was unconscious, or quite drunk, would come nearest to the Chinese ideal. How could a man in this completely negative state remember his earlier births and attain to the power of omniscience which was characteristic of the Buddhas? And how, further, could a man conquer his passions?

Jnânendra and dPal-dbyangs supported the arguments of the Indian teacher by pointing to the necessity of a gradual moral purgation and of a rise by degrees from one stage (bhûmi) of the Bodhisattvaship to the next higher, and finally to the tenth stage, the very highest. By following the Chinese way a man would also not be able to enter into the six perfections, the pâramitâ. It was nonsense to suppose that the Buddhaship could be attained swift ly. When a man climbed a mountain he could do so only step by step, and not by suddenly leaping to the top. If the advice of the Chinese were followed then it would be impossible to accumulate meritorious deeds, to purge the spirit, or even to pay attention to the tangible world, which would mean that to be logical one must die of hunger. How could one possibly attain to Buddhaship under such circumstances?

Tibetan sources record that the Chinese disputants, Hva-shang and its supporters, could find no reply to these arguments and were thus compelled to hand their garlands of flowers to Kamalashîla and admit themselves defeated. Some of them are even said to have laid hand on themselves. In any case, the king now ordered that henceforth no one should regard the teachings of sTon-mun-pa; and the writings of the defeated party were now collected and placed under lock and key. Henceforth the only binding and orthodox religion was the Nâgârjuna system. Man should henceforth zealously strive to uphold the ten moral laws and attain the pâramitâs. Perhaps we should add that the doctrine of Nâgârjuna here undoubtedly includes parts of the doctrine of the Yogâcâra school of Asanga. The views of these two religious teachers, though they may differ from each other in various points, comprise between them the fundamental canon of Lamaist philosophy down to the present day. The disputation organized by the king must therefore be regarded as an historical event of the greatest importance. It was, as P. Demiéville rightly calls it, a real Church Council. The result of the disputation decided that Tibet should not adopt the Chinese version of Buddhism, but the Indian Mahâyâna version. The statement of the sources according to which on his return to China Hva-shang Mahâyâna dispatched four hired murderers to Tibet to assassinate the Indian master Kamalashîla reads too much like a subsequent attempt to place the crown of martyrdom on the master's head, but at the same time it is not possible for us to say with any confidence that such behaviour was out of the question—the incident with the bricking-in of the anti-Buddhist Minister Ma-zhang Khrom-pa is a fair indication of the ruthless measures the Buddhists of those days were prepared to adopt. The important historical event represented by the expulsion of the Chinese Buddhist teachers from the country remains alive in the memory of the Tibetan people, but in a mythological form. In the religious Tsam mysteries performed in Tibetan monasteries the figure of Hva-shang appears in a grotesque form as the representative of the defeated teaching to be held up to the scorn of the children.[1] In the same way in similar religious masks the Black-Hat Sorcerer is the symbolic representative of the defeated and suppressed Bon religion.

But whereas the expulsion of the Chinese Buddhists represented an historical conclusion, the struggle with the Bon religion did not come to an end with the repressive measures introduced by King Khri-srong, since the Bon-po enjoyed the support of powerful Tibetan nobles. However, it appears that the trouble remained more or less underground during the last years of the reign of Khri-srong, and also during the reigns of his successors Mu-ne btsan-po (797-8) and Sad-na-legs (798-817). According to the *Annals of the Kings according to Bon Tradition*, many of those who were willy-nilly converted to Buddhism actually remained true to the old religion in their hearts—'whilst their bodies and their tongues practised Buddhism'. But one way or the other, nothing changed in the traditional leaning of the royal house towards Buddhism, or in its encouragement of the gradu-

[1] Filchner-Unkrig, *Kumbum Dschamba Ling*, p. 311; Grünwedel, *Mythologie*, p. 169.

ally strengthening Buddhist priesthood. The fifth Dalai Lama records in his chronicle that Mu-ne btsan-po inaugurated a special religious service in bSam-yas devoted to the sacred Tripitaka, the totality of the canonical writings, of which those devoted to the Sûtras, or doctrinal texts, were still in existence at the time of that High Priest of the church.[1] Sad-na-legs carefully maintained the holy places built by his forebears, continued the work of translating Buddhist texts, and himself built a new temple, rGyal-sde dkar-chung.[2]

But the Tibetan ruler who did most to strengthen the Buddhist prelacy was Ral-pa-can (817-36).[3] Tradition also credits him with the building of a new Temple, On-cang-rdo. But his most important service to Buddhism was undoubtedly the interest he showed—like his father Sad-na-legs before him—in the encouragement of Buddhist literature. During the course of generations a tremendous number of texts had been translated, but it was now seen that the lack of uniformity had resulted in something like chaos. It was not merely that the original texts had been translated from many languages—in addition to Sanskrit and the Central Indian dialects, also from Chinese and from the Khotan language—but, in particular, the up to then very primitive Tibetan language did not lend itself readily to the expression of complicated philosophic ideas. Further, foreign translators of very disparate backgrounds and religious traditions were involved, and they had translated the technical expressions of Buddhism in varying fashions. What now became urgently necessary was the creation of a uniform and generally valid literary language. The appropriate commission of scholars set up by Ral-pa-can's father Sad-na-legs tackled the difficult task with admirable skill, and apparently the work was completed during the reign of Ral-pa-can himself. The Indian pandits Jinamitra, Surendrabodhi, Shîlendrabodhi, Dânashîla and Bodhimitra were members of this commission, assisted by the Tibetans Ratnarakshita, Dharmatâshîla, Jnânasena (Tibetan Ye-shes-sde), Jayarakshita, Manjushrîvarman and Ratnendrashîla. The names of these men are part and parcel of the history of Tibetan literature. Even before beginning their work they created the Buddhist Encyclopaedia Mahâvyutpatti, which established the authorized

[1] Fol. 40a, 3.
[2] *Ibid.* Fol. 40b, 6 *et seq.*
[3] Se Bu-ston 117a, 1; Obermiller II, pp. 196 *et seq.*

translation of every Buddhist name and technical term.[1] In this period new translations of Hînayâna and Mahâyâna writings were made only from the Indian originals, and it is of great interest to note that in clear distinction from earlier periods no necromantic literature (sngags) was translated, and that from the Hînayâna writings only those of the Mûla-Sarvâstivâda sect were translated. The translations made in earlier times by other scholars were now subjected to a general revision, and amended to bring them into line with what had now been laid down as standard termonology. The totality of the sacred writings was not yet brought together in a recognized canon such as the later Kanjur, but a list of titles was drawn up of those books which had obtained the *imprimatur* of the commission.

Now although Ral-pa-can undoubtedly rendered a great service to history by his active support of the literary efforts of the Buddhist priesthood, his personal relation to religion was almost thraldom, and he left nothing undone to further their interests, strengthen their position, and afford them personal advantage. It was he, for example, who introduced the law that seven Tibetan families must make themselves responsible for the maintenance of one Buddhist monk. It is reported that his veneration for the priesthood went so far that he would humbly bow down at the feet of priests, and that he would fasten silk ribbons to his hair, attaching the other ends to the seats on which the priests sat. This exaggerated veneration offended Tibetan national feelings, but much more important than such outward signs of his slavish subordination was the fact that real power in the State was passing increasingly into the hands of the Buddhists; for example the chief minister under Ral-pal-can was a Buddhist monk named dPal-gyi yon-tan of Bran-kha. In fact, quite generally Buddhist influence was more openly flaunted in public life than was tolerable to Tibetan national pride. Not only the common people but also the nobles were compelled to conform, outwardly at least, to Buddhist standards of morality. In the end popular indignation and resentment finally burst out in violent anti-clerical demonstrations. But the purblind king supported the Buddhist priesthood recklessly and severely punished anyone who had been guilty of any offence against the overweening Buddhists.

[1] Obermiller, p. 197; cf., further, A. Ferrari, *Arthavinicaya* in Reale Academie d'Italia, 1944, pp. 540 *et seq.*; G. Tucci, *The Tombs of the Tibetan Kings*, Rome 1950, p. 15.

4 Gods and Demons guard the main temple of Lhasa

5 The highly-venerated image of the future Buddha Maitreya in Lhasa

Some of the offenders had fingers hacked off, and others even had their eyes put out. The effect of this brutal repression was to intensify the dangerous situation still further, and a conspiracy amongst the Tibetan nobles, who sympathized with the Bon-po, was led by the minister rGyal-to-re. Cleverly and systematically the conspirators intrigued to isolate the king before they delivered their decisive blow. Under various pretexts they succeeded in obtaining the banishment of the king's brother, who had himself become a Buddhist monk; and charges were made against dPal-gyi Yon-tan, the monk who had become chief minister, alleging that he was guilty of improper relations with one of the king's wives. The wretched Ral-pa-can fell into the trap, the accused minister was executed, and the lady in question committed suicide. When the nobles had succeeded in isolating the king and dispersing the Buddhist camarilla on which he had relied, they launched their coup: when the king was asleep after having drunk quantities of rice wine, assassins broke into his apartment and killed him in his bed.

The discontent of a long-suppressed opposition burst out in this reckless act of violence, but it also produced the inevitable reaction. The victorious conspirators put a new king on the throne, gLang-dar-ma (836-42), but his personality was no stronger than that of his predecessor, and he leaned towards the nobles and the Bon-po quite as much as Ral-pa-can had leaned towards Buddhism. All the influential posts were now, of course, occupied by the conspirators and their friends; for example, rGyal-to-re became chief minister—and immediately launched a fierce campaign of oppression against Buddhism, whilst at the same time doing everything possible to restore the Bon religion. Buddhist teachings were prohibited through the country, and the persecution extended even to the remotest parts. Of course, the work of translation which had been proceeding so promisingly was now stopped altogether, and even the premises on which it had taken place were destroyed. The solemn dedication of the new temple of On-cang-rdo built under Ral-pa-can did not take place as arranged, and even those sacred places which could already look back on some tradition, those built under Srong-btsan and Khri-srong, were now deliberately held up to public contempt. Their doors were bricked up, and the frescoes were painted over with pictures of beer-swilling monks in order to denigrate Buddhism in the eyes of the people. The numerous statues of

Buddha, including even those from the famous old temple of Jo-khang, were removed from their pedestals. The original intention was to throw them into the water, but on account of their weight the vandals contented themselves—as during the time of Khri-srong's minority—with burying them in the sand. The Chinese widow of Srong-btsan was declared to be an evil spirit, for it was she who had brought the most venerable of these statues from China. The Yo-khang itself was taken over as a cattle shed, and a rope was placed round the effigy of the 'Master of Secrets', Bodhisattva Vajrapâni. The wave of repression did not spare Buddhist literature, and many of the carefully translated texts were destroyed by fire or flung into the water. Fortunately it was possible to save some part of this literary treasure, and it was hidden away in caves in the neighbourhood of Lhasa.

The brunt of the fury was, of course, directed against the Buddhist monks in person. The Indian pandits, who but recently had enjoyed such respect and even veneration now had to flee for their lives, and many Tibetans fled with them. Rin-chen-mchog and Ting-nge-'dzin bzang-po, two of the best known of the Lo-tsâ-ba were killed in flight by hired murderers. Those who remained behind had to disavow their religion and their priesthood. The new authorities took a malicious pleasure in forcing the ex-monks to perform humiliating and unsuitable tasks, making them slaughtermen for example and sending them out with bows, arrows and dogs to hunt. It is also reported that many of them were provided with drums and tambourins and compelled to take part in the rites of the Bon religion.

But neither the campaign of repression nor the reign of gLang-dar-ma were destined to last long. A fanatical Buddhist hermit, dPal-gyi rdo-rje, killed the king with an arrow whilst the king was intently reading an inscription on one of the many big obelisks set up in Lhasa. As a true Buddhist Tantric, this murderer claimed that he had acted out of compassion: he wished to prevent the king from committing further crimes, and thus help him to a better re-birth. To Western minds this would appear grotesque hypocrisy, but it is a fact that such ideas are not unfamiliar in the philosophical outlook of the Vajrayâna and of Lamaism. The murderer made his escape unhindered, leaving the capital and the whole country in a state of utmost confusion. The fact that several kings had ended by assassination represented a dangerous threat to the reputation and prestige of the monarchy. The result was certainly not the restoration of Buddhism to its old position in the country, and generally speaking the consequences of these religious and political upheavals were negative. The religious confusion and the struggle between the monarchy and the nobles had weakened the once so powerful country to such an extent that it now began to disintegrate politically, and before long it broke up into numerous small principalities, whilst the authority of the central government was hardly operative outside the capital itself.

The collapse was also complete both culturally and religiously. Both Buddhism and the systematized Bon religion had received dangerous blows, and for almost a century and a half it began to look as though Tibet would fall back into the original anonymous and primitive condition from which the great Srong-btsan sgam-po had raised it. The disunity now manifested itself in the royal house too, and whilst one of the two sons of gLang-dar-ma, Od-srungs, showed Buddhist sympathies, the other, Yum-brtan, allowed himself to be guided by the aristocratic Tibetan party, which favoured the Bon-po. At first after the assassination of the king, this party must have held the leading strings, and chief power rested in the hands of the family of the old Bon minister Ta (or sTag) -ra klu-gong who had held office under King Khri-srong—as indicated by a contemporary inscription in Lhasa, which is drawn up in the terminology of the Bon-po.[1]

[1] *Journal of the Royal Asiatic Society*, 1910, pp. 1269 *et seq.*

CHAPTER V

THE SYSTEMATIZED BON RELIGION

As we have seen from our general sketch of the religious history of Tibet up to the close of the universal monarchy in the middle of the ninth century, the Bon religion, which was originally the national Tibetan version of North and Central Asian Shamanism and Animism, developed in Western Tibet, and particularly in Zhang-zhung; certainly under the influence of Buddhism and probably also under the influence of Persian and Manichaean teachings, into a syncretist system with a developed doctrine and a sacred literature. It was this changed and systematized Bon religion that the Tibetan nobles encouraged in their political struggle against the dynasty and against Buddhism. They brought in priests from Zhang-zhung and caused them to translate their texts into Tibetan, and they did their utmost to make the Bon religion into a State church. They were unsuccessful, and the anti-Buddhist reaction under gLang-dar-ma came too late to be effective, producing only a general collapse of Tibetan religious culture. Though the old, primitive Bon religion and customs still persisted amongst ordinary people, the new systematized Bon religion was no less damaged by the troubles than Buddhism itself, and had to be revived. The later history of the Bon religion is still unclear to us because the historical literature of the Bon-po has not yet been opened up, whilst the Buddhist chroniclers, whose accounts we were able to make use of in our previous inquiries, are not of much assistance later because they are just not interested in the fate of the hated heretics after their fall under Khri-srong lde-btsan. We shall now do our best to portray the character of the later Bon religion with the sparse material available, but we must make up our minds from the beginning that this form of religion was now operative only on the fringes of the spiritual life of the country, and no longer had any important influence (such as it possessed at the time of the universal monarchy) on the main line of development; that it was, so to speak, a moribund side channel of Tibetan cultural history—one capable of providing us with interesting indications with regard to the past, but not one which played any further role in shaping the life of the nation.

As was the case with Buddhism, the central figure of the Bon religion is that of its legendary founder, gShen-rab or gShen-rab mi-bo—'gShen-rab the Man' as he was called—who is credited with first proclaiming the religious gospel. But whilst Buddha was, in fact, a historical figure, the sources already available to us suggest that the founder of the Bon religion was a purely mythical figure whose alleged life story as we know it has obviously been spatchcocked together according to the pattern of the Buddha legend as contained in the Mahâyâna texts, with interesting literary and historical additions from other literatures and other religions. The name gShen-rab itself is not really a name at all, but a descriptive appellation meaning 'the most excellent of the Shamans' (gShen priest), something of which the Bon-po always remained aware.[1] We do not know whether there was perhaps the real person of some single prominent Zhang-zhung priest behind this mythical figure; some man who created the syncretic system as Padmasambhava created Padmaism, or whether the legendary figure stands in stead of a whole number of priests, representing their intensified and idealized personalities. The text containing his life history is fortunately available to us. It is entitled *gZer-myig*, which in the Bon-po language means *Key for Memory*.[2] About one quarter of it—Chapters I to VII[3]—has been translated into English by A. H. Francke. Let us review here the main features of the 'Life', which comprises 'Twelve Deeds or Main Events in the life of gShen-rab', much like the Lalitavistara of Buddha.

The first chapter deals in a summary form with the story of the teacher who went before gShen-rab in the present cycle of world development. This was (gShen) gTo-rgyal ye-mkhyen, who may be compared with Kâshyapa, the direct predecessor of Gautama Buddha. He and the ruling world god, (srid-pa) Mu-

[1] *Zeitschrift der Deutschen Morgenländische Gesellschaft* 1944, p. 347.

[2] Cf. the *Dictionary of Sarat Chandra Das*, 1108a.

[3] gZer—myig, a Book of the Tibetan Bonpos in *Asia Major* 1924. I am preparing a complete translation.

brgyud dkar-po, asigned to him, and the 'God of Wisdom', Sems-kyi sgron-ma-can, are tired of the circle of development and the laborious work of conversion, and withdraw in a state of the highest positive bliss into 'the place of perfect gShen'. It now becomes necessary for the brother of gTo-rgyal, who lived in a heavenly pre-existence under the name of gSal-ba in higher spheres, to come down therefrom after a certain time and continue the work of salvation in the cycle of development.

The second chapter concerns itself primarily with the earthly parents of the new saviour. Like Buddha, gShen-rab looks out from his heavenly world for a suitable place to be born in, and for suitable parents to be born of. He decides in favour of the land in which lie the sacred mountain Kailâsa (the Bon-po call it gYung-drung dgu-brtsegs), and the source of the four great rivers Ganges, Indus, Oxus and Sîtâ (Tarim), the land Ol-mo lung-rings, in which we must clearly recognize a district of Zhang-zhung, where the Palace Phar-po so-brgyad and the Bon temple Sham-po lha-rtse lie and where the prince rGyal-bon thod-dkar of the line of dMu dwells. The name of this line is interesting because it is at the same time the name of those heavenly spirits from whom, as we have seen, the Tibetan kings are supposed to spring. Now this king's son marries a beautiful maiden of low caste, who together with her parents is now raised to a higher eminence and receives the name of rGyal-zhad-ma. A Brahmin now appears on the scene as go-between. An interesting point is that before the wooing the king's son and all his retinue take a ritual bath in the sea. This suggests a connection with the Near Eastern baptist sects, one of which, the Mandaens, we already know something about. In India, on the other hand, we are told only of a 'sprinkling' (abhisheka), and that in connection with initiatory rites, such as the consecration of the king. Finally there is talk about the finding of fabulous treasures in a place to the north of the temple of Sham-po lha-rtse, which had been preserved and guarded by Jambhala, the god of riches. In consequence all the inhabitants of the country from which the maiden comes are made rich.

The beginning of the third chapter takes us into heavenly regions. The future saviour presents himself to the effective gods of this new cycle of time, the god of wisdom gShen-lha od-dkar ('gShen-God of the White Light') and the reigning world god Sangs-po 'bum-khri. The former insists that the saviour must be incarnated amongst men and not amongst gods, Asuras, animals, Pretas (Hunger spectres) and denizens of Hell. Heavenly beings declare themselves prepared to be the disciples of the coming Saviour. A last look is now taken by gShen-rab from the peak of the world mountain Sumeru down on to his future birthplace and his future parents. After which a white ray descends from Heaven, enters into the head of rGyal-bon and reaches his sexual organs, whilst a red ray similarly descends and enters the body of the mother.

In the twenty-second chapter of the *Report of the Ministers*, which belongs to Padmaistic literature, and which has unfortunately come down to us only in a truncated form, the happening is presented somewhat differently. From the body of gShen-rab five-coloured rays of light emerge and enter into the 'turquoise bird cuckoo' which is perched on the top of a sacred willow tree. This bird then flies on to the head of the future mother and flaps its wings three times, whereupon from its genitals a white and a light red ray of light enter into the woman. The growth of the foetus is described in *gZer-myig* according to the principles of Indian medicine. When the wonder child is born its voice is immediately heard like the voice of the turquoise bird cuckoo. According to the *Report of the Ministers* the child now takes seven steps—like Buddha. The Brahmin gSal-khyab, who had presided over the wooing of rGyal-zhad-ma, now wept aloud at the sight of the wonderful child because he knew that on account of his age he would never hear the preaching of the coming Saviour. Thus this Brahmin plays the same role as Asita plays in the Buddha legend, and as Simeon in the story of Jesus.

In the fourth chapter the young saviour is already beginning to preach. His pupils are heavenly beings. From his spirit springs the disciple rMa-lo, and from his words the disciple gYu-lo, who play the same role as Shâriputra and Maudgalyâyana in Buddhism. When gShen-rab reaches the age of three, the four great gShen elements emanate from his bodily orifices.

Chapter five describes gShen-rab's first great act of conversion. Amidst wondrous accompanying phenomena the incarnation of the world god Sangs-po 'bum-khri, namely 'the little son of the spirit', gYu'i zur-phud-can ('the one with the turquoise coloured hair knot') comes down from Heaven and calls on the teacher to convert the wild hunter gTo-bu do-te, a man who has killed innumerable animals, and has also murdered a number of human beings. The saviour gShen-rab now goes into the land of the sinner, and by magical means dissipates his murderous intentions, and takes him back as a disciple to Ol-mo lung-rings. However, the evil Karma of gTo-bu is so powerful that even after the three-year course in the tenets of the Bon religion he still sins, so that at the end of these three years he goes to Hell, whose torments are described after the Buddhist fashion most drastically and in great detail. Thanks to the performance of Tantric ceremonies and the recitation of the names of a hundred divinities, gShen-rab not only succeeds in extricating the sinner from Hell, but also, successively, from the phases of Preta, animals, humans, Asura and gods, through which he has to pass on account of his sins. Interesting in these ceremonies is the indicated spiritual presence of gTo-bu in the shape of a picture drawn on a sheet of shell-white paper between magic signs.

The sixth chapter deals with the sending of the disciple Zir-phud-can to the land of Hos-mo in the East. The whole story of Vairocana and the Queen Tshe-spong-bza as recorded in the *Report of the Queens*[1] is now tagged on to him, and quite literally, except that the authentic names of people and places from the time of King Khri-srong lde-btsan are replaced by names from the fantasy mythology and geography of the Bon-po. It is altogether an interesting example of how Buddhist texts were 'transformed' into Bon texts, and at the same time an indication that the borrowings were not confined to canonical Indian works, but that the later original Tibetan texts of the rNying-ma-pa were also plundered. The *gZer-myig* in its present-day form can thus not be counted as amongst those old works which were translated in the reign of King Khri-srong lde-btsan from the language of Zhang-zhung into Tibetan. The healing of the Queen from a magically-caused sickness offers a welcome opportunity for reciting the names of three hundred Bon goddesses.

The seventh and eighth chapters are also drawn up along the lines of the *Report of the Queens*. As the latter describes the marriage of Padmasambhava and the beautiful Khrom-pa-rgyan, the daughter of King Khri-srong, so in the corresponding passages of the Bon text the marriage of gShen-rab to Hos-za rgyal-med, the daughter of the King of Hos-mo and his sinful wife, who is afterwards cleansed by the Master, is similarly described. The eighth chapter informs us that the princess bore gShen-rab two

[1] Laufer, *Roman einer tibetische Königin*, Chap. 5–16.

sons; first of all gTo-bu 'bum-sangs, who corresponds to the figure of Ânanda in the Buddhist story, and then dPyad-bu. Both of them subsequently become disciples of the Master. Even in their early youth they are both of them learned and wise, and their discussions with gShen-rab offer a welcome opportunity to set out a great part of the Bon teachings. The discussions begin with relatively simple matters, such as the mystic-etymological interpretation of names, a pastime very popular in Tibet. In this case the names are those of gShen-rab, of his parents, of his palace, and so on. And from there the discussions proceed over the five moral poisons and various questions of Bon cosmology to the metaphysical heights of the doctrine of shûnyatâ, or voidness.

The ninth chapter tells us of King 'Bar-ba'i sgron-ma-can ('He of the Burning Lamp') who visited the Master gShen-rab in order to deal with his scruples of conscience. He tells a sad story of things which have happened in one of his vassal States. The son of Prince Khri-shang, one of his vassals, was stricken with an incurable disease. In despair the parents consulted a famous wise woman, who advised them to sacrifice the child of one of their subjects, a child born at the same time as the little prince, i.e. under the same astrological aspects. Such a child was found. The young prince himself rejected the idea of the vicarious sacrifice, and his father would have preferred to die himself so that his son should become healthy; but in her blind love for her son the mother sees no objection to such a sacrifice. Finally a Bon priest experienced in such ceremonies was called, and a stupid man, the 'black Har-dha', was given him to play the part of executioner. The sick prince continued to oppose the idea vigorously but, as his father hesitated, the terrible deed was carried out—as we have already described in Chapter I. But all to no purpose. Far from recovering, the young prince now died of his illness, whereupon father, mother, Bon priest, and the wise woman who had recommended the procedure in the first place all committed suicide, whilst the parents of the sacrificed youth took vengeance on 'the black Har-dha', and tore the heart from his body, after which they fled to the fortress of the vassal king. The Chief King 'Bar-ba'i sgron-ma-can now felt it incumbent on him to avenge this new crime, so he laid siege to the fortress with three thousand men, and when he took it he put the two parents to death.

Master gShen-rab can now, thanks to his divine eye, tell the king the fate of all the parties concerned in their next reincarnation. Each one has received according to the lex talionis the inexorable reward or punishment for all his deeds (Karma). Only the sick prince was born again in the blissful heavenly world, whilst all the others were thrown into various hells, the stupid Han-dha ending amongst the beasts. It is interesting to note that gShen-rab ascribes evil motives to the wise woman and to the Bon priest; both of them had no real knowledge, but acted from motives of self-interest. The king himself now became rather disturbed at his future fate and that of his three-thousand warriors, and asked where his and their re-incarnation would take place. He was told by gShen-rab that if he died now he would be re-born in a world of terrible struggle and war. The conclusion of this chapter, which contains long discussions on the Karma, is similar to that of the fifth and sixth chapters: by innumerable rites, and by conjuring a thousand gods of wisdom, world gods, and Bon teachers (gShen) the master secures the salvation of all concerned.

The three following chapters describe the many and various attacks on and persecutions of the Master and his followers by the Prince of the Devils, Khyab-pa lag-rings (Khyab-pa with the Long Arms). This Prince of Devils, who resembles Mâra, the tempter of Buddhism, is supported in these wrestlings—which, of course, gShen-rab wins in the end—by a host of subordinate demons (bDud). The activity of the Bon Saviour, who puts so many creatures on the right path and thus saves them from the devils, and who has also caused the four evil streams of devil's land to dry up, naturally infuriates the evil spirits. Khyab-pa lag-rings does book one great but temporary success: he manages to entice and carry off the daughter of gShen-rab, gShen-za ne'u-chung-ma. As a result of this adventure she bears the Prince of the Devils two children, but grandfather saves them from the Land of the Devils and purges them of all evil influences.

The Devil now robs the Master gShen-rab of his wonderful horses, and in the chase to recover this stolen property, the Master journeys from Zhang-zhung to Tibet, which he now converts. This 'missionary journey' seems to me of particular interest as a mythological reflection of those historical events we have already reviewed, which led to the missionary activity of priests of the systematized Bon religion from Zhang-zhung. It proceeded in much the same way as Padmasambhava's journey to Tibet, during which the great Tantric overthrew and subjugated the demons of the Land of Snows, thanks to his magic powers, and opened the country up to Buddhism. A typical example of the missionary work carried out by gShen-rab takes place in the wild woodland and gulchland of Kong-po. We are told that 'the entrance to the dark ravines of rKong-po were blocked by a black devil's mountain placed there by an infernal giant. When this gigantic devil had blocked the entrance in this way, he addressed gShen-rab: "Human, do not go beyond my stone! Although you wish to climb up, you cannot." The Master replied: "How much you people of rKong-po are to be pitied! The entrance is barred to me by this black mountain, is it? Just look and see whether I can be kept out!" And he then picked up the black mountain with his little finger and put it down again where three mountain passes met. And for this it received the name God's mountain Gyang-mtho, or High Earth Mound.'[1]

The thirteenth chapter is of particular interest. It describes how a further attack on the part of the Prince of Devils was brought to nothing, and this time the scene is in China. The story of the journey of gShen-rab to China is obviously related to the victorious China crusade of Ge-sar, the hero of the Tibetan national epic. The wise King Kong-tse—his name suggests a remote relationship with Confucius—had built a marvellous nine-storeyed Bon temple (gsas-mkhar) for the better dissemination of religion and the suppression of all evil spirits. This was, of course, a thorn in the side of the Prince of Devils, Khyab-pa lag-rings, and together with his host of supporting demons he did everything he could to destroy this temple. At first, thanks to his good deeds and the use of magic formulas, the king was able to ward off the attacks, but the situation became critical when Khyab-pa awakened the sea monster from its sleep on the ocean bed. In the hope of great booty this sea monster now swam with opened jaws towards the temple of the king in order to swallow it whole. Shaken with fear and in the direst distress, the king hurriedly uttered a prayer to Heaven. His prayer was heard by the Master gShen-rab, and as gShen-rab knew that the time had now come for the overthrow of the evil spirits he arrived before Kong-tse in all his shining glory accompanied by a vast host of terrifying gods. When the king had paid homage to gShen-rab, he was consoled by the latter, who raised his spirits by assuring him that he, gShen-rab, had come to ward off all evil. The

[1] *gZer-myig* II, 71a, 6 *et seq.*

Master then sat down in the meditative pose and uttered a mysterious formula. As a result a terrible monster with flaming eyes was conjured up. This was the dbU-dgu-pa, and with the assistance of four other monsters who differed from the first only by their colour, it now set off to do battle with the sea monster, whose attacks were beaten off and who was compelled to retire frustrated to his watery lair, so that thereafter the Bon religion could be preached in China without further hindrance.

The fourteenth chapter deals also with the preaching and spread of the Bon religions. The fifteenth chapter brings the Master's renunciation of the world. After such long reports concerning the numerous conversions carried out by the Master, the fact that he now withdraws from and renounces the world may seem rather strange, but for the Zhang-zhung priests, the creators of the gShen-rab legend according to Buddhist precedents, this is an essential part of the story of the Saviour. Despite the lamentations of his wives, to whom in the meantime the daughter of the Chinese King Kong-tse had also been added; despite the appeals of his son and his disciples; and even despite the great joy of the Prince of the Devils, who now feels certain of the final victory, gShen-rab leaves his house and all the comforts of this earthly life behind him.

'At that time and on that occasion', the text tells us,[1] 'the teacher gShen-rab mi-bo was no longer in the state of Samsâra. In order to attain to the real place of salvation he took the great work on himself in the three thousand one-hundredth human year and in the thirty-first year of a gShen-rab, and left his house to enter the spiritual state. He put on the wonderful "highest robe" (the monk's garment), the six-formed robe, and took the cleansing Hos horn in his hand.' The pictures in the manuscript of the *gZer-myig* now show gShen-rab as the enlightened Buddha in the garb of a monk, with one shoulder bare, and a sort of antilope horn in his hand, whereas previously he was always represented as a princely Bodhisattva with a crown and a sceptre decorated with swastikas. The wives and the disciples of the Master now followed his example, and they too are no longer portrayed as men and women of the world, but as ascetics.

We now see gShen-rab carrying out various forms of mortification. From time to time he lives only on a grain of corn and a little milk—the similarity to the Buddha legend is very obvious

[1] II 212a, 1 *et seq.*

here. He enters various heavenly worlds, including that of the King of the Apes, Ha-nu ma-'da (the Hanumat of the Indians); and in the end he even succeeds in converting the wicked Prince of the Devils, Khyab-pa lag-rings, and his host, who now make confessions of their guilt.

The sixteenth chapter tells us that as the simple renunciation of the world, and the living of the life of a monk no longer satisfied gShen-rab, he now, despite the objections of his disciples, amongst whom was now the former Prince of the Devils Khyab-pa, left his followers and withdrew to a place not visited by human beings in a wood at the foot of the sacred gYung-drung dgu-brtsegs (Kailâsa) in order to devote himself exclusively to meditation and mortification. However, from time to time he still gave lessons to his followers, for example concerning the thirteen stages of heaven. We have seen previously that the old Bon religion regarded these stages as literal material steps, but here in the *gZer-myig* the Master indicates that they are stages of moral and spiritual perfection leading from 'unconsidered belief', which is the first stage, to 'invisible glory', which is the thirteenth and highest stage.

The long seventeenth chapter deals with the Nirvâna of gShen-rab. Despite the pleadings of his followers the Master insists that the time has now come for him 'to leave the misery behind him'. And now, like Buddha in his last days, he is overcome by a serious illness. Although his son and disciple gTo-bu 'bum-sangs performs the normally effective ceremonies in order to bring about his recovery, their effectiveness lasts for three days only, when the sickness returns. The efforts of the other son dPyad-bu are no more successful, whereupon gShen-rab concludes that according to the world plan his departure is imminent. By means of many parables his disciple Yid-kyi khye'u-chung tries to persuade him to stay on in this earthly life. The Master, he declares, is like a precious field of gold, and all creatures represent the grass and trees growing out of it. But how should the grass and the trees continue to grow if the ground were withdrawn? The disciple also compares the Master to a sandalwood tree and all other creatures to its leaves, blossom and fruit; with a sea and the Nâgas, dragons and otters living in it; and also with a stream and the land which it waters. It is clear that the ideas behind these parables are similar to those behind the Christian parable of the vine.

The Master now consoles his disciple with the thought that

this Nirvâna is not a final disappearance, and that the Bon teachings will not perish. In order to teach renunciation to the indolent and avaricious, and to those who attach their hopes to the immutability of earthly things, he was, he said, giving them an example by his departure. A very interesting passage in the long speech of farewell is that in which the Master promises to return in a between-kalpa (world epoch), which reminds us of Jesus promising the coming of the Paraclete. Such Christian echoes suggest a familiarity of the Bon religion with Western ideas, probably passed on by the Manichaeans. Just as in the Buddha legend the disciple Mahâkâshyapa is not present at the death of the Master, so at the death of gShen-rab one of his best and most important disciples, A-zha gsang-ba mdo-sdud, is also absent, away meditating in loneliness and becoming aware of all kinds of evil portents. In a dream he sees the 'White A', a sacred letter for the Bon religion, disappear; the light of the sun and the moon goes out; the great rivers no longer flow downwards; flowers and curative herbs wither; and the earth shakes. On account of these signs he concludes mournfully that 'the light of the world' has gone out. And this was, in fact, the very moment at which gShen-rab moved into Nirvâna. A-zha wanders around searching for the Master, but he cannot find him either in the palace of Phar-po so-brgyad or in the temple of Sham-po lha-rtse, or on the sacred mountain gYung-drung dgu-brtsegs.

In the meantime the assembled disciples are unable to agree about the ceremonies to be held in connection with the death of the Master, and then gTo-bu points out that A-zha gsang-ba, whose spirit is 'akin to gShenrab's', is absent. Khyab-pa, the former Prince of Devils, is entrusted with the task of fetching him. When all the disciples are finally assembled the full pomp of the Bon burial ceremonies unrolls. 'A thousand and eight drums were beaten, a thousand and eight gongs were sounded, a thousand and eight conch horns were blown, a thousand and eight silk banners were flown, a thousand and eight incense fires were burned, a thousand and eight lamps were lit, and a thousand and eight sacrificial morsels were offered up.' Finally the coffin of gShen-rab, which faced the East, was closed down and the funeral pyre prepared. The details of the funeral ceremonies and the burning of the corpse as depicted in the miniatures illustrating the manuscript are identical with those purporting to depict the burning of Buddha. The relics were subsequently put into six containers, and thereafter held in the deepest veneration.

When the abandoned disciples now bend the knee at the four Stûpas which have miraculously appeared, and utter lamentations, demanding who shall now close the door of the circle of rebirth, and who shall place the ladder of salvation, gShen-rab hears their voices in the highest Heaven Akanishtha, where he is now imparting truths to the future Bon teacher, called Shes-pa in this heavenly pre-existence. According to the world law the third saviour of the Kalpa can appear only when the life of man has shrunk, owing to a general deterioration of conditions, to the span of ten years. But in order that the gospel shall not perish in the meantime, the previous teacher of the Asuras, Mu-cho ldem-drug, is sent down to earth to preach the gospel as the representative of gShen-rab. The promise of gShen-rab caused great delight amongst the people of the land of Ol-mo lung-rings, and at the determined time Mu-cho ldem-drugs comes down to earth, where he remains three years. During the first year he preached on the shores of the ocean dKar-nag bkra-gsal; in the second year in the palace of Khri-smon rgyal-bzhad; and in the third year in the palace of Phar-po so-brgyad, which had once been gShen-rab's headquarters on earth. 'Keeping to the words of the Master, he constantly preached the gospel, writing it down completely and fully', so the text informs us.

This note is of great importance as the first official report of the Bon-po concerning the creation of its sacred literature. Mu-cho now gathered together a large staff of translators to spread the Bon teachings throughout all countries as missionaries. Three Lo-tsâ-ba went westward into the land of Ta-zig, which stands for the empire of the Islamitic peoples, and in particular the eastern frontier district; whilst one each went to China, to India, to the land of Khrom, which can be identified as Turkestan, where King Ge-sar ruled, to Tibet, to the two countries lying between Tibet and China, namely Mi-nyag and Sum-pa, and, finally, to Zhang-zhung, the country where gShen-rab taught.[1] This interesting item of information, which must of course be regarded as legendary in this form, has in all probability a substratum of truth in it. We know already that beyond all question the syncretic Bon religion and related religions flourished in Zhang-zhung and the neighbouring western districts. G. Tucci dis-

[1] These translators are also mentioned in the *Crystal of Doctrinal Systems*; cf. also Hoffmann, *Bon Religion*, p. 329.

covered numerous abandoned sacred relics of the Bon-po in the Kailâsa districts and in Gu-ge, and particularly in the upper Sutley Valley, the 'Silver Palace', which the liturgical texts of the Bon-po celebrate as the birth and living place of the gShen-rab.[1] The Bon religion probably also had followers earlier on in the Indian and Chinese frontier districts, and we certainly know that it had in Eastern Turkestan, where texts have been found buried in the sands proving the presence of followers of the Bon religion in the country.[2] The facts which J. F. Rock has made known concerning the religion of the Na-khi and Mo-so in Yunnan, show quite clearly that the reports about a Bon mission have a factual basis. The sacred writings of the Mo-so reveal a clear literary dependance on the texts of the Tibetan Bon religion.[3]

We find a somewhat different version of the outward spread of the Bon religion in the book *bsTan-'byung* (*Story of the Gospel*), and I am indebted to Professor F. W. Thomas for a number of interesting passages from this Bon text. According to this version,[4] Heavenly Bon-po were sent out either by gShen-rab or Mu-cho to India, China, Udyâna, Eastern Turkestan and Tibet. The teachers for India are said to be incarnated in the line of the Shâkya, which is, of course, an attempt to document the alleged dependence of Buddhism on the Bon religion. The names of these teachers do not agree with those listed in the *gZer-myig*. However, it is interesting that they are referred to as 'Mu-cho', 'the Mu-cho who gathered the gospel' (bka bsdu mu cho). The name 'Mu-cho', in the name of gShen-rab's representative Mu-cho ldem-drug, is thus an appellation meaning 'teacher', and it is not out of the question that it comes from the Manichaean term 'Možag'.[5]

But let us return to the *gZer-myig:* when Mu-cho had preached the Bon gospel for the pre-arranged period of three years he returned, by means of his magic powers, to Heaven. The eighteenth and final chapter then takes us into the future, into a period when the life of man is no more than a short span of ten

[1] G. Tucci, *Santi e briganti nel Tibet ignoto*, pp, 57, 100, 129, 134-7.

[2] See the particulars given by me in the *Zeitschrift der Deutschen Morgenländische Gesellschaft*, 1940, p. 175, Note 3.

[3] *Ibid*, p. 179, Note 3; and Hoffmann, *Bon Religion*, p. 234.

[4] Fol. 261, 2 *et seq.*

[5] See the *Zeitschrift der Deutschen Morgenländische Gesellschaft*, 1938, p. 364, and *ibid.*, the correction 1940, p. 172. In the present state of our knowledge the connection between Mu-cho and Môžag seems worthy of consideration.

6 The main temple of bSam-yas, the oldest monastery in Tibet

7 Tantric Lama of the Red-Hat sect exorcising Demons

years. The former teacher gShen-rab has now left the Akanishtha Heaven, and is living in the highest and—unlike Buddhism—positive bliss 'in the sphere of perfected gShen, without return, equal to Heaven and extended in space'. But the new Bon teacher Shes-pa is already looking out over the world from the top of Mount Sumeru on to his future birthplace just as gShen-rab once did before him. He too is seeking for a father and mother, and the earth will soon once again be the scene of a new saviour's career, because according to the eternal world law a son of Heaven will always be descending into the world, and throughout a strictly preordained life he will save many creatures. The story of this Saviour is told in detail in *The Sûtra of the Origin of gShen-rab in the Three Periods*, of which, according to the note at the end of it, the *gZer-myig* is only an extract.[1]

Having examined the legendary story of gShen-rab we must now assemble what little historical evidence there is available concerning the later history of the Bon-po. For the moment the situation is not at all clear, and we shall know more only when texts such as the above mentioned 'bsTan-'byung' have been placed at our disposal. Notes compiled from Bon sources in the Buddhist historical work *rGyal-rabs* suggests that after the general religious and cultural collapse which followed the disintegration of the country, the systematized Bon religion had to be artificially revived too. This source attaches the revival of the Bon religion in Central Tibet to the name of a Bon priest named rNa-chen li-phyogs, who is said to have come from the East Tibetan province of Khams to Ü and Tsang (Dbus and gTsang), where he recovered writings which had been hidden in the rocks during the time of the persecutions, and founded a number of monasteries, four of which are mentioned by name. This building of monasteries in the Buddhist fashion was an innovation in the history of the Bon religion, because, as we have seen, the old Bon religion had no resident monasteries. But with this first founding of monasteries by rNa-chen a development began which brought the Bon religion closer and closer to Lamaism. The original religious fund from Zhang-zhung was now supplemented by a growing stream of newly borrowed teachings so that the gradually the Bon priests were in a position to offer their followers all that Buddhism could. The Bon religion now had monasteries occupied by monks who lived according to rules of an order along the lines

[1] *Zeitschrift der Deutschen Morgenländische Gesellschaft*, 1938, p. 361.

of the Buddhist Order, and who went in for philosophy, mysticism and new-fashioned magic, religious festivals and the carrying around of sacred objects in processions. But this all developed in an atmosphere of hostility to Buddhism. Just as the mediaeval Satanist desecrated the Host, so the Bon-po turned their sacred objects not in a dextral but in a sinister fashion. For example, the points of their holy sign the swastika did not turn dextrally as that of Lamaism do, but sinistrally, to left instead of to right. The Bon religion had become ossified as a heresy, and its essence lay largely in contradiction and negation.

Reports of Buddhist writers show that the Bon-po played a large part in religious life in the Middle Ages in Tibet but without lending it any new impetus. The text *Myang-chung* gives us a description of the unreformed religious instructions in the Nyang district, and mentions a number of monasteries of the Bon-po, and one or two well-known preachers of this religion. Referring to one of these holy men, the text[1] declares: 'He attained the "rainbow body" by means of which he could touch the glaciers of the river sources, because he was filled as a holy man with the "White 'A' Vehicle", "A" of the Samantabhadra (the highest Bon divinity)'. Up to the fifteenth century, that is, at a time when the red, unreformed Lamaist sects had the upper hand, and bore a striking inner resemblance to the Bon religion, there must have been lively competition between the two priesthoods for possession of the holy places, and for the profitable friendship of rich laymen. Particularly illuminating in this respect is the magic struggle of the Buddhist Mi-la ras-pa (who belonged to the bKa-rgyud-pa sect with which we shall deal in some detail later) and a representative of the Bon priesthood named Na-ro bon-chung and his magically-endowed sister for possession of the sacred mountain Kailâsa. We have already seen that the neighbourhood around Kailâsa, and the sacred lakes Mânasarovar and Rakas-tal, was once the famed centre of the Bon-po, and the place where according to its followers all the important happenings in the life of gShen-rab took place. It was thus a matter of very great importance when the Buddhist Mi-la claimed the essential domain of the Bon-po for Buddhism, particularly as it also enjoys the veneration of the Indian followers of Shiva. The wrestling for possession of these important places is reflected in the legendary reports of the *Hundred thousand Chants*

[1] *Bon Religion*, p. 309.

of Mi-la concerning a competition in magic between the two rivals, as a result of which Mi-la completely defeated his opponent and made himself master of the famous mountain.[1] According to Bon-po sources, however, the competition was won by their representative.[2] But one way or the other, the duel between Mi-la and Naro bon-chung opened up a development which ended in the complete disappearance of the Bon-po from its own most sacred neighbourhood. The *Crystal of Doctrinal Systems* has handed down an isolated but interesting report on a kind of Bon Concilium. This religious council, which must have taken place at the beginning of the Tibetan Middle Ages, was held in Mang-mkhar to the west of the famous monastery of Sa-skya; and Bon priests from the western districts (Ta-zig), India, China, and Tibet are said to have come to it in order to lay down a binding canon of magical formulas.

With the foundation of the reformed Yellow Church by Tsong-kha-pa in the fifteenth century, and its gradual development into the dominating spiritual and secular power in Tibet, the Bon-po found themselves increasingly restricted in their movements, and finally exposed to violent persecution. In the seventeenth century religion made another attempt to get itself recognized as an orthodox State religion; this time in the State of a small dynasty in Eastern Tibet, where even today there is still a Bon religious stronghold. This was Be-ri, one of the so-called Hor States on the Upper Ya-lung. A campaign of repression was begun there against Biddhism, and all the Buddhist Lamas, whether of the Red or Yellow sect, were thrown into prison indifferently. This anachronistic attempt at a Bon restoration did not last long; and the great fifth Dalai Lama, who was at that time completing the development of Tibet into a theocratic State under the dominance of the Yellow Tsong-kha-pa sect, had little difficulty in settling accounts with the heretics who had temporarily got the upper hand in Be-ri. The Mongol Prince Gu-shri Khan, who represented the secular arm of the Dalai Lama, led his forces against Be-ri, defeated its army, and threw its king into prison. The Buddhist monks were all released,[3] and a long period of persecution began for the Bon-po, a persecution which was practised not only by the Central Government in Lhasa, but

[1] I translated this chapter in my *Sieben Legenden des Mi-la ras-pa*, pp. 65 *et seq.*
[2] G. Tucci, *Santi e brigante nel Tibet ignoto*, p. 110.
[3] G. Huth, *Geschichte des Buddhismus in der Mongolei*, II, p. 251.

also by the Chinese, who felt impelled to intervene in the religious disputes in Tibet in the interests of their colonial policy under the Manchu Dynasty. The Chinese placed themselves completely on the side of the orthodox yellow church and suppressed the Bon-po, who had developed into the champions of Tibetan national independence in the border areas against Chinese westward pressure. The culmination of this development came under the Emperor Ch'ien-lung, when the Chinese subjugated the rebellious area along the Golden River.[1] As a result numerous Bon-po monasteries, complete with sacred relics were destroyed, including the famous gYung-drung lha-sding, which was stormed by the Chinese in 1775 and practically razed to the ground. However, at the instructions of the emperor it was rebuilt in the following years and handed over to the yellow orthodox church under the Chinese name of Kuang fa-sze, which means the Spread of the Faith. The well-known traveller Albert Tafel visited this monastery in 1907, and he notes in his subsequent travel book:[2] 'At the orders of the Manchurian officers the Bönbo murals in the old monastery were whitewashed over, whilst the Bönbo images and books were buried under the foundations of the Du Kang, and only sinistral swastikas and other symbols let into the floor were there to recall the forcible conversion of the place by the Mandchu.'

Although for the space of centuries the power of the State was brought into play against the hated heretics, the Bon-po managed to survive in Eastern and Northern Tibet, and they do right down to the present day. With the help of contributions from the faithful, new religious centres were set up to replace the old which had been destroyed. In Tibet proper, where the regime of the Dalai Lama is the strongest, these Bon centres are few and far between, and it is really only in backward districts such as the Chumbi Valley and the forest area of Kong-po that the Bon-po have managed to maintain themselves in any strength. On the other hand, frequent travellers reports show that both in the North and in the East there are still whole settlements of followers of the Bon-po.[3] The northern district is designated by a line from Dangra Yumtsho over the great lake districts and

[1] E. Haenisch, 'Die Eroberung des Goldstromlandes in Ost-Tibet', in *Asia Major*, 1935, pp. 262 *et seq.*

[2] *Meine Tibetreise II*, p. 230.

[3] I have provided a summary of the reports of Tibet travellers in my book *Quellen zur Geschichte der Tibetischen Bon-Religion*, pp. 236 *et seq.*

Nagchukha to the eastern Gyade (rGya-sde), and the eastern by a line from Amdo over the wild and inaccessible mountainous country Gyarong to Yunnan and the Burmese frontier.

It remains for us to review the patheon and the teachings and sacred writings of the Bon religion. Like the pantheon of Lamaism, that of the Bon-po has been tremendously extended, and all we can do is to give a general sketch of this world of gods as it is described in the *gZer-myig*, with the aid of occasional notes taken from other works. First of all we must bear in mind that in addition to the pantheon of the later Bon religion created primarily in Zhang-zhung under Western Asiatic and Buddhist influences, the old, so to speak, anonymous gods of the animist-shamanist era have remained alive in the minds of the common people. The highest principle of this religion and at the same time the transcendental Urguru from which all enlightened understanding comes, and which in type is similar to the Âdibuddha of many of the Vajrayâna systems, is called Kun-tu bzang-po, in Sanskrit Samantabhadra; in other words, it bears the same name as the Âdibuddha of Pandmaism, to which, of course, the syncretic Bon religion bears a close relationship. Philosophically considered, this Samantabhadra represents the ultimate absolute, the Dharmakâya, called here the Bon substance (Bon-sku), a concept which despite many positive characteristics (conscious bliss) seems to be largely the same as the mahâyâna 'voidness'. For example, gShen-rab was in the sphere of perfect gShen after his final departure from the highest heaven Akanishtha (og-myin) 'without return, equal to Heaven and extended in space'. According to the *gZer-myig*,[1] 'The Creator of the Spirit' (sems) is called Samantabhadra; the 'creatrix of the spirit' (yid) is Samantabhadrâ.

Thus side by side with the 'Âdibuddha' Samantabhadra there is also, as in related systems, his Shakti (the source of female energy) who is referred to here with the feminine form of her male partners name, but is usually referred to as 'the Great Mother' (yum chen) Sa-trig er-sangs. From the creative communion of these two there is produced in each Kalpa a 'God of Wisdom' (Ye-shes-kyi lha) attached to the 'Body of Pleasure' (in heavenly words), to the Sambhogakâya, and a 'World God' (Srid-pa) for the sphere of the 'Changing Body', the Nirmânakâya; and the latter guides and rules our visible world. From our

[1] I 23b, 5.

examination of the first chapter of the *gZer-myig* we discovered the appropriate two gods from the previous world era, which formed a trinity with the teaching Bon Saviour of the era gTo-rgyal ye-mkhyen. The trias, or trinity, of the current Kalpa consists of the God of Wisdom gShen-lha od-dkar, the World God Sangs-po 'bum-khri, and the Teacher gShen-rab mi-bo. In the conjuration formula of the *gZer-myig* this trinity is extended by the addition of the great Shakti Sa-trig er-sangs, who is not subordinate to the life circle of development, thus making a sacred Tetrad. This conjuration, which contains a description of the divinities and their attributes, and is obviously developed from inconographic material, as a comparison with the *gZer-myig* miniatures reveals, reads:[1]

'Therefore first veneration for our great mother!
The Mother of space Sa-trig er-sangs
Is like in colour to essence of gold.
Her finery, her clothing, her Heavenly Palace
Is golden and beautiful through golden light.
In her right hand she holds the heroic letters of the "Five Seeds",
In her left hand she holds the Mirror of Shining Gold.
She sits on the throne of two strong lions, who shine like jewels.
Through blessings she effects the well-being of creatures.
Veneration to the great Sa-trig er-sangs!

The God of Wisdom gShen-lha od-dkar
Is like in colour to essence of crystal.
His finery, his clothing, his Heavenly Palace.
Is of crystal, and beautiful through crystal light.
In his hand he holds an iron hook with which he guides through compassion.
He sits on the throne of two powerful elephants, which shine like jewels.
By his compassion he effects the well-being of creatures.
Veneration to the great gShen-lha od-dkar!

The best of the effective means (upyâya), the World God Sangs-po 'bum-khri

[1] *gZer-myig*, I, 174a, 6 *et seq*. I published the pictures of the four entities in question in my minor work *La religione Bon Tibetana*, Rome 1943.

Is like in colour to essence of silver.
His finery, his clothing, his Heavenly Palace
Is of silver, and beautiful through silver light.
In his hand he holds the Precious Banner.
He sits on the throne of two blissful garuda birds, which shine like jewels.
Through magical creation he effects the well-being of creatures.
Veneration to the great Sangs-po 'bum-khri!

The Teacher gShen-rab mi-bo, perfect in wisdom,
Glows in his colours like a jewel.
His finery, his clothing and his Heavenly Palace
Are like jewels, and beautiful through the lights of jewels.
In his hand he holds the Golden Sceptre.
He sits on the throne of Nine Degrees with the Wheel, which shines like a jewel.
By emitting rays of light he effects the well-being of creatures.
Veneration to the great gShen-rab mi-bo!'

The individual figures of the Trias—gShen-lha od-dkar, Sangs-po 'bum-khri and gShen-rab—appear in five-fold form (perhaps under Manichaean influences, and we have already pointed out the great significance of the Pentad in this religion). There is a gShen-rab of the body, of speech, of capacities (yon-tan), of merit ('phrin-las) and of the spirit (thugs). The corresponding five forms of the World God and of the God of Wisdom even have special names; for example, the World God of Speech is called Ye-bdal mu-khri. Part of these special forms of their divinity are graphically portrayed in the miniatures of the *gZer-myig*, and strictly distinguished inconographically by colour and attributes.

The so-called Gi-khod, or Gye-god, represent a special group of Bon gods. According to Bon belief they live on the peak of the sacred mountain Kailâsa, and comprise 360 divinities, a number no doubt astrologically arrived at. Na-ro bon-chung, the opponent of the Buddhist champion Mi-la appealed in a hymn to the Gye-god before he gave battle to the Buddhist, and one of those three Bon priests from Zhang-zhung, Bru-sha (Gilgit) and Kashmir, who were supposed to perform the funeral ceremonies of Gri-gum btsan-po in mythical antiquity was devoted to the cult of these 360 gods.

As in Lamaism, the number of the terrifying gods (Khro-bo, in Sanscrit Krodhadevatâ) is legion. They are represented with one or more human or animal heads. There are such gods with the heads of pigs, of horses, of bulls and of tigers. The non-plus-ultra monster is the 'Protector of the Doctrine' (Dharmapâla), a nine-headed enormity used by gShen-rab to fight against the demons who were trying to destroy the temple of the Chinese King Kong-tse: the 'King of Anger' dbU-dgu-pa. His terrible sister Srid-pa'i rgyal-mo (Queen of the World) has three eyes and six arms. She appears to be the Bon form of the Lamaist Shrîdevî, or the angry Târâ. And, above all, there is 'the Tiger God of Flaming Fire', sTag-lha me-'bar, whose terrible appearance is described to us by L. A. Waddell in his book on Lamaism.[1]

In its section devoted to the Bon religion the *Crystal of Doctrinal Systems* provides information concerning the Bon teachings on the origin of the visible world with its hierarchies of gods and creatures, which, of course, belong to the sphere of the 'Changing Body'. It is interesting to note in this connection that the Buddhist author declares that these dogmas of the Bon-po derive from the Tîrthika, the non-Buddhist, Hindu Indians. The reliability of the sketch provided by the Lamaist author has been amply confirmed by a discovery of my own in a Bon text *Origin of the Black-Headed Dwarflike Creatures* (*dbu nag mi'u 'dra chags*) which gives a detailed description of Bon cosmogony completely in agreement with the brief information provided in the *Crystal.*[2] In the beginning was 'voidness', nothingness, (ye-med), the state of pure Dharmakâya, from which the 'Being' (Ye-yod) gradually developed. This then gave birth to two principles, the one of which was bright and fatherly, the other sinister and motherly. Then cold developed, and after that, dull frost and glittering dew. From frost and dew developed a mirrorlike lake, which rolled itself up into an egg. Two birds were hatched from this egg. The one was called 'Rich Brilliance' and the other 'Tormented Darkness'. From the union of these two birds came three eggs, a white egg, a black egg, and a speckled egg. From the white egg came the line of World Gods (Srid-pa); from the black egg came 'the Arrogant Black Man', presumably the forebear of Asura; and from the speckled egg came an intercessional prayer. The World God Sangs-po 'bum-khri, and also Ye-smon rgyal-po,

[1] *The Buddhism of Tibet*, p. 520.
[2] Fol. 13a, 5 *et seq.*

had no control over the organs of sight, hearing, smelling, tasting, stretching and walking, but he had everything he needed, thanks to the 'Thinking Spirit'. The World God then called the whole habited and uninhabited world into being. 'To the right he laid gold and turquoise and spoke an intercessional prayer. From this developed a gold mountain and a turquoise valley, and the whole line of the Phya was born. To the left he laid a mussel and a precious stone, and spoke an intercessional prayer. From this developed a mussel mountain and a valley of precious stones, and the whole line of the dMu was born. Before him he laid a crystal and "a red light" (a precious stone?) and spoke an intercessional prayer. From this developed a crystal mountain and a sea of light, and the whole line of the gTsugs was born.' The Phya are human beings, the dMu, heavenly spirits, and the gTsugs, animals.

The Bon doctrinal canon as a whole is gathered into nine systematic sections, or 'Vehicles' (theg-pa) as with Padmaism. The first four, known as 'Vehicles of Cause', contain largely the teachings and practices of the old shamanist-animist Bon religion.[1] The first 'Vehicle' (P'yva-gshen) deals with the 360 gTo and the 84,000 dPyad ceremonies. Contained in them is the whole oracular side of the Bon-po, to which the greatest signficance has been attached from the earliest times. Whoever is acquainted with this Vehicle knows exactly which path leads to good and which to evil; how you can remove doubts as to the truth of a matter; and how you can obtain fore-knowledge of the things of daily life. The oracle is consulted by means of coloured ribbons, and the answers come through exclamations uttered in a Shamanistic trance, and are regarded as being inspired by the gods and spirits. Then there is the shoulder-blade oracle, a method which is still much used today, particularly amongst the followers of Lamaism. Shoulder-blades of sheep are cast into a fire, and from the shape of the cracks and so on caused by the heat it is believed that the future can be foreseen.

The teachings of the second Vehicle (sNang-gshen) are concerned with the four kinds of ritual recitations, the eight kinds of lamentation, and the forty-two methods of making thanksgiving offerings. The third Vehicle (Phrul-gshen) is devoted to the practice of magic, teaching the adepts how to make rain and to

[1] According to the *Crystal of Doctrinal Systems*, and the passage of the *Report of the Ministers* devoted to the Bon religion.

call down a curse on their enemies. The fourth Vehicle (Srid-gshen or Dur-gshen) must be regarded as of particular importance. In carrying out the rites of this necromatic Vehicle the priest arms himself with a sword or a knife. This Vehicle teaches the 360 ways to die, the four ways to arrange burial places, and the eighty-one ways to subdue evil spirits. These last-named rites are directed in particular against the so-called Sri spirits, to which we have already referred. These are fond of emerging from the ground, particularly in the neighbourhood of burial grounds. This Vehicle, or section, also concerns itself with rites for the protection of the living and for the observation of the stars, i.e. with Bon astrology.

The four Vehicles of Effect are quite different from the four Vehicles of Cause, and the former concern themselves with higher religious matters. They are not concerned with more or less worldly matters, such as oracular methods, good-luck ceremonies and the burial of the dead, but with the way to salvation, with the way to emancipation from the sorrowful life cycle of development from birth onward, quite in the Buddhist fashion. Vehicles Five and Six (dGe-gshen and Drang-srong) seem to be in accordance with the old Mayâyâna and its practice of the Bodhisattva virtues. When, according to their methods, a man has passed through three endless world periods (Asam khyeya-Kalpa) he arrives at salvation. However, the adepts of the seventh and eighth Vehicles—A-dkar (Vehicle of the White 'A' sacred to the Bon religion) and Ye-gshen—arrive at the same objective by reincarnation. These Vehicles include the Tantric teachings and the mysticism of Bon-po, and approximate to the Vajrayâna of the Buddhists. The non-plus-ultra Vehicle, hyad-par chen-po ('the greatest of all'), the ninth, contains the teachings of the so-called 'Direct Path', and is intended to help the seeker to merge with the Bon substance or essence, that is to say, with the highest absolute, even in this life. The old summary of the Bon doctrine in the *Report of the Ministers* mentions a tenth Vehicle (Ma-khu-ba), but nothing definite is known about it.

The aim of the Bon mystics, and the object of their conjuration and meditational practices, is unification with the original basic essence, the Bon essence, which is described as completely pure, unclouded by passions, void and shining. Although it is not a 'thing', it nevertheless shines as a 'thing'. It is not affected by recognition or non-recognition. It contains both good and evil (on this high stage they have both become pointless) and also the circle of rebirth and salvation as antitheses fully embraced in itself. Thus this mystic Bon belief is very closely related to the moral and metaphysical relativity of the Vajrayâna, and closer examination would in all likelihood reveal particularly close connections with the Padmasambhava sect. Characteristic here, it seems to me, is the significance of light. The Absolute, which is to be achieved by meditation, is practically the same as light. The *Crystal of Doctrinal Systems* declares: 'In the middle of the precious palace of the heart (citta) which is on the eight petals of the mystic arteries, there are five mystic saps. In their centre is a ball of the colour of the five wisdoms, like a sphere. In this centre is the Bon essence, a gathering of light. As its essence is void it is not subject to duration, and because it shines through knowledge it is also not subject to destruction. . . . Looking at its essence with fixed eyes, whereby contemplation and the contemplater are one . . . that is meditation.' The Bon-po distinguish three stages of meditation: the lowest, in which the distraction of the mind is gradually overcome, allows a persistence in concentration or its abandonment; the middle stage allows the thought of autosalvation to rise in the soul; and the third stage makes the soul of the meditating person one with space. 'At that time all spiritual pollutions (klesha) become knowledge, and the whole visible world is recognized as contained in the completely pure Bon sphere.'

Not all Bon mystics devoted themselves to such pure and selfless striving. Very often their efforts were directed to a lengthening of their own lives by the practice of magic, in which art, according to the historian Padma dkar-po, the rival of the holy Mi-la and sister of Na-ro bon-chung was very experienced. According to A. David-Neel, horrible things take place in connection with such practices, and some Bon priests are supposed to lengthen their own earthly days by appropriating the life force of others who die a painful death by starvation. However, these victims must be voluntary, as otherwise the sacrifice is of no effect.[1]

Before ending our examination of the syncretic Bon religion a few words must be said about the tremendous volume of literature which the priests of this belief have created throughout the

[1] A. David-Neel, *Magie d'amour et magie noire, Scènes du Tibet inconnu*, Paris 1938.

centuries.[1] When dealing with the religious historical events of the reign of King Khri-srong we met with the well-established ancient tradition according to which the systematized Bon religion originated in Zhang-zhung, whence also came the first sacred Bon texts, which were subsequently translated into the Tibetan language. But the Lamaist authors never cease to insist that even then, as well as later towards the end of the period of kings, Bon priests took Buddhist texts, merely making minor alterations in the names of persons and places, sometimes even turning the religious teachings in them into their own. In fact the *Crystal of Doctrinal Systems* gives us a whole list of Bon texts, comparing them in each case with the original Buddhist texts from which they were appropriated. These changes will, of course, have to be examined in detail when Bon texts become more readily available, but our own observations in connection with our analysis of the story of gShen-rab do suggest that there is some justification of the Buddhist charges of plagiarism. However, these can refer only to the teachings of the 'Vehicles of Effect', and the old Shamanist practices of the first four Vehicles are undoubtedly of ancient and authentic Bon origin, and it would hardly be possible to produce older Buddhist texts containing them.

From all this it must be regarded as highly probable that very few of the titles of the Bon works in the Zhang-zhung tongue are really authentic, but one day it will be very important for us to discover which actually are where the greater part of this literature is concerned, the alleged Zhang-zhung titles will probably prove to be fictitious, invented according to the laws of some mystic language—the sort of thing some Lamaists are quite familiar with. The famous Bon formula. On ma tri mu ye sa le du—the formula which represents and takes the place of the sacred Avalokiteshvara formula of the Lamaists—Om mani padme hum—is probably couched in some such 'language'. The Zhang-zhung tongue is obviously intended to serve the Bon religion as Sanscrit serves Buddhism, and the supplementary Zhang-zhung title is intended both to increase the authority of the texts and to vouch for its authenticity. We must also register the remarkable fact that some texts have ununderstandable titles, not in the Zhang-zhung tongue but in an idiom of the

[1] With regard to the literature of the Bon-po see my article in *Zeitschrift der Deutschen Morgenländische Gesellschaft*, 1940, pp. 169 *et seq.*

'Swastika' gods of Ka-pi-ta (this is the case in the *gZer-myig*), or in the language of Ta-zig or Mu-sangs ta-zig, which means 'heavenly Ta-zig'. Ta-zig was originally a name for the Arabs, who swept victoriously through Central Asia at the time of the Tibetan universal monarchy. Later on it came to refer exclusively to the Mahomedans to the west of Tibet, i.e. including the Persians. But as I have shown in another place,[1] a passage in the *gZer-myig* incidates that in the old days the frontier between Tibet and the western Ta-zig countries was regarded as lying only a little to the west of Lake Mânasarovar, so that Zhang-zhung was thus considered as belonging to the land of Ta-zig, so that the two language names are really one and the same. It is very difficult to decide today whether the Ka-pi-ta in the name of the third of these mysterious languages is only a mystic word, or whether it refers to the old area Kapisha, or Kapistân to the north-west of India. If the latter should turn out to be the case then a still further part of that area of North-West India will have been brought into connection with the Bon religion, an area which in the first thousand years after Christ was a remarkable centre for the development of syncretic religion.

Like the Buddhists, with whose canonical writings we shall deal in a further chapter, the Bon-po also codified its sacred literature in two great collections: the Kanjur (bKa-'gyur) containing the authoritative pronouncements of gShen-rab; and the Tanjur (bsTan-'gyur) containing the interpretative and expository literature. In 1931 the Tibet explorer George Roerich informed us in his book[2] that he had seen a complete set of each of these two collections in a monastery in Nub-hor, and that the Kanjur consisted of 140 volumes, and the Tanjur of 160. It would be a very good thing for religious history if these texts could now speedily be made available for expert examination. It remains to be seen in what relationship the Kanjur stands to another branch of the sacred Bon writings with which we are acquainted through the *gZer-myig*, namely those contained in four 'Bon-Gateways' (Bon sgo bzhi) and in a so-called 'Treasure' (mdzod). The 'Treasure' consists of four large didactic texts, one of which is that *Sûtra of the Origin of gShen-rab in the Three Periods*, of which the available *gZer-myig* is only an extract.[3] We

[1] *Bon Religion.*, p. 213. [2] *Trails to Inmost Asia*, Newhaven 1931, p. 357.

[3] *Zeitschrift der Deutschen Morgenländische Gesellschaft*, 1938, pp. 360 *et seq*; and 1940, pp. 170 *et seq.*

do not propose to list the titles of the numerous Bon texts contained in the *Crystal of Doctrinal Systems*, because so far they are mere names for us, and we know nothing of their content.

CHAPTER VI

THE RE-BIRTH OF BUDDHISM

We have already pointed out that the violent internal struggles during the last days of the Tibetan kings resulted in a general political collapse and a period of complete religious and cultural stagnation. The historian Bu-ston records that in this period the regular study of the sacred texts ceased, and that amongst the few Buddhist monks who had not become Bon-po or laymen the Order had fallen into a decline. The injunctions of Vinaya were complied with only in the summer months, whilst the degeneration amongst the Tantrics was complete. They no longer had any idea of the deeper significance of their mystic texts and ceremonies, and they abandoned themselves to a life of gross sexual indulgence. Everything now seemed to suggest that without the support of powerful kings, Buddhism would degenerate completely, disintegrate, and be absorbed by the old Bon religion. It is difficult for us to realize just how complete the religious collapse of those days really was. On the other hand, the development which set in within a few decades and led to a revival of the heavily persecuted belief and its ultimate victory showed very clearly that although Buddhism had remained restricted to a relatively small circle it had certainly taken root in the hearts of a real élite, so that the ending of powerful protection had not meant the end of all religious idealism. The period we are about to describe may therefore be properly regarded as 'the heroic age' of Buddhism in Tibet. High enthusiasm imbued those men who, without any outside encouragement, and impelled only by the faith in them, set to work to convert the Land of Snows once again, and to such purpose that in the end they were completely successful. The epoch of the kings, the epoch of 'the earlier dissemination of the gospel' (snga-dar), was chiefly marked by its receptive character, whilst the period of 'the later dissemination' (phyi-dar) was characterized by the exceptional vigour and independence of spiritual life.

The Tibetan chroniclers describe in glowing colours the story of those three spiritual leaders who saved the faith and handed on the torch to younger enthusiasts.[1] These three, gYo dGe-'byung, dMar Shâkyamuni, and gTsang Rab-gsal, were meditating in the hermitage of Chu-bo-ri when King gLang-dar-ma began his persecution of Buddhism. They observed with horror that monks were taking to hunting, and when they inquired the reason for this extraordinary happening they learned for the first time of the misfortune which had come upon Buddhism. Without hesitation they gathered the most important of the sacred texts, and in particular those relating to the maintenance of the Order, packed them on to a mule and fled to Western Tibet (mNga-ris), travelling at night and hiding during the day. But they could not stay in that area either, obviously because the wave of persecution had reached there too. They now journeyed through the land of the Turkish Karluk, 'took the northern road and went into the land of the Uigurians (Hor)', who at that time, after the collapse of their great steppe empire (840), had set up a small sub-principality in the eastern part of Eastern Turkestan, where both Buddhism and Manichaeanism were still flourishing. Although they were assisted there by a pious layman named Shâkyaprajna, and although they remained there for some time, they found great difficulties in propagating their faith in a district whose language was quite different. They therefore now went still farther eastward until they finally reached Amdo, where there was a Tibetan population. As the Tibetan State had disintegrated, the writ of the Central Government in Lhasa, which supported the Bon-po, did not run here, and they were therefore able to settle down in the neighbourhood of the Upper Huang-ho (Tibetan rMa-chu) and devote their lives to their religion.

The young man who inherited the teachings of the three elderly monks was to play a great role in the revival of religion in Central Tibet. He came from a Bon family in the province of 'Phan-yul, to the north of Lhasa. The rGyal-rabs records a touching story of how he (allegedly sixty years after the persecution begun by King gLang-dar-ma) came into an abandoned Buddhist temple in his own homeland and looked at the murals,

[1] Bu-ston 118b 3 (Obermiller II, p. 201); Pad-ma dkar-po, 104b, 1; dPag-bsam ljon-bzang, p. 177; rGyal-rabs B. 231b.

8 The exaltation of the Tantric Lama reaches its climax; he falls into a trance

9 Tantric deity in the sacred love embrace with his Shakti

which represented Buddhist monks going about their religious observances. He had no idea what the pictures represented—an eloquent indication of the extent to which the once powerful religion had disappeared from the memory of the people—so he questioned an old woman, who proved able to give him information. And with this a desire was born in him to become a Buddhist, so he asked the old woman how it was possible to do this. She replied that some of the monks who had been compelled to flee during the persecutions would probably still be in Eastern Tibet. This pleased the young man who immediately made his way 'without regard for life or limb' to Khams. Herdsmen told him how to find the three monks, and he begged them to instruct him. They gave him a Vinaya work to read, and when its teachings had struck root in him, gTsang and gYo accepted him as a novice. But when one year later he requested full ordination (Upasampadâ) the necessary quorum of five monks was unobtainable, so it was impossible to perform the ordination ceremony. The young man had heard that the assassin of gLang-dar-ma, dPal-gyi rdo-rje was living not far away in kLong-thang. He therefore hurried off to ask this priest to take part in the ordination ceremony, but the old ascetic made the interesting reply that as an assassin he felt himself unable to do so. However, in the end the young man succeeded in finding two Chinese monks—the story is set in the frontier district of Tibet and China—and the ordination finally took place, whereby gTsang took the important function of Upâdhyâya, whilst gYo acted as Âcârya and dMar as 'Teacher of Secrets' (Rahonushâsaka). The two Chinese monks assisted as members of the congregation. This young man subsequently became famous under his religious name of bLa-chen, or 'Great Lama', dGongs-pa-gsal, and he succeeded by his vigorous activity in gaining new pupils and spreading Buddhism throughout Central Tibet once more.

Within five years of his ordination a rumour had spread in Central Tibet of the existence of a small Buddhist centre in Khams, and ten further young enthusiasts, allegedly sent by the dynasties of the provinces of Ü and Tsang, made the journey to Eastern Tibet and applied to gTsang for admission into the Order. At first gTsang hesitated on account of his great age, whilst dGongs-pa-gsal hesitated because he had himself been ordained only five years previously. In the end, however, and in view of the exceptional circumstances gTsang gave his young pupil permission to carry out the ordination, and the ten young men, of whom Shîlaprajna of kLu-mes was particularly prominent, were ordained by dGongs-pa-gsal as Upâdhyâya, gTsang as Âcârya, and gYo as 'Teacher of Secrets', whilst the third of the old monks, dMar, and the two Chinese monks assisted. A younger brother of each of two of the ten also arrived, and then they all went back to their homeland to work for the propagation of the Buddhist gospel. The historian Bu-ston points out that whereas formerly Lhasa was the main centre for Buddhist monks these monks now went to bSam-yas, where apparently the writ of the Central Government did not run, whereas Buddhist monks were still being persecuted in Lhasa—obviously by the ruling Bon party. kLu-mes took up his quarters in the temple dbU-tshal, whilst his brothers in religion settled in the chief temple and in the other temples. From this centre they now disseminated Buddhist beliefs over the whole of Central Tibet, established a new doctrinal tradition, and building further temples and monasteries.

According to Bu-ston this revival of Buddhism came about seventy years after the persecutions carried out by gLang-dar-ma, whereas 'Brom-ston, who is quoted by the historian Sum-pa mkhan-po, puts it at seventy-eight years, and the historian Nel-pa Pandita, whose work is not yet fully available, speaks of 108 years. This latter figure is less convincing because it happens to be a favourite and typical schematic figure of the Buddhists. When Atîsha, who, as we shall see later, was working for the Buddhist faith from the West, was told of the achievements of dGongs-pa-gsal, he paid him the highest possible tribute, declaring that no ordinary man could have done it, and that dGongs-pa-gsal must be a Bodhisattva who had ascended the (ten) steps of holiness.

The courageous work of dGongs-pa-gsal and kLu-mes and their followers was to receive valuable support a few decades later from Western Tibet. After the collapse of the administration, a great grandson of gLang-dar-ma, named sKyid-lde Nyi-ma-mgon went there to found a new empire for himself in this area, which had been won for Tibet only during the time of the universal monarchy. When this man died his State was divided up between his three sons, of whom one received Ladakh, the second Pu-rangs (bordering on the Kailâsa district), and the third Gu-ge, including the old area of Zhang-zhung. In the following generation the two last-named areas were re-united under 'Khor-re, the grandson of Nyi-ma-mgon. The dynasty of this small kingdom in the Upper Sutley Valley became famous because of its zeal and enthusiasm for the cause of Buddhism. The king himself became a priest and took the religious name of Lha-bla-ma (Royal Monk) Ye-shes-od, and it is under this name that we meet him in the sources.[1] His two sons also became priests, and in consequence the government was handed over to the king's brother, Srong-nge. However, as Tucci points out, the king cannot have surrendered power completely, and Ye-shes-od remained the head of the State as Priest-King, whilst Srong-nge attended to the current business of government under the title of Viceroy (rgyal-tshab). This parallel functioning of a Priest-King and an officiating Viceroy was repeated in the next generation but one of the dynasty.

According to the sources it appears that Ye-shes-od regarded the philosophic teachings of the Mahâyâna (mtshan-nyid) as the authentic word of Buddha, whilst harbouring doubts as to whether the Tantras could be regarded as the authentic pronouncements of the Enlightened One. In particular he looked askance at some of the priests who upheld these latter doctrines for indulging in highly doubtful practices, above all those of an erotic nature. Just as other Tibetans in the days of the great dynasty, this royal monk felt the urge to establish direct contact with India, the sacred land of the Buddhist religion, and he therefore caused some of his own subjects to study under the great Indian masters. These young Tibetans were exhorted to bring back sacred texts and, if possible, some of the representatives of contemporary Buddhism to Gu-ge.

Ye-shes-od chose twenty-one youths from the pick of the land. They were not younger than ten, and not older than twenty, and these he divided into three groups according to their capacities. Amongst them was Rin-chen bzang-po (958-1055) who was to give a tremendous impetus to the new development of Buddhism thanks both to his translations and his religious building activities. The party of twenty-one youths set off for Kashmir, which, together with Magadha in the East, was at that time an important

[1] The revival of Buddhism in Western Tibet is described in Bu-ston 123*a et seq.* (Obermiller II, p. 212); Pad-ma dkar-po 107a, 3 *et seq.*, and dPag-basm ljon-bzang, pp. 181 *et seq.* In addition there is an excellent study by G. Tucci on Rin-chen bzang-po entitled *Rin c'en bzan-po e la rinascità del Buddhismo nel Tibet intorno al mille*, Rome 1933.

centre of Buddhism from which many of the most noted of teachers and mystics of various schools originated. As in many previous cases, the young Tibetans could not stand up to the very different climate of India, and after seven years only Rin-chen bzang-po and one companion, Legs-pa'i shes-rab, returned safely home. However, the success of this first of Rin-chen's great journeys was complete. The unusually talented young priest, who was afterwards to receive the title of 'Great Translator' (lo-chen), had studied Buddhist philosophy and many Tantras under various masters, including in particular the important Guhyasamâja according to the two ways of interpretation ascribed to Nâgârjuna and Buddhajnâna, the Tattvasamgraha according to the commentaries of Ânandagarbha (not to be confused with the philosophical work of the Shântirakshita), and also the Kâlacakra, with which we shall deal later. It was due largely to him that famous masters such as Shraddhâkaravarman, Padmâkaragupta, Kamalagupta and Ratnavajra came to the new Buddhist centre in Western Tibet and co-operated with the Great Translator in turning a tremendous number of Buddhist writings into the Tibetan language. The list of these translations, which represent the life's work of Rin-chen bzang-po, comprises seventeen titles of canonical works, thirty-three systematic exegetical texts to the Sûtras, and 108 to the Tantras.

It is clear from this that, far from being neglected, the study of the Tantras was vigorously furthered. However, these mystical-magical studies were no longer regarded in the coarse and morally doubtful fashion which King Ye-shes-od had condemned, but from an elevated philosophical viewpoint. Rin-chen bzang-po renounced the world at the early age of thirteen, but according to Padma dkar-po he was forty-nine before he was fully ordained. He is said to have studied under no less than seventy-five Indian Pandits, and to have made three journeys to India, the second of which took him to the holy places of Magadha, and the third once again to Kashmir. But it was not only through the great Lo-tsâ-ba that the spiritual forces of India now streamed into Western Tibet, and the king succeeded in securing a visit from the famous Pandit Dharmapâla of Eastern India when the latter was on a visit to Kashmir. Dharmapâla was a great authority on the Vinaya, and through the three pupils he was able to ordain in Tibet—Sâdhupâla, Gunapâla and Prajnapâla—he became the founder of a special West-Tibetan school of the Vinaya.[1] King Ye-shes-od appointed Dharmapâla his special master (Upâdhyâya). The historian Pad-ma dkar-po declares that Rin-chen bzang-po also studied under the famous Pandit Nâro-pa (Nâdapâda), but this does not seem likely because amongst the works translated by the great Lo-tsâ-ba there is not one by this leading figure of contemporary Buddhism, who was to obtain great influence in Tibet but only later, first through his pupil Atîsha, and then through Mar-pa and the sect founded by him.

The importance of Rin-chen bzang-po is by no means confined to his translation work, which, incidentally, included the revision of the old translations made in the reign of Khri-srong; and he was also the moving spirit in the building of numerous temples and monasteries begun by King Ye-shes-od and his successors. His name is still alive in Western Tibet today, and all the more or less ancient holy places in this part of the country are still ascribed by the people to his activities. Amongst the new buildings with which he was connected are said to be the temples of Kha-char and Rong, and in particular the later centre of West-Tibetan Buddhism, the gSer-khang, or 'Golden House', in mTho-ling, probably the capital of the country, which was erected in the days of Ye-shes-od. According to Padma dkar-po, this holy place was built after the model of bSam-yas, and received its name because on its eastern side stood a golden stûpa which caught the rays of the rising sun and reflected them on to the gSher-kang.

One or two reports strike me as important as indicating that all this vigorous activity of the Buddhist enthusiasts did not pass without opposition. It will be remembered that Zhang-zhung was the stronghold and centre of the systematized Bon religion, and at the time of Rin-chen bzang-po it must still have been powerful there. It was only the victory of Mi-la ras-pa over the Bon-po at Kailâsa, which occurred several decades later, that gave Buddhism its final predominance. According to the sources, Rin-chen bzang-po subdued the Nâga (kLu) sKar-rgyal at Guma in Mang-yul, because the building of many temples angered the local spirits, i.e. the Bon priests. Incidentally, this sKar-rgyal seems to have been something more than a mere local deity, for Sum-pa mkhan-po mentions the teachings connected with his name, together with those of the actual Bon-po, as

[1] dPag-bsam ljon-bzang, p. 183; and Tucci, p. 29.

amongst those heresies he has no intention of describing.[1] Quite generally, Rin-chen bzang-po seems to have defeated and refuted a good many followers of heterodox magical practices. The Great Translator passed on his tradition to numerous pupils, amongst whom four were particularly close to him as his spiritual sons. One of them was his companion on his first journey to India, Legs-pa'i shes-rab, who is called 'the Little Translator' to distinguish him from his more renowned master.

It would seem that the Viceroy Srong-nge ruled only for a relatively short time, because even during the lifetime of the Royal Monk Ye-shes-od his nephew Lha-lde became Viceroy. This ruler also showed himself to be favourably inclined towards Rin-chen bzang-po and gave him the title of High Priest and of Vajrâcârya, or teacher of esoteric doctrines. Further, he presented him with lands and the appropriate revenues in the district of Pu-rangs.

The Royal Monk Ye-shes-od continued to work untiringly in the cause of Buddhism. When he heard tell of the fame of Atîsha, one of the leading scholars and mystics of the Buddhist university Vikramashîlâ in Magadha, the stronghold of the faith, he decided to invite the famous master to Tibet, because he was by no means satisfied with the results of his own efforts to purify and consolidate Buddhism in his own country. His first messenger to Vikramashîlâ was unsuccessful, although he had been instructed to offer Atîsha a bar of gold. However, the king sent him to Vikramashîlâ once again to act as observer on the spot and keep the matter in view. In the meantime the king, who was, as we learn in this connection, still the commander of the army of Gu-ge, despite his religious condition organized expeditions into the neighbouring lands for the purpose of collecting large sums of money in order to be able to invite Atîsha and other Indian pandits to his country. With this intention he also penetrated into the land of Gar-log, a name used to describe the Turkish Karluk, or perhaps just Mohammedan unbelievers in general, but there he was defeated and taken prisoner. The King of Gar-log declared himself prepared to release his important captive and allow him to return to his own country, but only on condition that he became a vassal and adopted the religion of Gar-log. Should he be unwilling to do this he could ransom himself with his weight in gold. At this misfortune the followers of Ye-shes-od, and in

[1] P. 406.

particular his great-nephew Byang-chub-od, who was also a religious, were cast into deep gloom. At first they thought of rescuing the king from captivity by armed force, but because such an action might well result in the death of the captive they decided against the attempt. Instead Byang-chub-od organized the collection of gold throughout Tibet in order to raise the ransom. When he had succeeded in gathering what he took to be the required amount he went with an escort to the court of the king of Gar-log. On arriving there, however, it was discovered that the amount of gold available was sufficient only to ransom the captured body of the king, but not his head as well. But at least Byang-chub-od obtained permission for a short interview with the captured king, and the moving scene which now unrolled may be regarded as typical for the spiritual exaltation and religious enthusiasm of the time.[1]

The prince found his great-uncle sick and depressed as a result of the long time he had been kept in a dungeon. He did his best to console him and raise his spirits by telling him that he would go away to collect more gold, and return when he had sufficient for the ransom. But the heroic Ye-shes-od replied that as he was now an old man and broken by illness his life was no longer of value. The young man should therefore use the gold he had collected to invite Indian pandits to the country. He, Ye-shes-od, had never in any of his earlier reincarnations sacrificed his life for the sake of religion, and now this unique opportunity offered itself to be of some use to Buddhism by his sufferings and death. It should therefore be taken advantage of. Byan-chub-od parted in tears from his great-uncle, and returned to their land to do his will and invite Atîsha, and this time his efforts were successful. King-Monk Ye-shes-od was murdered in prison.

The great master, who was to establish the Buddhist religion in Tibet once and for all, and whom the Tibetans usually call 'the Nobleman' (Jo-bo-rje), or Atîsha, was born in the town of Vikramapurî in the Bengal district of Sahora during the reign of King Mahîpâla as the son of a prince.[2] He married and became the father of nine children, but even early on his interest was drawn to the Buddhist teachings and he soon abandoned his princely rights.

[1] See my translation of the description of these events in Pad-ma dkar-po, Oriens 1950, pp. 205 *et seq.*

[2] His life is described in a biography ascribed to his pupil 'Brom-ston, which is available in several editions of varying length.

In a very short time he mastered the knowledge of his day, and became well versed in grammar, philosophy, art-handicraft and medicine. He chose the female Bodhisattva, Târâ, the great saviour, as his protective deity, and he consulted her in all the problems of his life. Before long he had penetrated into the depths of Buddhist philosophy and mysticism, and in his twenty-ninth year he renounced the world for religion, entering the monastery of Otantapurî where he received the name of Dîpamkarashrîjnâna. Amongst his teachesr were some famous Tantrics such as Shânti-pa, Nâ-ro-pa, the younger Kusali, Avadhûti and Dombhi. Apart from the face of Târâ he is also said to have looked on the face of the Tantric deity Hevajra. As his fame spread he was summoned to the famous university of the monastery of Vikramashîlâ, in which he soon occupied a prominent position together with the Sthavira Ratnâkara. Amongst those pupils whose numbers increased rapidly and must have been very great was, as Sum-pa tells us, Pi-to-pa, who is said to have introduced the Kâlacakra system to India during the reign of King Mahîpâla of Bengal.

When the princely monk Byang-chub-od prepared to carry out the wish of his great-uncle and invite Atîsha, he looked around for a suitable person to whom he could entrust the important mission of bringing Atîsha to Tibet, and his choice fell on the translator of Nag-tsho, Tshul-khrims rgyal-ba, who was a master of Sanscrit and already had one successful journey to India to his credit. This man was now sent off to India with five companions and a great deal of gold. The gold was intended partly to facilitate the path of the deputation, and partly to be given to Atîsha as a present when the formal invitation was conveyed to him. After having successfully beaten off an attack by heretical supporters of Hinduism, who coveted their gold, the party arrived safely in Vikramashîlâ after having crossed the Ganges in the night. There they met the earlier messenger of the King of West Tibet whose mission had not been successful, but who had in the meantime taken advantage of the opportunity afforded him by his stay at one of the main centres of Buddhism to acquaint himself very thoroughly with its teachings. Atîsha was much impressed by the persistence of the Tibetans, and deeply moved by the heroic death of King Ye-shes-od, so he consulted his protective deity, Târâ, in the matter, and when she told him that although the journey would shorten his life it would nevertheless be to the benefit of numerous creatures, he decided to accept the invitation. The gold that was now presented to him he used to maintain the leading Indian holy places of the Buddhist religion. Finally the opposition of Sthavira Ratnâkara to the journey was overcome, and Atîsha departed for Tibet; but on the understanding that he must return within three years, which, however, subsequent circumstances did not allow him to do. He left Vikramashîlâ with his companions in 1040, was in Nepal in the following year, and arrived in Western Tibet in 1042. In the meantime Od-lde, the brother of Byang-chub-od, had become king, and he received Atîsha with the highest honours.

It is reported that at his first meeting with Atîsha, which took place in the 'Golden House' of mTho-ling, the old translator Rin-chen bzang-po, who was already in his eighty-fifth year, did not bow. When the great Indian master then showed his supreme knowledge of Buddhist teachings by songs of praise to all the deities represented on the walls of the temple, the old translator became his pupil and was initiated into the deepest Tantric secrets. We are told that he looked upon the faces of the Tantric gods Guhyasamâja and Cakrasamvara, and that before his death at the age of ninety-eight years he had become a 'sky goer'.

Atîsha now worked with great success in mTho-ling for the cause of Buddhism, purifying the degenerated form of Tibetan Buddhism, and whilst by no means seeking to abolish the study of the Tantras, yet endeavouring to balance the requirements of religious discipline, philosophy and mysticism as perfectly as possible. There were many pupils at his feet, including the royal monk Byang-chub-od, and he devoted himself in particular to the work of translation, so that in the extant Lamaist encyclopaedias we find numerous texts whose Tibetan version we owe to the joint efforts of Atîsha and Rin-chen bzang-po. Atîsha also did literary work of his own, and its most important fruit is certainly the small but highly important work *Bodhipathapradîpa* (*Lamp for the Way of Enlightenment*), which was written for Byang-chub-od and translated immediately with the help of its author into the Tibetan language. The book is informed with the purest spirit of an elevated Mahâyâna, such as inspired the best representatives of the Buddhist world. The book begins in an impressive fashion with the classification of men into three groups. Those in the first and lowest group strive only for the happiness of Samsâra and are self-seeking; those of the second and intermediary group devote themselves to a virtuous life in the interests of their own purification; whilst those of the third and highest group desire to obtain salvation for all.

At the invitation of some of his followers, Atîsha now went to Central Tibet in order to further the cause of Buddhism there too, and to consolidate the work begun by gGongs-pa-gsal. The most urgent task in these provinces was to bring the Tantric and non-Tantric aspects of Buddhism into right proportion to each other. In Pu-rangs Atîsha met the important pupil whose coming had been prophesied by his protective deity. This pupil was rGyal-ba'i 'byung-gnas of the 'Brom family, a rich layman who was to consolidate the tradition of Atîsha and found a sect to perpetuate it. From Pu-rangs Atîsha now went on to Tibet proper, where, at the invitation of his numerous followers, including in addition to 'Brom, Khu-ston and bLo-ldan shes-rab, the translator of rNgog, he successively visited the famous holy places of Ü and Tsang: Phan-po-che in Yar-klungs, bSam-yas, Yer-pa and Lhasa. Everywhere he conferred mystic initiations on his pupils, including significantly that of Cakrasamvara according to the tradition of the older Indian Siddha Lûi-pa. Even the father of his pupil 'Brom sat at his feet. After remaining in Tibet for a space of thirteen years he died at the age of seventy-three in sNye-thang on the river sKyid-chu, to the south of Lhasa, after having passed on his tradition to 'Brom (1054). It was Atîsha and his followers who finally succeeded in establishing the Buddhist teachings in Tibet once and for all. His work was crowned, so to speak, after his death when the King of Western Tibet, rTse-lde, the nephew of Byang-chub-od, called a Dharma (chos-'khor), or great council, in the holy place of mTho-ling, to which Buddhist priests came from Western, Central and Eastern Tibet (Khams).

But there is one important achievement of Atîsha which has not yet been mentioned, namely his revision of the Tibetan system of chronology.[1] According to the Re'u-mig reckoning, he wrote his work on chronology in Central Tibet in the year 1051. In the previous centuries dates were reckoned only according to the well-known animal cycle of twelve (hare, dragon, snake, horse, sheep, monkey, hen, dog, pig, mouse, ox and tiger), which

[1] Cf. Grünwedel, *Mythologie*, p. 58; and Pelliot in the *Journal Asiatique*, 1913, pp. 633 *et seq.*

was in use throughout Central Asia, but which was at best a very primitive method of computation. Thanks to the addition of a further cycle of constituents made up of combinations of the five elements, fire, earth, iron, water and wood, a cycle of sixty years was introduced which allowed a much more accurate time computation. The first year of the first cycle of sixty years represents our year 1027 AD. This suggests that Atîsha did not actually introduce the new chronology, but merely systematized and simplified it. The Re'u-mig ascribes its actual introduction to the translator of Gyi-jo, Zla-ba'i od-zer, and its actual introduction was connected with the adoption of the Kâlacakra system in Tibet, on which the whole new chronology was based. Atîsha was also an adept of this new system, and he had received his initiation into its secrets, which obviously greatly excited the Buddhist world at the time, from his teacher Nâ-ro-pa, one of the first important interpreters of the new truths. The history of the Kâlacakra, the ultimate phase of Buddhism in India, is still largely unknown and it will represent an important subject for future research. However, we must deal briefly here with what little we do know about it, because it has played an important role in the life of Tibet down to our own day.

Literally Kâlacakra means 'the Wheel of Time', and, as B. Laufer has pointed out,[1] must originally have represented the animal cycle of twelve already referred to. Astronomy and astrology are the basis of the whole system, but the elements of astrology are deified and raised to the status of means to salvation. At the back of the Kâlacakra lies also the ancient belief in the identity of the microcosm and the macrocosm, whose most condensed expression is contained in the famous magic device of 'the Powerful One in Ten Forms' (dashâkâro vashî) which can be seen everywhere in Tibet. Its symbolism embraces simultaneously all the powers of the world and of the human body and the human spirit.[2] From the standpoint of religious history the Kâlacakra represents the last attempt to revive the slowly declining and degenerating Buddhism of India by liberal borrowings from the powerfully developing systems of Shivaism, and, in particular, of Vishnuism, and also from foreign, western teachings, thus increasing attractions for both the priesthood and the laity. Up to a point the attempt was successful, but at the

[1] *T'oung Pao*, 1907, p. 403.
[2] Cf. A. Grünwedel, *Der Weg nach Sambhala*, p. 96.

same time the new development contained the seeds of death in it, because Buddhism had to abandon so much of its own essence, and had to adapt itself so closely to other contemporary religions that there was no longer any real necessity for its own continued existence, so that when it suffered the shock of the Mohammedan irruption into Eastern India in 1193 it was no longer strong enough to survive it.

The basic Tantra (Mûlatantra) itself, from which gradually a voluminous literature has developed, belongs to the class of so-called 'Mother Tantras,' which occupy themselves with the transmission of teachings concerning transcendental wisdom (prajnâ), whilst the 'Father Tantras' are devoted to the active realization of the ideal of compassion. Kâlacakra is also personified as a pale deity, such as that of Cakrasamvara and Guhyasamâja, but this bloodless creation has never played any great role, and it has been quite overshadowed by the powerful potentialities of the original Buddha, which, as in related systems, takes first place and generally remains nameless.

According to the Tantra texts,[1] Buddha himself preached the Kâlacakra teachings on the famous vulture peak near Râjagriha after his proclamation of the Mahâyâna, the methods of transcendental wisdom (Prajnâpâramitâ); and again at Dhânyakataka in southern India not far from the famous sacred mountain Shrîparvata, which is closely associated with the legend of Nâgârjuna. There was a most sacred Stûpa there, which has been described for us in Tibetan literature.[2] According to the sparse indications available, Dhânyakataka must have been an important centre of Buddhist Tantrism. In his eightieth year, or in the year of his Enlightenment (the Tibetan sources differ on this point) Buddha is said to have preached the esoteric teachings there in the presence of numerous Bodhisattvas and deities; by some mysterious means, King Sucandra of Shambhala was also present, and he asked the Buddha for the text of his teachings. One year later the Mûlatantra (basic text) of 12,000 verses was recorded and preserved in Shambhala. This Sucandra is regarded as the incarnation of the 'Master of Secrets', the Bodhisattva Vajrapâni,

[1] The Mûlatantra (Basic Tantra) of 12,000 verses has not been preserved, but a manuscript of the shortened version Laghu-tantra (abridged Tantra) is extant; see Hoffmann, *Festschrift Schubring*, Hamburg 1951, p. 146. I am preparing an edition of this. The *Sekoddeshatîkâ* issued by M. Carelli, Baroda 1941, quotes the Mûlatantra, pp. 2-4.

[2] Works of kLong-rdol-bla-ma, Essay 7.

and as the inspirer of numerous mystic Vajrayâna teachings. The land of Shambhala is undoubtedly somewhere outside India, and originally it was in all probability a real area, whereas as time went on it faded into the idea of a purely mythical kingdom. According to the unanimous indications of the sources it was situated somewhere to the north of the river Shîtâ. Csoma has tried to identify the Shîtâ, the most northern of the four great streams which according to Buddhist cosmography originate in the sacred lake Mânasarovara, with the Iaxartes, but some of the magically embellished descriptions of the way to this mysterious Shambhala rather suggest Tarim in East Turkestan. So far only later Tibetan descriptions, i.e. second-hand sources,[1] of this way have been made available, whilst an older one translated from the Sanscrit and contained in the encyclopaedia of the Tanjur has so far attached no research. Shambhala is described as being surrounded by snow-capped mountains. In the centre of the country lies a tremendous city with the King's Palace Kalâpa, and to the south of this is a great park in which there is a Mandala of the Kâlacakra. This is said to have been built by King Sucandra, whilst a smaller one is ascribed to one of his successors Pundarîka (White Lotus). The connection of the Kâlacakra tradition with a strange Central-Asian land, from which—as we shall see—the teachings are said to have been introduced into India, is highly significant. There is also at least a probability that the Kâlacakra existed in areas outside India before it penetrated into the land of Buddha. An analysis of the still extant briefer review of the Tantra and of the texts based on it will provide us with information concerning the foreign teachings which contributed to this final syncretic system on the basis of Buddhism.

According to tradition, Sucandra was the first of a line of seven 'Priest-Kings' of Shambhala, who were succeeded by a line of twenty-five rulers known as 'Kulika' or 'Kalki', each of whom reigned for one hundred years. The neatness of this arrangement makes it quite clear that behind the formality of these figures there must be some definite astrological symbolism which we are not yet in a position to unravel. The Kulika who came to the throne in 1927 of our chronology was named Aniruddha, and the twenty-fifth and last ruler 'Rudra with the Wheel' (cakrin) will come to the throne in the year 2327, and his task will be to destroy the hated Mohammedans in a tremendous

[1] Cf. *T'oung Pao*, 1907, pp. 404 *et seq.*

battle, a sort of Armageddon, which is described in glowing eschatological colours. After this a new Golden Age will dawn for Buddhism. These future hopes are alive in the minds of many Tibetans and Mongols even today. Incidentally, the religion of the Mohammedans is often mentioned in the Kâlacakra, which suggests that it must have been of some importance in the place where this system originated.

The story of the conversion of thirty-five million seers (Rishi) led by Sûryaratha (Sun Chariot)[1] is also of historical religious significance, as it is obviously a reference to a clash with some foreign religious system. We are told that the first Kulika, Manjushrîkîrti, preached the Vajrayâna to all his subjects one moonlit night. But the Seers desired to stay loyal to the teachings of Sûryaratha, and they preferred banishment. When they had made off in the direction of India the king was filled with mortification at being unable to win them for the cause of Vajrayâna. He sank into meditation, and thanks to his magic powers he obscured the consciousness of the Seers and caused them to be brought back by demons in the form of Garudas. The Kâlacakra was now preached to them in a shortened form, whereupon they understood it, meditated upon it and reached understanding.

The historians are in agreement concerning the introduction of the Kâlacakra from Shambhala into India sixty years before its arrival in Tibet. As the year 1026 is accepted as the time of its official introduction into Tibet, this would mean that it penetrated into India in the year 966, a date which can be more or less reconciled with the reports that the 'Wheel of Time' became effective in India under King Mahîpâla of Bengal (*c.* 974-1026). However, very little is known about the person of the master who first brought the new teachings to India, and there are contradictions even in the accounts of one and the same historian. Sum-pa mkhan-po[2] writes: 'The Kâlacakra was brought from northern Shambhala by Tsi-lu-pa, Pi-to-pa or the great Kâlacakrapâda, which may be correct'. Now Pi-to-pa, whom we have already met as one of the pupils of Atîsha, and who is also described by Târanâtha as a disciple of Nâ-ro-pa,[3] can hardly

[1] Grünwedel, *Weg nach Sambhala*, p.76; kLong-rdol bla-ma, Essay 5. Grünwedel's translation is in need of some corrections however. The sources mentioned are based on the description in the Vimalaprabhâ ('Immaculate Lustre'), the as yet unpublished great Kâlacakra commentary.

[2] dPag-bsam ljon-bzang., p. 134.

[3] *Edelsteinmine*, p. 79.

have been the first Indian interpreter of the new system, because according to the unanimous reports of the sources, Nâ-ro-pa first had knowledge of the Kâlacakra through that original representative in India, whoever he was. The fact that the Indian mystics received a new name after each new initiation greatly increases the difficulties of identification, but it seems likely that Tsi-lu-pa and the great, i.e. the older, Kâlacakrapâda are identical. The story of this master is given to us by Padma-dkar-po as follows:[1]

A Yogi of a blue colour with a third eye in his forehead, and carrying a Vajra of acacia wood in his hand, appeared to a female Yogi at the time of her menses. This woman was a seller of alcoholic spirits in the land of Bengal. He bought some of this spirit, and in the night he sought the love of the female Yogi. But in the morning he had gone into the Vajra so that the woman could no longer see him. When she now hesitantly picked up the Vajra it gave out a blue light which went into her arms. After a year a son was born to her. When seven years later she went on a journey with the child she met a handsome monk (bhikshu) who begged her to let him have her son. She agreed and he took the boy as a novice, and as the lad was quick of understanding he introduced him to the Tantras. Finally he told the boy to hold tightly to his gown, and then he bore him through the air to Vajrapâni, who then acquainted him with the preaching of the Kulika in Shambhala. When the boy came back the monk told him to go to Eastern India, where he was to disseminate the Kâlacakra. This monk was Avalokiteshvara, the Yogi who had produced the boy in the first place. The significance of these two Bodhisattvas in the Kâlacakra system is worth mentioning because a preference for certain Bodhisattvas and Buddhas always permits valuable conclusions to be drawn as to the teachings of a mystic school.

The young man, whose name as a monk was Tsi-lu-pa, travelled in later years to southern India where a minister, a Brahmin and a linguist became his pupils. As the traditional teachings had not yet been written down, he now performed this task. Then he went to Nâlandâ, which was, together with Vikramashîlâ, the most important centre of Buddhism in those days. It is reported that Tsi-lu-pa wrote the macrocosm-microcosm symbol of the Kâlacakra, 'The Powerful One in Ten Forms',

[1] Fol. 67a, 1 *et seq.*

over the gate of the monastery, and below it the thesis: 'Whoever does not know the Âdibuddha he also does not know the Kâlacakra. Whoever does not know the Kâlacakra, he also does not know how to utter the (mystic) names perfectly. Whoever cannot utter the names perfectly he also does not know the body of wisdom of the Vajra bearer (of the perfect Yoga). Whoever does not know the body of wisdom of the Vajra bearer he also does not know the Vehicle of Magic Formulas (Mantra). All those who do not know the Vehicle of the Magic Formulas, they exist only in Samsâra and are remote from the path of the illustrious Vajra bearer. Therefore, every good master must proclaim the highest Âdibuddha, and each good pupil who seeks after salvation must listen to his words'.

Now in those days the great Pandit Nâdapâda, called Nâ-ro-pa by the Tibetans, was the abbot (Upâdhyâya) of the monastery. With five hundred monks of his following he entered into a disputaton with Tsi-lu-pa, but was defeated, whereupon he paid homage to the bearer of the new teachings and studied the Kâlacakra under him, soon himself becoming a prominent interpreter of the teachings. The only work of the Kâlacakra so far published in its original Sanscrit form is a commentary by Nâdapâda on the sprinkling or initiatory rites (seka). In another place[1] Padma dkar-po mentions that Tsi-lu-pa is also known as the 'Great Kâlacakrapâda', whilst Nâdapâda is also known as 'the Lesser Kâlacakrapâda'. Later on Tsi-lu-pa is said to have initiated Nâdapâda into the mysteries of Kâlacakra and Vajrapâni in a monastery named Phullahari.

It would seem that the whole further tradition of Kâlacakra derived from these two, not only in India but also in Tibet. Amongst their pupils were obviously the already mentioned Pi-to-pa, who is also, and perhaps more correctly, known as Pindo Âcârya, and, as one of the most famous interpreters of the system, the 'greater', or 'elder' Vajrâsana, also called Amoghavajra. The introduction of the Kâlacakra into Tibet[2] took place more or less simultaneously through various channels about sixty years after it became known in India. We have already mentioned the introduction of the 'Wheel of Time' by the translator Gyi-jo, who studied under Bhadrabodhi, a pupil of Tsi-lu-pa, with whose assistance he carried out a translation of the condensed

[1] Fol, 78a, 6.

[2] Pad-ma dkar-po 126b, 2 *et seq.*; Sum-pa mkhan-po, p. 145.

10 Image of the 'White Târâ' in the monastery of Tashilhunpo

11 An ancient Stupa (Chorten) near Daithang

'essence' of the shorter Tantra (*Laghutantra*), and of two exegetical works. Although this master taught the Kâlacakra in Tibet for a long time, he had only four pupils, and even they did not maintain the tradition after him.

However, a second and more important chain of teachers began with the Kashmiri Somanâtha, a pupil of Nâdapâda. Being assured of a present of 100 ounces of gold, this master of the Kâlacakra went to Tibet in order to induct Ye-shes-mchog of gNyos. As, however, the promise was not kept—we have already seen what an important role gold played as a present from pupils amongst the Indian pandits—Somanâtha stopped his work on the translation of the great representative commentary *Vimalaprabhâ* (*The 'Immaculate Lustre'*) and went to the province of 'Phan-yul to the north of Lha-sa, where Shes-rab-grags, the translator of 'Bro, became his pupil. With his assistance the translation of the great commentary was now completed. Ye-shes-mchog was very angry at the defection of his teacher, and used black-magical means against his rival, the translator of 'Bro. But it is reported that one hundred terrible Gods could not frighten the pupil of Somanâtha, nor could a hundred graciously smiling goddesses turn his thoughts to love. Somanâtha initiated no further pupils in Tibet, and those who subsequently offered themselves as disciples were instructed only in the moral regulations. The tradition established by Somanâtha and carried on by his pupils is known to the Tibetans as the school of 'Bro.

The second important tradition, the school of Rva, was founded by Chos-rab of Rva. It is reported that he went to Kashmir and studied there for five years, ten months and five days under a local pandit named Samantashrî, who was a former pupil of Nâ-ro-pa. It is interesting to note that this master also came from Kashmir, where an important centre of the Kâlacakra seems to have formed. Chos-rab presented his teacher with three hundred ounces of gold and succeeded in persuading him to make the journey to Tibet. In joint work they now translated numerous Kâlacakra writings. The Rva school was to take on particular significance, because its tradition formed the basis for the study of the Kâlacakra by the important sect of the Sa-skya-pa and its daughter sect the Jo-nang-pa, to which the well-known historian Târanâtha belonged. In the chain of teachers now set up were such famous names as those of the Sa-skya Pandita (1182-1251), 'Phags-pa (1235-80), who played an important role in the Mongolian period, and finally that of the omniscient Bu-ston, the author of the highly-valued *History of Buddhism*, and supervisor of the *Buddhist Encyclopaedia* of Tibet. We have devoted so much space to the history of the Kâlacakra because it maintained its importance in the further history of the Lamaist religion in Tibet. Tsong-kha-pa made a close study of it, and his scholarly pupil mKhas-grub-rje wrote an important sub-commentary to the Tantra; and even down to this day it represents one of the most important fundamentals of the dominant Yellow Church in Tibet.

CHAPTER VII

THE RISE OF THE LAMAIST SECTS

The work of Rin-chen bzang-po and of Atîsha laid the foundation for the further religious development of Tibet. However, we must not think of the spiritual face of those decades as being similar to that of Lamaism since the year 1300. In those days there were no sects in the proper sense of the word attached to particular monasteries. The relationship with Indian Buddhism was much too intimate for that. The leading Tibetan spiritual figures of the eleventh and twelfth centuries were almost all in the closest contact with the country of origin of Buddhism, and they merely transplanted the various teachings of the Indian Gurus to their own now ultimately converted homeland. Close contact with the main stream of Buddhist religious thought did not yet allow any self-isolation of the Tibetan monasteries or the development of any specific sectarianism. On the other hand it is true to say that all those great figures whose traditions led later to the foundation of schools lived in those centuries. Figures like that of Mar-pa and the old lamas of Sa-skya were themselves in a stream of freer religious development constantly fed from India. But when Buddhism received the death blow in its own stronghold of Bengal, contact was broken off, and in consequence the religious forms in Tibet, which would no doubt have shown themselves capable of adaptation under persistent outside influence, now tended to become rigid, or at least to continue a line of development already implicit in its main direction. However, at the beginning of the thirteenth century there was apparently still a certain amount of direct teaching by Indian Buddhists, and the presence in Tibet of the famous 'Pandit of Kashmir', Shâkyashrîbhadra, from 1204 to 1213 may be regarded as cogent proof of this. But then this fructifying contact gradually grew less, and the last Tibetans who had been initiated by Indian

Buddhists were elevated by their spiritual successors to be the leaders of schools.

Atîsha himself founded no school or sect in Tibet, and his pupil 'Brom-ston (1005-64) was regarded as the leading personality from which that sect derived whose beliefs accorded most closely with the traditions of Atîsha.[1] This sect received the name bKa-gdams-pa because, according to Sum-pa mkhan-po, it held fast to the authoritative word (bka-gdams) of Atîsha as laid down primarily in his work *Lamp for the Way of Enlightenment* and its commentary. The successors of the master were also called 'the earlier bKa-gdams-pa' because later on Tsong-kha-pa adopted their traditions, and his sect was therefore referred to as the later or new bKa-gdams-pa. 'Brom, who met Atîsha when in his forty-first year, received the whole teaching tradition from the master and was regarded thereafter as his spiritual son and 'viceroy', though in fact he always remained a layman. He had already taken the vows of a lay follower with one of the pupils of kLu-mes, who, as we have already seen, came from Eastern Tibet and disseminated the faith in Ü and Tsang. In addition to Atîsha 'Brom studied under four other spiritual leaders, and he himself was venerated as the reincarnation of Avalokiteshvara. On the death of Atîsha he was clearly the one called upon to celebrate the funeral obsequies of the master, held at the end of one year. When 'Brom left sNye-thang, the death place of his master, in order to devote himself to contemplation in the North of the country, he took the bones of his teacher and other relics with him, and they found their final resting place in a monastery which 'Brom founded in the year 1057, a monastery which was to become very important as the stronghold of the bKa-gdams-pa. It was called Rva-sgreng, and henceforth it was the seat of the leader of the sect, who was the apostolic successor of 'Brom. 'Brom was succeeded by three of his pupils and closest collaborators in turn; these were the so-called 'spiritual brethren' (sku-mched), and the third abbot in line, Po-to-ba, who died in 1082, was probably the greatest of them. He, like his two predecessors, had actually been taught by Atîsha, but they nevertheless obtained the greater part of their spiritual training from 'Brom-ston. Po-to-ba founded a monastery in the 'Phan-yul area to the north of Lhasa, and it was named after him. Quite a considerable number

[1] See also the rather sparse information in the handbooks, and in particular dPag-bsam ljon-bzang, pp. 197 *et seq.*; and Roerich, *The Blue Annals*, pp. 241 *et seq.*

of bKa-gdams teaching centres arose in this neighbourhood in the course of time, so that 'Phan-yul is now regarded as the classic stronghold of the sect. Po-to-ba preached the six main texts of his religion, the most important was Atîsha's *Lamp for the Way of Enlightenment*, and he is said to have reached a high degree of spiritual enlightenment and to have looked upon the faces of numerous Bodhisattvas and Tantra gods. After his death there was at first no one who was worthy to take over the abbotship of Rva-sgreng, and the sources term the time of vacancy the days of 'religious indigence'. The one thing which is reported about the abbot who was finally inducted into the vacant chair is that he introduced a very strict disciplinary regulation forbidding women to enter monasterial precincts.

In general, the religious institutions of the bKa-gdams-pa school were noted for their strict moral rectitude; and in this respect they were certainly following the tradition of Atîsha, who had made it his particular task to purify Buddhism, which had degenerated under the influence of shady Tantric practices, and to introduce stricter religious discipline. But this did not prevent the followers of the sect from enjoying a high reputation as experts on ritual who had penetrated deep into the philosophically-based Tantric teachings. It is reported of most of these Lamas that in their meditation they had looked on the faces of numerous gods. The followers of 'Brom-ston regarded the seven basic elements (chos) of their doctrine as consisting of the three parts of the Buddhist doctrinal collection (Tripitaka); the person of the historic Buddha Shâkyamuni; the great God of Mercy, Avalokiteshvara; his female counterpart, the goddess Târâ; and, as their special protective deity, Acala, the 'King of Religion'. Avalokiteshvara and Târâ also retained their importance amongst the successors of the old sect; and down to this day the Dalai Lama, the 'Pope' of the orthodox Yellow Church in Tibet, is regarded as the reincarnation of Avalokiteshvara.

The bKa-gdams-pa played no role in the material development which transformed Tibet into a theocratic State, and neither did another school which was founded at about the same time, that of the Zhi-byed-pa.[1] This latter school derived from the teachings of the Indian master Pha-dam-pa sangs-rgyas ('Illustrious Father Buddha') and his Tibetan disciple Chos-gshes of rMa, who met the master in the year 1073. Pha-dam-pa came from southern

[1] dPag-bsam ljon-bzang, pp. 374 *et seq.*; Roerich, *The Blue Annals*, pp. 867 *et seq.*

India and became a monk in the famous monastery of Vikramashîlâ. He was introduced to mysticism by numerous teachers, including Suvarnadvîpin, who, as his name indicates, came from Indonesia. Pha-dam-pa now devoted himself to meditation and the conjuration of Tantric gods in many parts of India, including Vajrâsana, near the spot where Buddha received Enlightenment, on the banks of the Ganges, and the famous funeral place Shîtavana, which is already known to us from the story of Padmasambhava's life. Through this way of life he mastered not only the lower Siddhis, which consist in the ability to perform vulgar magical tricks, but also the highest ones pertaining to a perfect holy man; and he is said to have looked on the face of twelve gods, including Manjushrî, Avalokiteshvara and Târâ.

According to one tradition, Pha-dam-pa paid seven visits to Tibet, though other sources say only three; and he is also said to have gone to China in some mysterious and wondrous fashion. He founded a monastery near Ding-ri in the neighbourhood of Mount Everest, and he died in 1118, according to the Re'u-mig chronology—though according to the Deb-ther sngon-po it was a year earlier. 1113 is given as the last year in which he was in Tibet. Amongst his spiritual successors one in particular is worthy of mention: a female disciple, Ma-gcig lab-sgron ('Unique Mother, Lamp of Eloquence'), who founded a centre of the Zhi-byed-pa in the south of Ü. The sect has never become particularly prominent because it attaches more importance to mystic perfection and meditation in isolation than to formal organization. It was an Order of typical Yogis, and a number of highly reputable mystics belonged to it, but at the time of Tsong-kha-pa it seems to have become practically extinct, and today, in any case, it no longer has any followers at all. Its main teachings referred to abscission (gCod) of the roots of Klesha, or spiritual pollution, by destroying the evil spirits which lead men to sin; this being brought about by certain meditational practices. It remains to be discovered to what extent the gCod of this Zhi-byed-pa sect differs from the ritual of the same name practised by the followers of Padmasambhava. The second main doctrine of the school taught by Pha-dam-pa related to the 'Section for the achievement of Peace" (zhi-byed skor) from which the school took its name. According to this method the mystic strives in isolation to bring all suffering to an end by Mantras, thus attaining perfect equanimity. 'When evil omens occur, take them as good fortune' is one of the typical axioms of Pha-dam-pa, as quoted by Sum-pa. It would seem also that the teachings of the Indian Father of the Church Âryadeva played a particularly important role in the life of the Zhi-byed-pa.

The Sa-skya-pa school, which still has numerous followers in Tibet,[1] played a much greater role in Tibetan spiritual life than either of these two previous schools. The spiritual founder of its teachings was 'Brog-mi, a contemporary of Atîsha, who studied in Vikramashîlâ for eight years, embracing religious discipline, Prajnâpâramitâ and the secret teachings, under a famous 'Keeper of the Door' of that monastery named Shânti-pa. He was also initiated into the mysteries of the Tantra deity Hevajra by one of the pupils of another great Siddha, Virûpa. He then returned to Tibet where in 1043 he founded the monastery Myu-gu-lung in the province of Tsang and thereafter he instructed numerous pupils in his doctrine of 'The Way' (lam) and 'The Fruit' ('bras). A direct contact with India was established when 'Brog-mi succeeded in persuading a famous scholar and mystic of Bengal, Gayadhara, to come to Myu-gu-lung in return for five hundred ounces of gold as a pupils' present.

This 'Brog-mi was the chief teacher of dKon-mchog rgyal-po of the family of 'Khon in the mystic studies, although four other well-known religious teachers are also mentioned as his masters. 'Brog-mi based the study of Buddhist mysticism on the 'new' Tantras; that is to say not on those which were already known in the days of Padmasambhava and accepted by the rNying-ma-pa; for him the only authentic Tantras were those translated by Atîsha and Rin-chen bzang-po after the re-introduction of Buddhism. The Tantric demon Vajrakîla was venerated as the protective deity of the new chain of tradition, whilst the Bodhisattva Manjushrî was also of great significance, as seen from its traditional beliefs that seven reincarnations of Manjushrî will appear in the line of dKon-mchog rgyal-po. In the year 1073 'Brog-mi founded the monastery of Sa-skya ('Fallow Land') which was later to become so famous. Its long line of abbots included a number of highly important hierarchs. An inclination towards magic is characteristic of this Sa-skya-pa school, coupled

[1] Cf. Grünwedel, *Mythologie*, pp. 61 *et seq.*; Waddell, *Buddhism of Tibet*, pp. 69 *et seq.*; and in particular the biographies of the Sa-skya Lamas in Huth, *Geschichte des Buddhismus in der Mongolei*, II., pp. 106 *et seq.*, and the description in dPag-bsam ljon-bzang, pp. 359 *et seq.* The important Sa-skya 'reports' (yig-tshang) are unfortunately not accessible.

with the fact that their abbots are permitted to marry. The founder of Sa-skya was followed in office by his son, and thereafter it was quite common for the leadership of the sect to pass from an uncle to a nephew. A great number of Sa-skya Lamas won considerable literary renown for themselves.

Amongst the famous Sa-skya hierarchs was Kun-dga rgyal-mtshan, usually known as Sa-skya Pandita (1182–1251). This man was not only an important abbot in the long line, and the leader of one of the most powerful of the Lama sects, but also, it appears, the king of large parts of Tibet. The Sa-skya Lamas first established that idea of a priestly monarchy, which was later so successfully adopted by the Great Lamas of the Yellow Church, though as upholders of strict religious celibacy these latter had no natural line of succession. Kun-dga rgyal-mtshan is credited with being particularly learned and knowledgeable. As a linguist, for example, he mastered not only the languages and literature of India, but also the idiom of Bru-sha (Gilgit). His spiritual education, which was concluded with his ordination as a full monk under the supervision of the already mentioned great Pandit of Kashmir, Shâkyashrîbhadra, in the year 1208, was remarkable for its many-sidedness, and it is particularly noteworthy that he not only mastered the traditions and secret teachings of his own sect, but also those of the Zhi-byed-pa, the bKa-gdams-pa and the 'six Dharmas of Nâ-ro-pa', the spiritual predecessor of bKa-rgyud-pa, and, in addition, the Kâlacakra. With the aid of Manjushrî, whose incarnation he, of course, was, he triumphed in disputation against certain Indians on the borders of Nepal who were followers of Hinduism. The fact that Sa-skya Pandita established relations with the rising world power of the Mongols was to prove of great importance. The Mongol armies never seem actually to have entered Tibet, and the correspondence which is supposed to have passed between the great conqueror Gengis Khan and Sa-skya Pandita is probably only a pious legend. On the other hand, Sa-skya Pandita was invited to the court of the Mongol Prince Godan, where he is supposed to have cured him of a serious sickness by reciting a Dhâranî. According to Re'u-mig, this meeting with Prince Godan took place in the year 1246 in the West Chinese town of Lan-chou. The great hierarch succeeded in obtaining the friendly interest of this descendant of Gengis Khan in the cause of Buddhism, and henceforth Buddhism was to become as important for the Mongol nomads as it had been for the Tibetans in the days of Srong-btsan sgam-po. The hierarch made himself particularly useful to the Mongolians by providing them with written characters for their language along the lines of that Duktus of Syrian origin which was in use amongst the Turkish Uigurians in the west of Eastern Turkestan.

The nephew of Sa-skya Pandita, the famous Lama 'Phags-pa (1235-80), completed the work of his uncle, and succeeded in obtaining the unconditional recognition of the secular dominance of the Sa-skya Lamas over the whole of Tibet.[1] The great admiration to which this gave rise in Tibet is reflected in a legend concerning the wondrous events in the life of the father of the great man before the latter's birth. The God with the Elephant Head, Ganesha, borrowed from Hinduism, took hold of the father in his trunk and set him down on the peak of the world mountain, Meru. At first the father was afraid and did not dare look down. When he finally did so he saw the provinces of all Tibet spread out below him. Ganesha then prophesied that one day they would all be ruled by his descendants, saying that he, the father, had lost his chance of this brilliant future by his preliminary hesitation. 'Phags-pa, who, like his uncle, was a master of all the religious knowledge of his day, accepted the invitation of the Mongol emperor Khubilai (1260-94), the first of the Mongol emperors to rule over the whole of China. 'Phags-pa visited the Emperor at his court and, according to the legend, he conducted himself proudly, insisting on his equality in rank with the Emperor. Thanks to the mediation of one of Khubilai's wives, the two finally came to an understanding whereby in all spiritual and Tibetan affairs the Lama should take precedence, whilst in all secular affairs of concern to the great Mongol empire the Emperor should be supreme.

An interesting discussion between the Emperor and the Lama on historical matters is recorded. In order to stress his high position 'Phags-pa reminded the Emperor that the kings of Tibet once ruled over 'two-thirds of Jambudvîpa', that they had defeated China, and that on the re-establishment of peace a Chinese princess had journeyed to Tibet with the famous Buddhist image Jo-bo. Thus 'Phags-pa showed himself very knowledgeable in the earlier history of his country, and we may well credit his

[1] *Geschichte des Buddhismus in der Mongolie* by 'Jigs-med Rig-pa'i rdo-rje (wrongly called Jigs-med nam-mkha) translated by G. Huth contains a detailed biography of this Lama, II, pp. 139 *et seq.*; see also dPag-bsam ljon-bzang, p. 362.

biography in this point because we know that in addition to numerous other writings, 'Phags-pa was also responsible for a *Genealogy of the Tibetan Kings.*[1] The Emperor doubted what 'Phags-pa had told him, and he caused his scholars to consult the historical documents in the case, probably the annals of the T'ang dynasty, whereupon they found the statements of the hierarch brilliantly confirmed. Thereafter the Emperor had full confidence in his guest, and allowed himself to be received into the Buddhist religion by 'Phags-pa; and together with a number of his notables he received the ordination of Hevajra. He also appointed 'Phags-pa 'Imperial Tutor'. This report is also quite credible because although for political reasons the Mongol rulers tolerated and even encouraged all religions, including Islamism and Nestorian Christianity, they did show a special leaning towards Buddhism, with which they were already acquainted through their Uigurian subjects.

In gratitude for the religious instruction given to him by 'Phags-pa, the Emperor now gave him and his successors secular jurisdiction over the whole of Tibet. He also proposed to enact a law compelling all Buddhists to follow the Sa-skya teachings, but 'Phags-pa dissuaded him, beseeching him to leave everyone to follow his own conscience according to ancient Buddhist custom. The privileges which the Emperor bestowed on 'Phags-pa must not be regarded as mere empty gestures of friendship—they were of very real significance. For example, 'Phags-pa specifically obtained the exemption of the monasteries from all taxation; and at the same time an order to the famous Mongol couriers that henceforth they should no longer use the houses of Buddhist priests as posting stations. These privileges were continued under the successors of Khubilai, but they were no longer so powerful or independent and they had fallen under Buddhist sway to a dangerous extent. The result was a great increase in the number of Buddhist monasteries on Chinese soil, and, in particular, an enormous increase in the number of Buddhist monks. This gave rise to lively resentment amongst the Chinese, who were themselves heavily burdened with taxes by the Mongols, whilst having to watch these spiritual drones leading comfortable and even prosperous lives.[2]

[1] Cf. G. Tucci in *India Antiqua*, Leyden 1947, p. 310.

[2] E. Haenisch, 'Steuergerechtsame der chinesischen Klöster unter der Mongolenherrschaft' in *Reports of the Saxon Academy*, Leipzig 1940.

The Emperor was also delighted with 'Phags-pa in his capacity as a sorcerer, because although he, the Emperor, was a statesman of high quality, he was not, as the descendant of nomads, altogether free from a lurking primitive belief in necromancy. 'Phags-pa also provided the Mongols with a new alphabet to take the place of the one Sa-skya Pandita had devised, but the new alphabet proved rather cumbrous and unpractical. Sa-skya Pandita had taken the Uigurian alphabet as his basis, but 'Phags-pa devised his characters from the Tibetan, and arranged the letters of these so-called 'quadratic' characters in such a fashion one below the other so that in double language pronouncements the Mongol version could stand side by side with the Chinese, which is written from above downwards. This new alphabet was used in official documents and inscriptions, and for books, but after the year 1300 it was increasingly discarded in favour of an improved version of the first alphabet originally introduced by Sa-skya Pandita, devised with the help of another Sa-skya Lama, Chos-sku od-zer.

'Phags-pa is also said to have visited the famous holy centre of Buddhism in West China, Wu-t'ai-shan, or the 'Five-peaked Mountain'. The veneration of Manjushrî was very prominent here, and, as we have already mentioned, the traditions of Sa-skya are very closely connected with the cult of this Bodhisattva. The contact between Lamaism and this Chinese centre was subsequently maintained, and right down to the present day this legendary mountain is a favourite object of pilgrimage for Tibetans. The journey of 'Phags-pa to the Mongol capital brought the Grand Lama so many presents from the Emperor himself and from the faithful, that 'Phags-pa was able not only to decorate his own monastery very richly, but also to present religious objects to other holy places, for example, Mahâbodhi (Bodh Gayâ) in India.

In the thirteenth century there was a split in the Sa-skya-pa school, and a new sect was founded which was in course of time to play a very important role in Tibet. This was the Jo-nang-pa sect, named after the monastery Jo-nang or Jo-mo-nang, which lies about a hundred miles to the north-west of Tashilhunpo. Its master, Phyogs-las rnam-rgyal, whose teaching was based on that of the famous Kâlacakra master Dol-po-pa (1292-1361), is said to have preached a version of the Shûnyatâ somewhat different from that accepted by the other schools. This new sect attained particular fame through one of its Lamas, Târanâtha, who was born in the year 1575, and made himself a great name as a historian. Thanks in particular to his *History of Buddhism in India*, Târanâtha provided European research into the Vajrayâna with a very much more reliable basis than would ever have been possible with the sparse historical material of the Indian writers. Like the Sa-skya-pa school from which it derived, the Jo-nang-pa sect, as the example of Târanâtha shows, was based chiefly on Tantric magic teachings. Although the reformer and founder of the Yellow Church, Tsong-kha-pa, studied the Kâlacakra under a Jo-nang Lama, in the seventeenth century, the great fifth Dalai Lama took up a hostile attitude to this sect and forcibly incorporated its monasteries into his own Order. He also seized and had sealed the plates containing the Jo-nang texts, so that with the exception of two historical works by Târanâtha, the writings of this sect became very difficult of access. However, we do know that the study of the Kâlacakra was constantly encouraged, because there is a work translated by Târanâtha in the encyclopaedia of the bsTan-'gyur concerning the way to the mythical land of Shambhala, whilst Târanâtha himself devoted a number of books to the system.[1]

The moral status of the Sa-skya-pa does not seem to have been particularly high in those centuries. The exhortations of Atîsha for sterner monastic discipline and for strict celibacy were largely ignored by these representatives of Lamaism. In general the monks of the big monasteries conducted themselves in a very worldly fashion. The big religious communities were less centres of religious study than strongholds in the struggle between the rival sects. On occasion the Grand Lamas and their monks even gave veritable battle to their enemies. For example, in the year 1290 the Lamas of Sa-skya captured and sacked the monastery of 'Bri-gung.

Another school, that of the bKa-rgyud-pa was certainly not the equal of the Sa-skya-pa in worldly power, but equally certainly it was superior spiritually. The name of this sect indicates that it represents a school of oral tradition in which the secret mystical teachings are passed on from teacher to pupil by word of mouth. The sect was founded by Mar-pa of Lho-brag, who, according to Sum-pa, lived from 1012 to 1097. This sect also developed from Indian traditions, and as we are better informed than usual about

[1] Cf. G. Tucci, *Tibetan Painted Scrolls.*, p.128.

its inspirational sources from the literature of the sect, we know something about these Indian Yogis. The most important teacher of Mar-pa in India was one of the most famous teachers and mystics of later Buddhism, Master Nâdapâda, or, as the Tibetans call him, Nâ-ro-pa, whom we have already met as one of the first interpreters of the Kâlacakra system. Nâ-ro-pa received his own initiation at the hands of the Bengalee Ti-lo-pa. The literature of this sect has preserved biographies of all the great Gurus in this chain of teachers. There are even several biographies of some of them, and the information is sometimes contradictory. The harvest in authentic facts concerning the earthly lives of these holy men—at least of the first two, the Indians—is relatively sparse, but the legendary details provide us with such interesting information concerning their fundamental spiritual attitude and their teachings that the time spent with these very symbolic stories is not wasted.

Ti-lo-pa the first of the line[1] was born in Eastern India of a Brahmin family. In his youth when he was looking after the cattle he met the Master Nâgârjuna, who was so impressed by the boy that he determined to test him to see whether he was a suitable vessel for the secret teachings of Buddhism. He made as though to wade across a small and shallow stream near by. The youth immediately hurried up and offered to carry the holy man across. The master accepted the offer, but when they were in the centre of the stream he used his magic powers to make the water swell so greatly that the lad was in danger of drowning. But despite the danger the lad showed no fear or regret, and his trust in the master was unshaken. Nâgârjuna then ordered the waters to subside, and when he reached the other side he went off leaving the boy, who had been found worthy, to play for a few more years with his companions. This story is very significant, because it indicates that personal courage and steadfastness were regarded as essential conditions for the taking of the mystic 'Direct Path'.

Years later Nâgârjuna reappeared in the neighbourhood and found the youth playing with his companions, taking the part of a king and sitting on a branch with two girls, as though on a throne with his Queens. Around him were his playmates as ministers and subjects. When the youth saw the master he immediately sprang down from the branch and paid him his respects. The master then asked him whether he liked playing the role of king, to which the

[1] Based primarily on Pad-ma dkar-po, Fol. 70a, 5.

youthful Ti-lo-pa replied that he certainly did, but that he could never be a king because by an unkind fate he had been born a subject. Nâgârjuna then promised that he would obtain the royal dignity for him. For seven days the master now performed mystic ceremonies with his water jug; then he wrote down the names of the play king, his wives, and his ministers in the game on a piece of paper and placed it in the water jug. As a result of this the land lost its king, and the State elephant placed the water jug with the holy water for the consecration of the king on the head of the young Ti-lo-pa. However, the officials of the palace did not regard him as their lawful king and were unwilling to pay him homage. But once again Nâgârjuna was not at a loss. He caused the young king, his notables and his subjects to assemble in a great park, and there he struck a tree which immediately turned into a great concourse of soldiers all subject to the orders of the king. Thereafter everyone regarded him as rightful king.

After a long reign Ti-lo-pa grew tired of the life circle and its pleasures, and he had himself been ordained as a priest by his uncle, who was in charge of a temple of the Tantra deity Heruka near the funeral place of Somapurî in Bengal. One day when he was pursuing his religious studies a horrible bearded old woman appeared before him and asked whether he would like enlightenment concerning his studies. Ti-lo-pa immediately recognized this old crone as a Dâkinî—we have already seen what an important role these sorceresses play at the initiation of Vajrayâna saints and—he therefore begged her for instruction. The old woman now observed that the teaching of moral perfection by stages by means of the pâramitâs, which he was now zealously studying, was extremely onerous, that numerous hindrances would certainly arise along the way, and that in general he would find it extremely difficult to reach the perfect enlightenment of a Buddha in this way. On the other hand, she pointed out, the path of the Vehicle of the Magic Formulas (Mantras) was very much easier, and required little asceticism, and involved fewer hindrances. She therefore proposed to initiate him into its mysteries. She then initiated him into the Mandala of Cakrasamvara which appeared in the air before him in a mysterious fashion. Subsequently the 'God of Wisdom' Cakrasamvara, whose favourite domicile was on the sacred mountain of Kailâsa, became the highly-venerated protective deity (ishtadevatâ) of the bKa-rgyud-pa sect.

In order to emancipate her neophyte from all worldly lusts the Dakinî now taught him the secrets of the mystic stages of Utpattikrama; and in order to release him also from the joy of the gods she taught him the ode of the Sampannakrama. Finally she caused him to talk in the language of a drunkard or a madman, to divest himself of his ordinary clothes and to abandon the sign of his caste in order that he should now proceed along the secret way of the Direct Path. Having done all this the strange crone now became invisible. This story is very typical of the initiation of a mystic in those days. In the further course of Ti-lo-pa's life the Dâkinî reappeared at his side again and again.

Other information concerning the life of Ti-lo-pa according to which his initiation came direct from the Âdibuddha Vajradhara, 'the Thunderclub-Bearer', need not be regarded as in contradiction with this tradition, for the Dâkinî are to be regarded merely as mediators of the initiation. In any case, all the sources are in agreement that human Gurus were not of great importance in the life of Ti-lo-pa, and that preliminary revelation was made to him which he then passed on as the first of a mystic line to a series of spiritual successors. David-Neel quotes another source with a further symbolic initiation story.[1] According to this the Dâkinî instructed Ti-lo-pa to go into the land of her queen, and in order that he should survive this adventurous and highly dangerous journey unscathed she taught him a magic formula which he had to repeat constantly in order to make himself deaf and blind to all the terrors and temptations of the way. Terrible deserts, tumultuous waterfalls and fearful chasms were amongst the many obstacles he had to overcome, whilst murderous demons beset him and wills of the wisp sought to deceive him. Though tortured by hunger and thirst, he was not allowed to slake his thirst at a fresh stream, or to eat of tempting and lucious fruits on the way. He also had to resist the blandishments of beauteous maidens. After long trials and tribulations he finally made his way to the court of the Dâkinî queen, whose palace walls of metal gave forth a tremendous heat and brilliance. But neither this nor other terrors dismayed him, and he forced his way into the enchanted palace, passed through an endless succession of splendid apartments until finally he reached the queen of the Dâkinîs, who sat on her throne in superb beauty, loaded with jewels, and smiling gently at the gallant adept. But he kept re-

[1] *Heilige und Hexer*, p. 173.

peating his magic formula, ripped off the jewellery and clothing of the queen and raped her. This fantastic story, a reflection of meditative experiences, may also be regarded as typical, and recalls parallel stories in the legends of other peoples.

According to Pad-ma dkar po, Ti-lo-pa then wandered throughout India being inducted into numerous Mandalas and mystic practices. For example, in South India a Yogi revealed the secrets of Guhyasamâja to him. Amongst his teachers were the bearers of famous names, for example, Krishnacârin and Vajraghanta. He also experienced the mystic warmth (canda, Tibetan gtum-mo), a sign that he could draw breath from the two side arteries of mystic Indian-Tibetan physiology and press it into the main artery, Dhûti. This mysterious ability was later transferred to a high degree to his spiritual successor the Tibetan Mi-la ras-pa, who, thanks to it, was enabled to live for months in the bitter cold of the upper mountains clad only in a thin cotton garment. Ti-lo-pa lived for a long time unrecognized in Bengal as a crusher of Sesam (tila), and it was from this activity that he received his name Tilli-pa, or Ti-lo-pa. But in the end he was seen in a lonely place in an aura of light surrounded by twelve lamps and twelve women. With this the master was recognized, and he now disseminated secret teachings in certain mystic verses (Vajra-Dohâ), and from that time on he is said to have been able to walk on the heavens. With this he had become equal to the Dâkas and the Dâkinîs.

Later he appeared in various parts of India in order to defeat and humble non-Buddhist heretics and arrogant scholars. In the neighbourhood of Udyâna a king had called a council of magis, a so-called Ganacakra, and he appointed a Yogi named Mati to be their leader because his magic was the most powerful of all. But then an old crone, who bore the 'Eighteen Marks of Ugliness', demanded entry into the council and declared that Mati was not worthy to be the leader of the Ganacakra. When she was asked who was then worthier than Mati she replied 'My brother'. When she was asked where her brother was she replied that he was at a certain burial place, and that she would fetch him. Whereupon she disappeared in a mysterious fashion and returned after a while with Ti-lo-pa, who then had to set his magic against that of Mati. When he succeeded, seated on a lion, the typical riding beast of the Yogi, in drawing down the sun and the moon to the earth, and causing the four continents of the world to appear upon his body, Mati admitted defeat. These examples of the wonders performed by Ti-lo-pa clearly indicate the strange and degenerate character of Indian Buddhism in the tenth century. Vulgar and meretricious magic performances of this kind played a suspiciously important part in the cult. Nevertheless, such stories proved again and again to be only the colourful vessel of deep metaphysical doctrines.

Ti-lo-pa's pupil, Nâ-ro-pa[1] was born into a high-caste family of Kashmir Brahmins who are said to have had kingly rank. Having familiarized himself with all Brahmanist knowledge in his youth, his heart turned to Buddhism, and with the permission of his parents he renounced the world. At the spiritual university of Nâlandâ he was initiated into the depths of the Mahâyâna doctrines by a number of famous masters, and gradually his own reputation as a prominent teacher spread until finally he was paid the honour of the appointment as abbot of the monastery of Nâlandâ. He also made a name for himself as a writer on all matters of Buddhist doctrine. It would appear that, although Nâ-ro-pa was very proud of his fame and his position, the life as scholar in the purlieu of a great monastery did not satisfy him, and in consequence, attracted by the mysteries of the 'direct path', he turned to the occult sciences. The story of his calling to higher things is somewhat similar to that of Ti-lo-pa's. One day when he was studying the Vajrayâna teachings a black shadow fell over his book. He looked up and saw the ugly, witchlike old crone, who had formerly appeared to Ti-lo-pa as a Dâkinî. The old woman asked him whether he understood the sense of the words he was reading. When he answered in the affirmative she laughed. But when he declared that he also understood their deeper significance, she wept, since this was untrue. Nâ-ro-pa now asked eagerly who did understand the secret significance of the text, and she replied that her brother Tilli-pa did. Then she disappeared. Nâ-ro-pa was not certain that this was an authentic Dâkinî revelation, so he performed a conjuration of the protective god Cakrasamvara at a burial place. When he had muttered the appropriate formulas for seven days there were tangible signs

[1] Our account is based primarily on Pad-ma dkar-po, which contains certain interesting details not dealt with in the more official and formal biography translated by Grünwedel *Die Legenden des Nâ-ro-pa*, Leipzig 1933. Grünwedel's work is weakened by pre-conceived opinions and should be used only with the corrections provided by G. Tucci; see the *Journal of the Royal Asiatic Society* 1935, pp. 677 *et seq.*

that the conjuration was successful. The earth shook, a light flashed up, and a voice announced from heaven: 'Go into Eastern India! There you will find Tilli-pa, the leader of the Yogis, who will accept you as his pupil.' Nâ-ro-pa then gave up all his monasterial privileges and with the reluctantly granted permission of the community of monks he made his way eastward, without knowing where in particular he would find the teacher he now sought. In a kingdom of the east he was recognized as the great Pandit Nâ-ro-pa, and the king made him the highest of the scholars in the land. But Nâ-ro-pa had now completely adopted the customs of the ascetics of the Diamond Vehicle. When he came across a maiden with the appropriate bodily signs he lived with her, and used her as his Mûdrâ in secret rites. This created a scandal—from which we see that public opinion still demanded that a Buddhist monk should live a pure life—and the king reproached the sorcerer with harsh words and expelled him from the land.

Now Nâ-ro-pa was a typical Indian ascetic of a wrathful and vengeful nature, and he determined to punish the king by magic incantations. Following the paths of the most sinister black magic he made his way to the peak of a jungle-covered mountain, where he built himself a grass hut and devoted himself once again to a protracted conjuration of Cakrasamvara according to a ritual deriving from Udyâna. When after seven months of this his success was made tangible in the shaking of the earth and of the mountain he collected the paraphernalia he needed to bring down his curse upon the king. But then two Dâkinîs appeared to him and warned him that the course he proposed to adopt could only lead to hell. They also repeated the information that the teacher intended for him was in Eastern India, specifying Bengal.

Nâ-ro-pa now set out in desperate yearning to find his teacher. The sources report that Ti-lo-pa deceived him by adopting twelve different guises in order to show Nâ-ro-pa, who was still proud of his scholarliness, his spiritual purity and his Brahmin origin, that he would have to surrender everything if he desired to venture on the path of the Vajrayâna occult mysteries. On the first occasion Ti-lo-pa appeared in the form of a leprous woman who barred the way along a narrow rocky path so that no one could pass without stepping over her loathsome and evil-smelling body. With great difficulty the seeker mastered his revulsion and stepped over her. Whereupon the leprous woman disappeared and a voice from Heaven announced: 'If you are troubled with scruples how will you hope to find your teacher?' Finally Nâ-ro-pa was fated to find his teacher in the monastery of Otan-tapurî. The monks there recognized the great abbot of Nâlandâ and received him with high honours. But when he asked at once after Ti-lo-pa, the leader of the Yogis, the monks were unable to answer, but they recalled that there was a beggar of that name in the monastery kitchen. When Nâ-ro-pa entered the kitchen he saw a completely naked Yogi whose body had been dried out by the sun, and whose blue-black hair had not been cropped in the fashion of the monks, but was worn bound high on the head. This man was doing something quite outrageous for a Buddhist monastery: he was frying living fish on the fire which had been lit to cook the food of the monks. When the monks observed this flagrant violation of the Buddhist law which prohibits the harming of any living creature they rushed at the offender to strike him. But the beggar asked: 'Does this not please you?' Then he murmured 'Lu-hi ja-ja', whereupon the fishes all flew up to heaven completely unharmed. Everyone now recognized that this beggar must in reality be a great Siddha, whilst Nâ-ro-pa realized that he had found his master at last. Such stories are very typical in connection with the occult teachings of the Vajra-yâna. The representatives of this path are never tired of pointing out the relativity of all moral injunctions, and that although such injunctions are necessary and beneficial for those still on a lower stage of development, they are no longer valid for the perfected adepts, who have progressed beyond the Samsâra.

Ti-lo-pa, the naked ascetic, now went to the roof of the temple, and Nâ-ro-pa followed him in order to beg the master to teach him. Ti-lo-pa demanded: 'Is there anyone here who will spring down from this roof?' Nâ-ro-pa looked round, and as there was no one else to whom the words could have been addressed, he took the challenge to himself and sprang down from the roof, falling heavily to the ground and lying there with broken bones. The shocked monks hurried up, thinking that he had gone mad, but the suffering man muttered: 'I have done this to follow the instructions of the master.' Ti-lo-pa now came up and asked the injured man in a mocking tone whether he had injured himself. Nâ-ro-pa showed no regret for what he had done, and was quite prepared to take the consequences of his obedience to the words of the master. Ti-lo-pa now passed his hands over the injured man's body, murmuring 'Ro-ka na-hi', whereupon Nâ-ro-pa became completely whole and well again. This was the first of twelve very severe ordeals to which the master subjected his pupil in order to test his confidence and his devotion before he consented to initiate him into the occult teachings Nâ-ro-pa longed to learn in order that he might be emancipated from the cycle of development from birth to death. Nâ-ro-pa had to cast himself into the burning fire. He had to rob and steal for the Guru, whereby he was almost beaten to death. He had to stay in a pool full of leeches which sucked his blood, let burning torches be pressed into his body, and finally he had to offer up his own body in the consecration of a Mandala.

All these symbolic stories are very well known and popular in Tibet, and they are frequently graphically depicted on the walls of the monasteries of the bKa-rgyud-pa sect. They illustrate what a master of the mystic way can and must demand of his pupil, and even today Tibetan mystics still often require strange and astonishing things of their pupils in order to train them spiritually—'to make them supple', as David-Neel puts it. After terrible sufferings Nâ-ro-pa finally attained the highest aim of a super-being beyond all the dangers of Samsâra, and becoming the leading pupil of Ti-lo-pa, who passed on all the mystic initiations and teachings to him.

The Tibetan who was privileged to prepare a permanent resting place in his homeland for the mystic revelations of Ti-lo and Nâro, and thus found the school of the bKa-rgyud-pa, was Mar-pa of Lho-brag (1012-97).[1] Even the relatively formalized descriptions of Tibetan hagiography show him to us as a man of definitely choleric temperament and great strength of character. Early on his father prophesied that the lad would perform outstanding things both spiritually and materially if he turned to the right path, but that he would do great harm should he choose the evil path. At the age of twelve Mar-po turned to Buddhism and received the spiritual name of Dharmamati. At the age of fifteen he learned sanscrit from 'Brog-mi, the founder of the Sa-skya tradition, and then learned the art of translation, bringing it to a high degree of mastery. As a result of this he was known by the honorary title of Lo-tsâ-ba, the Translator. Despite the vigorous

[2] Cf. J. Bacot, *La vie de Marpa le traducteur*', and also Pad-ma dkar-pa, 131b 6 *et seq.;* and dPag-bsam ljon-bzang, p. 363.

opposition of his parents, the young man sold all his possessions and obtained gold in return, and with this gold, and a companion less idealistic than himself known as gNyos, he made his way to India. In Nepal they met two pupils of Nâ-ro-pa, and Mar-pa was so deeply impressed by what he heard of their teacher that he turned his footsteps towards Eastern India to meet Nâ-ro-pa. We may also regard the example of Mar-pa as typical. Like him, in those days many enthusiastic young Tibetans made their way to the land of Buddha to get themselves initiated, and then returned to Tibet bringing sacred books with them to be translated.

Mar-pa found Nâ-ro-pa in Phullahari not far from Nâlandâ. He was given a joyful reception, because his arrival as a spiritual son had already been announced in a wondrous fashion, and Nâ-ro-pa gladly initiated him into the profound doctrines of the Vajrayâna. His period of study seems to have passed without noteworthy incident, and to have been in no way like that of his master. Although even at that time Nâ-ro-pa was himself an adept in all the secret doctrines, he sent his pupil to other ascetics from whom he had also received instruction. In this way Mar-pa was initiated into the doctrines of Guhyasamâja by Jnânagarbha in West India; whilst in South India he was initiated into the Tantric secrets of the 'Great Illusion' (Mahâmâyâ) by the strange and holy Kukuri (the 'hound ascetic'), who had thick hair over his whole body, and whose lower face was like that of an ape. This holy man lived alone on an uninhabited island in the middle of a poisonous lake. All these teachings were similar in their fundamentals, and they differed only outwardly in such matters as the exact hierarchy of their gods, and their Mandalas. The objective to be attained in constantly new ways was not merely a knowledge of the irreality of the world of phenomena, but an actual experience of it; and each teacher had worked out his own path to this end. Mar-pa is also said to have received initiations at the hands of a funeral-place Dâkinî, and of Mai-tri-pa, a pupil of Nâ-ro, who taught the doctrine of Mahâmudrâ, or the 'Great Symbol'. The training in Mahâmudrâ is also a Yoga way, using special breathing technique and various physical exercises, and purporting to lead to a consciousness of the identity of the soul with the Absolute, the 'Void'. A text dealing with this doctrine was written by Pad-ma dkar-po, a successor of Mar-pa in the sixteenth century, and it has been translated into English and

German.[1] After Nâ-ro had also assisted his Tibetan pupil in the carrying out of these teachings, together with instruction in the six Yoga exercises which have become famous as the 'Dharma of Nâ-ro',[2] Mar-pa returned to his own country.

On the way home, and when crossing the Ganges, a misfortune occurred. At the instigation of the unworthy gNyos, his Tibetan companion, a fellow traveller threw Mar-pa's precious mystical books into the river. Finally, however, gNyos agreed to allow Mar-pa to copy his own manuscripts. When Mar-pa arrived back in Tibet he found that both his parents were dead. The ensuing period he used to translate Sanscrit texts into Tibetan, to collect gold for another journey to India, and to obtain his first pupils, to whom he taught the words of Nâ-ro. At the age of forty-two he took bDag-med-ma to be his Mudrâ, his sensual-suprasensual companion. His sect did not therefore uphold celibacy, as 'Brom-ston, and later Tsong-ka-pa did, but followed the practices of the Tantric Buddhists of India. His wife significantly bore the name of the Shakti of the Âdibuddha of his sect, the Vajradhara, bDag-med-ma, which is a translation of the Indian name Nairâtmâ. This woman played a great role in his life, and was something more than a wife to him. Mar-pa had numerous sons, of whom the dearest was Dar-ma. Later on he attempted to make this Dar-ma the inheritor of his most profound teachings.

A second journey to India brought him once again to the presence of the venerated Nâ-ro-pa, and to that of other Gurus, and had as its object the consolidation of the lessons he had already learned. Finally he prepared himself for a third great journey to India because Nâ-ro had not yet initiated him into a particularly important mystery, the Grong-'jug, or the ability to enter into a strange corpse, and to transfer consciousness from one body to another.[3] Whilst still in Tibet Mar-pa met another great Indian master, Atîsha, who had at one time exchanged Upadeshas (mystical doctrines) with Nâ-ro. Atîsha passed on the sad news to Mar-pa that his master Nâ-ro was already dead. However, Mar-pa continued his journey, and he was rewarded by receiving the desired initiation at the hands of Nâ-ro-pa, who,

[1] W. Y. Evans-Wentz, *Yoga and Geheimlehren Tibets*, pp. 95 *et seq.*

[2] *Ibid.*, p. 156.

[3] Cf. the above-mentioned work of J. Bacot (passim), and also Evans-Wentz, pp. 183 *et seq.*

although dead, appeared to him in a wondrous fashion. According to the instructions of his master Mar-pa should really have passed on these teachings to his main pupil, the famous Mi-la ras-pa, but his love for his son Dar-ma mdo-sde persuaded him to initiate him in the Grong-'jug instead. This disobedience was punished by the sudden death of his beloved son, who was thrown from a horse into a precipice, where he died. As the death was unexpected there was no other human corpse in the neighbourhood, and tradition has it that the best Mar-pa could do in the circumstances was to use his art to make the spirit of his son pass into the body of a dove. This dove then flew off to India and perched beside the dead body of a Brahmin child which was about to be burned. But the dove died and the child came to life, and grew up to be a great ascetic. Mar-pa himself died at the age of eighty-six years (according to Tibetan reckoning, which includes the actual year of birth) leaving his spiritual son and pupil Mi-la as his successor.

Mi-la ras-pa, that is to say, Mi-la, the 'One Clothed in Cotton Garments' (1040–1123), came from the land of Gung-thang in the west of Tibet not far from the Nepalese frontier.[1] His youth was saddened very early on by the death of his father, which also left the family poor. When Mi-la's mother refused to marry her late husband's brother, this man seized the whole property of the family, leaving the widow and her children in great distress. The widow, a temperamental and picturesque character, lived on now with only one object in mind—revenge on her enemy—and she brought up her son in this spirit. When the boy Mi-la had grown to be a youth she sent him out into the world to look for a Guru who could teach him magical means with which to destroy his enemies. The youthful Mi-la actually found two much-feared Magis who taught him their black art—once they had assured themselves that the youth and his mother really had suffered bitter injustice. From them Mi-la learnt the art of killing people by means of the Tantric magic circles, and also developed the ability to conjure up hailstorms to destroy the

[1] As sources we have in addition to the short descriptions in Pad-ma dkar-po, Fol. 144a, 1, and dPag-bsam ljon-bzang, p. 394, the biography (rnam-thar) probably falsely ascribed to Ras-chung, a pupil of Mi-la, and the *Hundred-thousand Chants* (mgur 'bum) of Mi-la. The biography has been translated by J. Bacot, *Le poète tibétain Milarépa*, Paris 1925; and also by W. Y. Evans-Wentz, *Milarepa, Tibets grosser Yogi*, Munich 1937; H. Hoffmann *Mi-la Ras-pa, Sieben Legenden*, Munich 1950, gives a selection from the *Hundred-thousand Chants.*

crops of his enemies. The description of these ceremonies is not without ethnological interest. When his conjurations in an underground cave had been successful, as his biography reports, the terrifying spirits he had conjured appeared carrying the bloody heads of his enemies in their hands. At the same time the victims in question perished in Mi-la's homeland because their houses collapsed above their heads. In order to demonstrate his powers still further and to prevent the villagers from taking vengeance on his mother, Mi-la now conjured up a tremendous shower of hail which destroyed the crops in the common fields.

The mother expressed her delight and satisfaction in a wild song of triumph, but Mi-la himself found no pleasure in his victory. The successful Magi was seized with deep remorse for the fearful crime he had committed, and he now longed to free himself from the burden of guilt. According to the laws of Karma his next reincarnation was sure to be in hell, and only by the dangerous 'Direct Path' of the Vajrayâna could he now hope to evade the fate he had prepared for himself through his own fault. He therefore now had to raise himself to a stage in which neither sin nor virtue was of any significance. His pupilship with a certain rNying ma-Lama did not bring him the inner peace he desired. But in his thirty-eighth year he became the pupil of Mar-pa, in whom he soon had the greatest confidence. Mar-pa made him serve a probationship of six years during which he tormented him cruelly, just as Ti-lo-pa had once tormented Nâ-ro-pa, who had also committed the offence of dabbling in black magic. Mar-pa promised to give his pupil the saving initiation when he, Mi-la ras-pa, had succeeded in building a house of many storeys without outside assistance. But each time the house was nearly completed the relentless teacher had it pulled down again on one pretext or the other and ordered his pupil to start again elsewhere. When Mi-la begged for the promised initiation he was driven off with abuse and blows. As a result of the carrying of heavy stones, the pupil's back developed into one festering wound. In his desperation he made several attempts to escape from his persecutor, and on one occasion he even attempted to take his life, but he did not succeed in loosing the bonds which bound him to the one man from whom he hoped for the initiation. In these difficult days Mar-pa's wife and Shakti bDag-med-ma stood mercifully by the pupil's side, and regarded him and loved him as her own son. But not even she could save him from the temperamental outbursts of anger on the part of her choleric husband; and in any case although the sufferings Mar-pa imposed on his pupil were very real they were also necessary and they all had a hidden significance. In the end the 'cleansing' and the ordeals came to an end, and Mar-pa rewarded his best and most heroic pupil with the longed-for initiation into the profoundest secrets. Then he released him to live the life of a hermit in the neighbourhood of Gung-thang.

The rest of Mi-la's life was now devoted to lonely meditation in the Tibetan mountains, on rocky slopes and in hidden grottos, for the benefit of all living creatures. The *Hundred-thousand Chants* are devoted to this period, and they clearly reveal the unique personality of this noble man, whose character was very different from that of Nâ-ro-pa or of Ti-lo-pa, neither of whom was exempt from sinister characteristics. The difference between the good-natured and frugal living Mi-la and his corpulent and married teacher Mar-pa, who was also given to the consumption of large quantities of Tibetan malt beer (chang), was also very striking. A harsh fate had turned Mi-la into a real 'anima candida', whose character is movingly reflected in the *Hundred-thousand Chants*. This voluminous work describes the experiences of the master after his Enlightenment, his wanderings and his conversions, and it is written in a traditional contemporary style and with impressive imagery. It also contains numerous hymns or chants in which Mi-la describes his material and spiritual experiences, and we should not, I think, go far wrong in assuming that the greater number of these chants actually are the work of the great ascetic. His spiritual personality is so clear-cut and so outstanding that it seems unlikely that the whole of this book of chants is the work of later writers, particularly as we know that the master himself was a real poet. It was no uncommon thing in India for mystics to describe their spiritual experiences in verses which were often most paradoxically phrased (Vajra-Dohâs), but the style of the chants of Mi-la differs from that of the Dohâs by something unmistakably personal. For example, they contain matters relating to the outside world, and to the life of the Tibetan people, and also entrancing descriptions of nature in the high mountains of Tibet. For all their spirituality these chants are very human too, and their graphic character has made them a popular book so that down to this day many of the verses of Mi-la are still to be heard on the lips of ordinary

Tibetans. The following is a typical example, and it conveys something of the magic of this hermit poet even in translation:

'This is the hermitage, called the "Palace of Enlightenment";
Above towers the high white glacier mountain of the gods;
Below are many faithful bringers of gifts;
Behind the mountain is a veil of white silk;
Before me grow the wish-fulfilling woods;
Meadows and green valleys stretch far away;
Over the lovely and scented water lilies,
Buzz and swarm the insect folk.
At the edge of lake and pool,
Water fowl crane their shapely necks.
In the spreading branches of the trees,
Swarms of birds sing sweetly.
Moved by the wind, the bearer of scents,
The foliage dances in the air.
High in the crowns of the trees
The monkeys twist and turn.
On the soft green carpet of fields
The four-footed creatures browse,
Whilst the herdsmen their masters
Sing songs and pipe the melancholy flute.
Below the slaves of worldly greed
Busy themselves with their follies.
But I, the Yogi, look down on it all
From my perch on these glorious mountains
And take the inconstant world as a parable.
Earthly goods are to me as a reflection in water;
Life is the deceit of a dream.
And my pity goes out to the unenlightened.
The vastness of space is my banquet,
No distraction disturbs my meditation.
That all diversity is encompassed in my spirit,
That all the things of the three-world circle
Although irreal are yet visible, how wonderful that is!'

In the first years after his initiation by Mar-pa, Mi-la avoided almost all contact with human beings. Even in the icy Tibetan winter he remained in the caves of Mount Everest and other Himalayan giants, snowed under, cut off from all human aid and clothed only in a light cotton garment. The 'Blissful Warmth' (gtum-mo) of the Yogis, which Mar-pa had taught him to generate must have done him great service. He had now become the heir of all the teachings of the bKa-rgyud-pa, since all that Marpa had passed on to his son was the Grong-'jug initiation, the power to enter into a strange corpse, and with the death of the son that power had been lost. The hermit of the mountains is said to have lived for nine years in the utmost frugality nourishing himself only on herbs. But gradually he became better known and much loved, so that pious laymen began to regard it as an honour to be allowed to supply him with flour and butter. Like the lives of all Yogis, his own was soon surrounded with an aura of wondrous stories. He was said to be able to turn himself into any animal he pleased, and also to be able to fly through the air. We have already dealt with his most famous achievement, the defeat of a Bon priest and the latter's extraordinary sister on the sacred mountain Kailâsa. After bringing about innumerable conversions and performing many beneficial deeds he died in his old age in the year 1123 after having drunk poisoned milk given to him by an envious Lama.

Mi-la ras-pa had gathered numerous pupils around him in his lifetime to carry on the tradition after his death. The story of their meeting with the master is set out at full length in the book of legends. Particularly popular amongst the Tibetans is the story of the conversion of the wild hunter mGon-po rdo-rje, whose whole life was devoted to the destruction of life. In the *Hundred-thousand Chants* there is a marvellous description of how Mi-la subdued this wild fellow by the sheer power of his personality and made him into one of his most devoted disciples. Many representations of Mi-la show the holy man in a grotto, one hand cupped behind his right ear, whilst before him the wild hunter, his bow and arrows cast aside, pays homage together with his dog and the game he hunted. Amongst the host of Mi-la's pupils were eight 'spiritual sons', and thirteen lesser sons (upaputra). Amongst the former group were two in particular who are compared to the sun and the moon, whilst all the others are given the rank of attendant stars. The disciple whose spiritual light is compared to that of the moon was Ras-chung-pa (1084-1161) who came from the same neighbourhood as Mi-la ras-pa, and met the master when he, Ras-chung-pa, was only eleven. In his fifteenth year Ras-chung-pa was struck with leprosy, and together with three companions he set off for the holy land of India, a country which his master never knew. In India he was initiated by the Indian master Balacandra into the gTum-mo and other esoteric practices, and was cured of his leprosy. Later on Mi-la sent him to India once again in order that he should be initiated into the 'Nine Circles of the Dâkinî Teachings' by a pupil of Nâ-ro-pa and of Maitri-pa, and bring back this knowledge to his own master. Ras-chung appears to have been a rather self-willed person who was more interested in the practical experience of the secret teachings than in church organization.

In consequence the main stream of the bKa-rgyud-pa tradition was not transmitted through him, but through the 'Doctor of Dvags-po' (Dvags-po lha-rje), also known as sGam-po-pa, or 'The Man of sGam-po', after his later hermitage. This sGam-po-pa, who lived from 1079 to 1153, first studied the teachings of the bKa-gdams-pa, and then the Mantras under a Tantric teacher in Western Tibet. In his thirty-second year he heard from the lips of a beggar about the fame of Mi-la ras-pa and soon became his most important pupil. After esoteric training lasting for the space of thirteen months Mi-la transmitted all his teachings to him, including the gTum-mo, the Six Principles of Nâ-ro and the Mahâmudrâ. After this the disciple returned to his own home in Dvags-po in the south eastern part of the province of Ü, where he engaged in meditation for a number of years in various hermitages, including one on the famous mountain O-de gung-rgyal. In the latter days of his life he carried out important literary activity, and in particular he wrote certain mystic dissertations. He also founded a monastery at sGam-po. His pupil, Phag-mo gru-pa (1110-1170) who inherited the apostolic succession, came from Eastern Tibet. He studied the teachings of the bKa-gdams-pa and the Sa-skya-pa, but he regarded sGam-po-pa as his chief teacher. From amongst his pupils developed the various sub-sects of the bKa-rgyud-pa into which the previously uniform tradition split up. Even today in Tibet they still enjoy a reputation, for scholarship and the successful practise of the magic arts. A pupil named 'Jig-rten mgon-po (born 1143) founded the sub-sect 'Bri-gung-pa, so named because its stronghold was in 'Bri-gung, north-east of the later State monastery, dGa-ldan, where Tsong-kha-pa is buried. The hierarchs of the 'Bri-gung sect were to become serious political rivals of the

Grand Lamas of Sa-skya. At the time of the Chinese Ming dynasty they and two other sect leaders were given the same rights as the leaders of the Sa-skya. A break-away sect, the sTag-lung-pa, so called after its chief monastery, was founded by another pupil of Phag-mo gru-pa, a monk named sTag-lung thang-pa, who founded the monastery sTag-lung ('Tiger Valley') to the north of the Brahmaputra. A further important sub-sect, the 'Brug-pa, was founded by a third pupil, gTsang-pa rgya-ras-pa (1161-1211). The name 'Brug actually means thunder, because when the founder of the sect was building his monastery 'Brug in the province of Tsang he is said to have been surprised by extremely violent thunder and lightning. In the seventeenth century, followers of this sect did missionary work in the Himalaya land of Bhutan, and they were so successful that today this neighbourhood is the stronghold of the 'Brug-pa sect. The fourth and final sub-sect worthy of mention here is that of the Kar-ma-pa, and it honours another pupil of sGam-po-pa, Dus-gsum mk'yen-pa (1110-93) as its founder. The seat of the Karma hierarchs, built by the founder of the sect, lies to the west of Lhasa and is called mTshur-phug. A number of the abbots of this monastery, like the Lamas of Sa-skya, were called to the court of the Mongol Emperor, whilst the fifth in line was also invited by the Ming Emperor Yung-lo to his court. All four branches of the bKa-rgyud-pa were influenced in their teachings by the Padmasambhava school.

The period from the tenth to the fourteenth century, which we have just reviewed, saw the final consolidation of Buddhism in the spiritual life of Tibet, and the rise of various special groups and sects, though, owing to the breaking off of direct contact with India, the main lines of their development soon hardened. Not only was religion, as such, definitively consolidated, but the beginning of the fourteenth century can also be regarded as an important concluding stage in the history of the sacred writings. A first collection of all the Buddhist Tibetan translations was made in the thirteenth century and deposited in sNar-t'ang.[1] The completion of the work of codification as far as the literature of the commentaries is concerned is connected with the name of one of the most famous of the Lamaist scholars, Bu-ston (1290-1364), who worked in the monastery Zha-lu not far from Tashilhunpo, where he collected the innumerable translations made

[1] Cf. Roerich, *The Blue Annals*, p. 337.

not only during the time of the universal monarchy but also in the period of 'the later dissemination of the gospel', translations which had in the meantime, often been revised and amended. In particular he worked for the general adoption of the new uniform Tibetan orthography. This was very necessary because there was a good deal of confusion: some of the sacred texts were still as they had been copied in the orthography of the monarchical period, whilst the main body of the translations was already in the new orthography. Incidentally, the writings of the heretical Bon-po are still to some extent in the old orthography even today. The famous *History of Buddhism* of Bu-ston, from which we have already quoted frequently, has a final part which has unfortunately not yet been thoroughly studied. It contains a review of the whole canon and the exegetical literature as it was available to the great scholar at the time.

In theory this canon is regarded both by the Tibetans and the Hînayâna Buddhists as the 'Threefold Vessel' or Tripitaka, containing the three sections of the Vinaya (discipline of the Order), the Sûtra (the doctrinal texts) and the Abhidharma (systematic philosophy), but in fact it has tremendously exceeded this limitation since it also contains the whole Mahâyâna literature and the Tantras, and they, just as much as the old Hînayâna texts, rank as the authoritative word of Buddha (bka). The official name of this collection is, in fact, *bKa-'gyur*, or in the present-day pronunciation *Kanjur*, which means *Translations of the Word* (*of Buddha*). The arrangement of the parts differs amongst the various schools, but the most usual one—the one used in the printed editions of the present dominant Yellow Church—contains the following sections: 1. 'Dul-ba (Vinaya in Sanscrit) or the discipline of the Order; 2. Sher-phyin (Prajnâpâramitâ), the 'Perfection of Wisdom'; 3. Sangs-rgyas phal-po-che (Buddhâvatamsaka) 'Collection of the Buddhas'; 4. dKon-brtsegs (Ratnakûta) 'Peak of Jewels'; (2 to 4 contain only the Mahâyâna texts); 5. mDo (Sûtra) Doctrines of the Large and Small Vehicles; and 6. rGyud (Tantra), the Magical Literature. In some editions a special section Myang-'das (Nirvâna) is extracted from the fifth section, and contains the reports on the death of Buddha. The sections relating to the Sûtra and the Tantra are by far the most voluminous.

Unlike the *Kanjur*, the second great collection of Lamaist literature, the *bsTan-'gyur* (*Tanjur*) or *Translations of the Text-*

books is regarded as semi-canonical only. It contains the philosophical and exegetical works of the great Fathers of the Church translated from the Indian; and, in addition, a number of more worldly Indian writings dealing with the auxiliary sciences such as grammar, the theory of poetry, the theory of the creative arts, logic, mathematics, chronology, astrology and medicine. The Mahâyâna philosophy and the ancillary sciences are contained in the mDo (Sûtra) section, the rest consists of commentaries on Tantra literature, rGyud—apart from a small cycle of divine hymns (bsTod-tshogs, Stotra), which is at the beginning of the enormous collection.

In the centuries which followed the time of Bu-ston, these two great collections were produced on wooden matrices by a number of monasteries. The first printing of the *Kanjur* was not in Tibet but in Pekin during the reign of the Ming Emperor Yung-lo, and it was completed in the year 1411. Fine Kanjur reproductions were also turned out under the Manchurian Emperors K'ang-hsi and Ch'ien-lung.[1] The first editions produced in Tibet were at sNar-thang, the *Kanjur* in 1731 and the *Tanjur* in 1742.[2] Others were subsequently produced in the printing works of the Dalai Lama at Lhasa, and in the monasteries of Eastern Tibet sDe-dge (Derge), bLa-brang (La-brang), sKu-bum (Kumbum) and Co-ne. One, which has so far remained unknown, was also produced in the Bhutanese town of Punakha. Most of the *Kanjur* editions comprise a hundred great volumes. One was produced in Derge by the Red sect, unaffected by the Tsong-kha-pa reformation, and this edition had 108 volumes. So far all the editions of the *Tanjur* which have become known consist of 225 volumes, and they were produced in sNar-thang, Derge and Co-ne.

[1] B. Laufer, 'Die Kanjur-Ausgabe des Kaisers K'ang-hsi' in the *Proceedings of the Petersburg Academy*, 1909.

[2] Cf. G. Tucci, *Harvard Journal of Asiatic Studies*, 1949, pp. 477 *et seq.*

CHAPTER VIII

THE TSONG-KHA-PA REFORMATION AND THE PRIEST-STATE OF THE DALAI LAMAS

The picture presented by Lamaism in the fourteenth century was that of a chaos of numerous schools and sects. The bKa-gdams-pa had, it is true, inspired by Atîsha, made an attempt to purge and discipline the priesthood and purify the teachings of Tibetan Buddhism, but it had lost ground against the Sa-skya, the 'Bri-gung and the stag-lung sects, particularly because their rival hierarchs had succeeded in securing temporal power over Tibet. On the whole, therefore, the Buddhism of those days displayed a number of disagreeable features, one of which was a more and more blatant urge on the part of the priesthood towards temporal power, and another the predominance of magical arts according to Tantric rituals. In other words, the appeal of Atîsha for a real Buddhist outlook and way of life had found no effective echo amongst the majority of the priesthood, and his work had to be done all over again.

The man who was destined to carry out this task was the great reformer Tsong-kha-pa, whose name as a monk was Sumati-kîrti. He is also known to the followers of the new church he called into being as, 'the Precious Ruler' (rje rin-po-che).[1] This greatly venerated master, whose followers honour him with a highly-developed cult of prayers and Mantra recitations, and who never utter his name without coupling it with expressions of the utmost devotion, was born in the year 1357 as the fourth son of poor parents in the east of Tibet, in the district Tsong-kha, or

[1] The authoritative biography comes from the pen of a favourite pupil of the great religious teacher, mKhas-grub-rje. Unfortunately it is not available. A certain substitute is offered by the detailed account in dPag-bsam ljon-bzang, pp. 210 *et seq.* See also Grünwedel, *Mythologie*, pp. 70 *et seq.*; Schulemann, *Geschichte der Dalailamas*, pp. 58 *et seq.*; Filchner-Unkrig, *Kumbum Dschamba Ling*, pp. 171 *et seq.*; Huth, *Geschichte des Buddhismus in der Mongolei*, pp. 176 *et seq.*; and in particular Obermiller's monograph *Tson-kha-pa le Pandit.*

12 Lamas sunk in meditation in the main temple of Lhasa

13 The Potala, the official Residence of the Dalai Lama

'Onion Valley', in the area of Amdo. At the place where he was born a sacred tree now stands, and writing is said to appear miraculously on its leaves. All around today extend the enclosures of the monasterial area of Kumbum (sKu-'bum). The lad is said to have been initiated into the Buddhist religion at an astonishingly tender age by the Karma hierarch Lalitavajra, but his real teacher from his third year was Don-grub rin-chen of his own neighbourhood. Before long he was honoured with Tantric initiations of the Hevajra, the Cakrasmavara and the Vajrapâni, whereupon he was given a mystical initiation name—Amoghavajra. He was seven years old when he took the vows of the novitiate. When the industrious young pupil was sixteen years old his teacher considered it essential for his further studies that he should go to the famous monasteries of Central Tibet. This teacher worked out a systematic plan of study for the youth, and urged him in particular to devote himself to the teachings of the great Indian Fathers of the Church Maitreya, Dharmakîrti and Nâgârjuna. These exhortations were to prove of decisive importance for Tsong-kha-pa's further studies, and they obviously fitted in well with his own inclinations. Although in 'Bri-gung he began with an introduction to medicine, he devoted the following decisive years exclusively to the study of the fundamentals of the Mahâyâna philosophy. He successively visited the most famous centres of scholarship of the various schools, and studied in Sa-skya, Jo-nang, sNar-t'ang and Lhasa, and also in the leading monasteries of Yar-klungs. Red-mda-pa was to be particularly important to his career, teaching him logic and philosophy in the tradition of the Sa-skya. It was characteristic of Tsong-kha-pa that unlike the other great religious teachers, such as Bu-ston, he attached great importance to the science of logic (pramâna) taken over from the Indians, and regarded its mastery as essential. It was not very long before Tsong-kha-pa outstripped all his fellow students. In his eighteenth year he could recite an important Maitreya work by heart, and in the following years he took part in philosophic disputations with great success. In the end he completely mastered the five spheres which are regarded down to this day as essential by the Lamaist masters: logic, the doctrine of the perfection of wisdom (Prajnâpâramita), the 'middle teaching' of Nâgârjuna which is based on it, the body of scholastic philosophy according to the Abhidharmakosha of Vasabandhu, and finally, significantly, the discipline of the Order.

Tsong-kha-pa's interest in the Vinaya naturally brought him into touch with the tradition of the old sect of the bKa-gdams-pa, and a Lama, Mar-res spyi-po-lhas, introduced him to the regulations of this school, for which Tsong-kha-pa thereafter always retained a liking. When we consider, so to speak, the spiritual 'general line' of Tsong-kha-pa as expressed in his course of studies and as it determined his subsequent teaching activities, we cannot but agree with Obermiller who sees the great man primarily as a pandit, as an eminent scholar. The character of Tsong-kha-pa seems to have been a mixture of prudence and cool severity, and he lacked that special religious charisma which was particularly marked with Mi-la. He was not a man of warm and impulsive sympathies, but a stickler for discipline and order; and one must recognize that at the time no qualities were more beneficial to the Tibetan prelacy. However, the young scholar also clearly felt the necessity for an all-round study of the Buddhist teachings, as evidenced by the fact that in the monastery of Zhalu he had himself initiated in the Tantric traditions by a personal pupil of Bu-ston, Chos-kyi dpal, and in particular in the Kâlacakra. All in all, Tsong-kha-pa can be described as a man of the middle; a man of moderation, opposed to all extremes.

His mother appealed to him to return to his home in Eastern Tibet, but after giving her request careful consideration he decided not to accede to it, and he sent her a letter pointing out that it was impossible for him to interrupt his studies, and asking her to erect a Stûpa over the miraculous sandlewood tree which was growing at his birthplace. In his twenty-fifth year he was ordained a full monk, and from then on his constant study was paired by teaching activity of his own. His favourite subjects remained logic and the Mahâyâna philosophy, but in addition there was now his efforts to perfect himself in the auxiliary sciences of medicine, mathematics and stilistics, in which he schooled himself according to a famous Indian textbook *The Mirror of Poetry* by Dandin. He also continued his close study of the Tantras. A Lama named dbU-ma-pa afforded him mystic communication with the Bodhisattva of sciences, Manjushrî, as whose incarnation Tsong-kha pa is often regarded. In particular the great scholar was fascinated by the representative commentary on the 'Kâlacakra', known as the 'Immaculate Lustre' (Vimalaprabhâ), and he him self delivered a number of lectures on it. An observation in the great biography of his pupil mKhas-grub-rje, which we quote here in Unkrig's translation,[1] throws an interesting light on his attitude to the Tantras, which, according to official dogma, are regarded as an authentic part of the word of Buddha, and on his leaning towards a balanced consideration of all parts of the Buddhist gospel: 'In so far as the majority of the present day, that is to say, the studying Lamas, turn with their understanding towards the mTshan-nyid school (philosophy), they have abandoned the idea of entering the Tantra faculty. Everything is done to turn even the students who listen to lectures here away from it. Certain listeners even consider, as soon as the slightest vestige of respect for the Tantra system evinces itself in them, that for this reason the Pâramitâs section is superfluous and inferior. . . . The guilt of such an attitude is very great, and its development evinces itself in the form of violent suffering. . . . Nowadays one seldom meets people who wish to master the Sûtras and the Tantras, though both were proclaimed by the victorious Buddha.' In his desire to master the Tantra teachings completely in addition to his other studies, Tsong-kha-pa included not only his favoured Kâlacakra, but also the Guhyasamâja with the great commentary of Nâ-ro-pa, the 'Six Dharmas' of this master, and the cycle of the Cakrasamvara according to the tradition of the Indian Lûi-pa. The Tantric system developed by Tsong-kha-pa, which was to remain binding for the church he founded, regards Vajradhara as the Âdibuddha, as also does the bKa-rgyud-pa, whereas out of the Bodhisattvas Manjushrî and Avalokiteshvara are considered to be equally significant. The most important Tantric 'protective deity' (ishtadevatâ) is Bhairava ('The Terrible)', also called Yamântaka ('Executioner of the Death God'), the terrifying form of Manjushrî influenced by Shivaism. But in accordance with the practice of Tsong-kha-pa neither Cakrasamvara nor Guhyasamâja are excluded.

Tsong-kha-pa garnered the results of his scholarly and religious studies in a great number of important writings. The collected edition of his works, which was printed in the monastery of Kumbum, consists of sixteen volumes containing 313 different treatises. His first great work was a commentary on a book by the Indian Maitreya (Abhisamayâlamkâra) devoted to the Prajnâpâramitâ philosophy, and it has become famous under the title *Golden Wreath of Helpful Dicta*. But the most popular and

[1] *Kumbum Dschamba Ling*, p. 177.

the most renowned are the two concluding compendia which deal with the gradual rise of man with the aid of the Pâramitâ teachings on the one hand and the Tantra doctrines on the other. The first of these works, *Steps to Enlightenment* (Byang-chub lam-rim), was completed in 1403 in the old chief monastery of the bKa-gdams-pa in Rva-sgreng. In this book Tsong-kha-pa describes the rise of man and his spiritual cleansing according to the principle of the Pâramitâ teaching, beginning with resort to a spiritual teacher and ending in the highest spheres of profound spiritual peace (shamatha). He points out that this step by step way to moral purification is also binding on the followers of the Tantra system. The basis of this book can be seen in the *Entrance to the Bodhi Way* (Bodhicaryâvatâra) of the Indian Shântideva, and, above all, in Atîsha's *Lamp of the Bodhi Way* with the commentary of Po-to-ba. Both these works were liberally quoted by Tsong-kha-pa. From Atîsha he also took the classification of men into three groups, though he finds the needs of the spiritually inferior and their demand for the preaching of the 'Common Way' insufficiently considered, and this he makes up for in his own work. For those who cannot aspire to the highest spheres of religious life he prepared a special extract *The Smaller Stage Way* in 1415. The master regards only the noblest and highest class of men to be worthy of the 'Perfection of Wisdom'. The other important book is entitled *The Great Stage Way to the Occult Sciences* (sngags rim chen mo) and it sets out in an authoritative manner for his own school the four basic systems. The avowed intention is to cleanse Tantrism as practised in Tibet, and to prevent evil men from exploiting the study of the Tantras in order to satisfy their lower instincts.

It was inevitable that the great scholarship and the blameless personal life of Tsong-kha-pa should attract an ever growing number of pupils, and these subsequently formed the body of the new sect, or, better, church. This religious community, known as the Sect of the 'Virtuous' (dGe-lugs-pa), or the Yellow Church, was soon to win a decisive position for itself in Tibet. The latter name comes from the fact that the Lamas who follow Tsong-kha-pa do not wear the red monk's hat of the followers of the old unreformed church, but use a yellow hat instead. In the year 1393 only eight pupils listened to the teachings of Tsong-kha-pa, but by 1409 his following had grown enormously and there was no longer any question about the great importance of his new school, which, incidentally, professedly aimed at no more than continuing the old tradition of the gKa gdams-pa. The old and sacred Buddha image in the main temple at Lhasa became the objective of solemn processions at which votive offerings were made. The temple itself was cleansed of all misuses, alms were distributed to 8,000 clergy, and for the first time the Tibetan New Year's celebration (at the beginning of February) was held in conjuction with the great sMon-lam or Feast of the Intercession (which has since become obligatory) for the well-being of all living creatures. In order to demonstrate symbolically the rule of the Yellow Church, the abbots of the three dGe-lugs-pa State monasteries near Lhasa exercised police powers in the capital during the religious feast days.

In the same year, 1409, Tsong-kha-pa, and his pupil rGyal-tshab-rje ('Crown Prince' or 'Representative') founded a new monastery to the north-east of Lhasa to accommodate his tremendously increased following. This monastery, dGal-ldan, 'the joyful', which was also a Tushita Heaven on Earth, became the chief monastery of the new church, and Tsong-kha-pa was its first abbot. A little later, in 1419, another prominent disciple, Byams-chen chos-rje founded the Mahâyâna monasteries Se-ra (Se-ra theg-chen-gling), and 'Bras-spungs ('Heap of Rice') in 1416. This latter was a copy of the South Indian Dhânyakataka, whose name was translated into Tibetan with 'Bras-spungs. The names of these two latter monasteries were intended to underline the close connection of the dGe-lugs-pa with the Kâlacakra system, for Dhânyakataka is traditionally the place where Buddha is said to have preached the Kâlacakra to King Sucandra.

Tsong-kha-pa himself never left Tibet, though he is said at one time to have harboured an intention of visiting the holy places in India, but finally decided not to in consequence of a revelation from Manjushrî, who ordered him to remain in Tibet and purify religion there. In any case, a journey to India could no longer have borne such fruit as at the time of Rin-chen bzang-po, or even in 1200 in the period of the great Sa-skya Lamas, because since then Buddhism had lost ground in its homeland as a result of the Mohammedan persecutions. A proposed journey to China also did not come about. Having heard of the fame of the Tibetan priest, the Ming Emperor Yung-lo (1403-24) sent a delegation to Tsong-kha-pa to invite him to visit the Chinese capital. Unlike the hierachs of the Sa-skya and 'Bri-gung sects, Tsong-kha-pa could see no advantage in such a journey. He was not interested in worldly honours, and he regarded his great task as the spiritual training of those who had been given to him as pupils. However, his pupil Byams-chen chos-rje, the founder of Se-ra, did go to China, where he spent a few years at the court of the Chinese Emperor, and was loaded with honours.[1] Naturally, the new religious community founded by Tsong-kha-pa was not without its enemies. The Grand Lamas of Sa-skya in particular regarded Tsong-kha-pa as a competitor who was particularly dangerous to them because of his personal moral purity and his strictness in religious matters. According to the Russian scholar Potanin, the leaders of the Red Church made an attempt to curb the activities of the great Reformer, only to be put to shame by him.[2]

What most disturbed the representatives of the older sects about the activities of Tsong-kha-pa was his puritanism, and his determination to restore the unambiguous requirements of Buddhism, particularly in the matter of religious discipline, to their old authority. The restitution of the Vinaya alone and the almost pedantically regulated daily lives of the monks were quite sufficient to win for Tsong-kha-pa the title of 'Reformer of Lamaism'. Nothing was farther from his thoughts than to change in any way the basic teachings of what was regarded as Buddhism in his day, and perhaps to return to the teachings and practice of the old Buddhist texts, which have maintained themselves in a more or less original state in south Buddhist countries such as Ceylon, Siam and Burma. He re-introduced the old prohibition of intoxicating liquors, and he insisted on the strict observation of celibacy for the priesthood—two points in which the practices of the new dGe-lugs-pa differed most strikingly from those of the Red Church. He also forbade the Yellow priests to take an evening meal, and to sleep too long or at inappropriate times. The practices of the cult were strictly regulated down to the smallest details and in this way the monks were kept busy almost all day. There is no doubt that Tsong-kha-pa set himself a very serious and high ideal, and similarly there is no doubt that his achievement was of tremendous value for the spiritual restoration of Buddhism of his day. On the other hand, there is also no doubt that he imposed a certain narrow uniformity, a pedantic medi-

[1] Huth, *Geschichte des Buddhismus in der Mongolei*, pp. 191 *et seq.*
[2] Schulemann, *Geschichte des Dalailamas*, pp. 63 *et seq.*

ocrity, on the spiritual attitude that he inaugurated, thus making it very different in character from the Tibetan Buddhism of earlier times. Tsong-kha-pa was a brilliant scholar, and that is also true of his immediate pupils; and right down to the present day his followers have produced a number of first-class all-round scholars. But we shall look in vain for a religious genius of the calibre of Mi-la ras-pa amongst them. The founder of the Yellow Church also did everything possible to restrict the practice of magic and the use of the Tantras, and to reduce them to their proper canonical proportion. However, he did not succeed in this without having to compromise, for the practices were very deeply rooted. His followers were forbidden to practise certain branches of the magic art, but in order to satisfy the deep-rooted desire of the people for such things, each monastery took a representative, often a married man, of the old unreformed Red Tantra sects into its community for the performance of the suspect rites, though generally speaking his living quarters were outside the monastery precincts. We meet such a 'Protector of Religion' (Chos-skyong) in the person of the Oracle Lama of gNas-chung, attached to the State monastery 'Bras-spungs. It is therefore not too much to say that the new State Church system is based on a compromise between the Red and the Yellow sects.

In 1419 the great reformer died amongst his pupils in the new metropolitan monastery of dGa-ldan, after having given his pupil rGyal-tshab Dar-ma rin-chen his hat and cloak, thus clearly appointing him his successor as abbot of dGa-ldan and head of the sect. Apart from the already mentioned Byams-chen chos-rje, the founder of Se-ra, other prominent pupils were dGe-legs dpal-bzang-po, commonly known as mKhas-grub-rje, and Tsong-kha-pa's nephew dGe-'dun grub-pa, of whom the last-named was by far the youngest. The pupil mKhas-grub-rje, who is said to have seen a vision of his teacher who had come down from Tushita Heaven after his death—a vision which has become famous—established a veritable cult in memory of the departed teacher and master. Every year since then the Yellow Church has solemnly marked the anniversary of the death of Tsong-kha-pa by reciting special hymns devoted to his glorification. This mKhas-grub-rje was hardly less of a scholar than his master, and his works are still held in the highest regard amongst the dGe-lugs-pa, and in particular his sub-commentary to the Kâlacakra written in 1434. In 1431 mKhas-grub-rje succeeded rGyal-tshab as abbot of dGa-ldan, and retained that office down to his death in 1438, when dGe-'dun grub-pa, the nephew of the Reformer, became the leader of the sect. This dGe-'dun grub-pa was an unusually clever man but at the same time he was an intriguer and a somewhat arrogant personality who did everything possible to consolidate the hierarchical system of the Yellow Church. It was he who founded the first monastery outside the old central district of the dGe-lugs-pa around Lhasa. This was the monastery Tashilhunpo (bKra-shis lhun-po) near Shigatse in the province of gTsang, where he installed bSod-nams phyogs-glang as the first abbot, who was then regarded as the reincarnation of mKhas-grub-rje. It would appear that this dGe-'dun grub-pa played an important role in the development of the reincarnation dogma which was henceforth to play such a dominant role in the Yellow Church. It is true that Tsong-kha-pa himself is credited with the statement that he would be reincarnated innumerable times and in many different places, and there is also the prophecy that his disciples mKhas-grub-rje and dGe-'dun grub-pa would appear again and again in a ceaseless series of reincarnations; nevertheless it looks as though the ultimate acceptance of reincarnation as a dogma took place only after his death.

The idea that gods and famous holy men could appear in other bodies was already familiar to Indian Buddhism, although in this popular form it naturally contradicted the authentic and strict Buddhist teaching of the non-existence of a permanent ego. Already in the pre-birth stories of the Jâtakas earlier births of Buddha Shâkyamuni are reported as a human being, a god, and even as an animal. King Sucandra of Shambhala was regarded as the reincarnation of Bodhisattva Vajrapâni, whilst in Tibet the old minister Thon-mi was regarded as a reincarnation of Manjushrî, and the Chinese and Nepalese wives of Srong-btsan were held to be reincarnations of the White and Green Târâ. Similarly, King Ral-pa-can was held to be a reincarnation of Vajrapâni. In the series of natural successors to the Grand Lamaship of Sa-skya from father to son or from uncle to nephew, Manjushrî is supposed to have been reincarnated no less than seven times. The natural wish to exploit the prestige of such a line of reincarnations for one particular monastery, and at the same time the impossibility of the mysterious reincarnation taking place in the case of physical succession as practised by the Sa-skya, played a big role in the development of the famous special form of the reincarnation dogma adopted by the Yellow Church. After the death of each Grand Lama the dead man is supposed to be reincarnated, usually after the passage of forty-nine days, in the body of a new-born baby, which, of course, first has to be found. This reincarnation dogma declares that the special protective deity of Tibet, Avalokiteshvara, is constantly reincarnated in the chain of priest princes beginning with dGe-'dun grub-pa, and they all bore the title rGyal-ba ('Victor)' or rGyal-dbang, which later became known in the Mongolian title Dalai Lama. At the same time the so-called Pan-chen rin-po ('Precious Teacher'), the hierarchs of the monastery of Tashilhunpo, are the reincarnations of Amitâbha, the Buddha of Infinite Light. Thus we can regard dGe-'dun grub-pa as the first Dalai Lama, although he was not known by this title. Similarly, the first abbot of Tashilhunpo may be regarded as the first Pan-chen, although it was only his second successor who actually adopted this title. European sources describe mKhas-grub-rje as the first hierarch of Tashilihunpo,[1] but this is incorrect if only on account of the fact that he died before the monastery was founded. Subsequent developments greatly increased the importance of the successors of dGe-'dun-pa, until finally they obtained temporal power over the whole of Tibet, whilst at the same time the Pan-chens, though all interesting and valuable personalities, remained more or less within their spiritual office and gradually decreased in importance by comparison with the Dalai Lamas.

The institution which had first been adopted by the leading prelates of the country and which became generally known by a Mongolian expression as the 'hubilganic succession' soon became so popular that every important monastery—and not only those of the Yellow Church—strove to establish a similar sacred procedure. The reincarnation of the Dalai Lama in his successor is carried out in the following fashion: generally speaking it is supposed that the soul of the dead Dalai Lama occupies the body of a new-born baby forty-nine days after his death. But this baby has to be found. It very often happens that the old Dalai Lama gives some general indications concerning the neighbourhood in which he will reappear, but usually the State oracle has to be consulted. Further, it is important that the baby should possess certain physical characteristics, and that certain signs and wonders

[1] Grünwedel, *Mythologie*, p. 76; and Schulemann, *Geschichte der Dalailamas*, p. 91.

should have accompanied its birth; for example, the blossoming of a tree in cold weather, or the healing of sickness amongst people who have been in some contact with the child. In cases of doubt, for example the existence of several candidates, the decision is arrived at by casting lots. The finally chosen child is then brought in triumph to Lhasa, where for the time being he continues to live with his parents. From his seventh or eighth year he is given a systematic spiritual education. Somewhat earlier the child is subjected to a kind of test to make sure of its authenticity. Amidst numerous other belongings some of the old Dalai Lama's are presented to the child. If it succeeds in recognizing those which belonged to the dead Dalai Lama, i.e. those which are its own as it is the reincarnation of the dead man, then the authenticity of its claim is proved beyond a peradventure. David-Neel was present at the finding of a number of babies supposedly representing the reincarnation of dead Lamas, though they were not particularly famous ones. She describes the procedure in her book *Heilige und Hexer*[1] The Grand Domo of such a sPrul-sku (Tulku in contemporary pronunciation) was enjoying the belongings of his dead master, which is the custom until the reincarnation of the dead prelate is discovered. In such circumstances, of course, he is in no particular hurry to find the child. Amongst other things this Major Domo used the precious snuff-box of his dead master. On one occasion he was invited to take tea with one of the lessees of the monastery. Producing his snuff-box afterwards he was startled when a small boy who had previously kept in the background now came forward and asked reproachfully: 'What are you doing with my snuff-box?' At that the Major Domo was appropriately moved and flung himself down at the feet of the child and acknowledged him as his new master. When this boy had been brought to the monastery in solemn procession he asked for certain other belongings of the dead Lama which at first no one knew about, but which were ultimately found—amidst enormous astonishment. It is, of course, not surprising to learn that this principle of succession has often been manipulated in the interests of certain families, or that, particularly with the higher reincarnations, such as those of the Dalai Lama and the Pan-chen, the Chinese overlords have often played a suspicious role in the matter in furtherance of their political interests.

[1] pp.122 *et seq.*

However, at the time of dGe-'dun grub-pa and his successor dGe-'dun rgya-mtsho (1475-1542) the political importance of the new church and its hierarchs was not very great, but before long it began to spread throughout the whole of Central Tibet and to squeeze out the old Red Church. It is quite likely that it was in this period that the Red Lamas began to move away, a process which was later greatly accelerated by the vigorous repressive action of the fifth Dalai Lama, and ultimately led to the evangelizing of the Himalaya countries—Sikkim by the Karma-pa, and Bhutan by the 'Brug-pa. The dGe-lugs-pa also spread steadily in Eastern Tibet too, where a milestone in the general development was the founding of the Kumbum monastery at the birthplace of the great Reformer, though this did not take place until 1578. Under dGe-'dun rgya-mtsho the monasteries of the Yellow Church increased considerably in number, and influence, and it became necessary to create the office of sDe-pa, or Major Domo, for their administration, an office often entrusted to a layman. At 'Bras-spungs this second rGyal-ba built the famous dGa-ldan pho-brang ('Palace of Joy'), and later on when the hierarchs became the temporal rulers of Tibet this was their official residence and the seat of government. Today this is reflected in the fact that the name of this palace appears on Tibetan coins as the authoritative minting place. This dGal-ldan pho-brang means 'Tibetan Government', although today the Dalai Lama resides in the Potala or 'Park of Jewels' (Nor-bu gling-ka).

The third rGyal-ba bSod-nams rgya-mtsho (1543-88) was of considerable importance in the history of Lamaism, because he succeeded in converting the Mongols for the second and definitive time.[1] Since they lost control of China in 1368 the Mongols broke up once into numerous tribes which were constantly fighting each other. The original work of conversion carried out by Sa-skya hierarch 'Phags-pa had not lasted, and the successors of Gengis Khan had fallen back into their old Shamanist religion. One of the most important of the Mongol princelings, the Altan Khan, of the tribe of Tümet, captured a number of Lamas of the Yellow Church, and these captives seem to have used the occasion to make propaganda for their beliefs. The result was that the Mongol prince sent a deputation to the centre of the dGe-lugs-pa to invite the Grand Lama to visit him. At first the Grand Lama

[1] See the biography, Huth II, pp. 200 *et seq.*; Grünwedel, *Mythologie*, p. 80; and Schulemann, *Geschichte der Dalailamas*, pp. 109 *et seq.*

did not accept the invitation but at least he sent a representative whose task was obviously to discover the lie of the land. The Mongol Khan then sent a second and more pressing invitation, and this the Grand Lama felt bound to accept so he journeyed over Rva-sgreng and Nag-chu to Mongolia, where he arrived in 1578. The legend has it that on the way the Grand Lama met the war demon Beg-tse and other Mongol gods, whom he promptly converted and made into 'Protectors of Religion', just as Padmasambhava and Rin-chen bzang-po had once converted the popular gods of Tibet, and ranged them in the pantheon of Lamaism. The Altan Khan received the Grand Lama with great ceremony, and thereafter he adopted Lamaism, in the form of the Yellow Church, as the official religion of his people. From now on the Mongols remained quite fanatically attached to Buddhism, and their conversion was a very important event in the history of Lamaism, because its sphere of influence was now greatly extended, particularly as the West Mongols (Oirat, Dsungaria and the Kalmucks) also soon came over as well. The same year saw the founding of Theg-chen chos-'khor-gling, the first Mongol monastery. This event was quickly followed by the founding of others. During the visit the Grand Lama recalled the first period of Buddhism amongst the Mongols, when he had been 'Phags-pa, and the Altan Khan had been Khubilai. It was on this occasion that the Altai Khan conferred the title of Dalai bLama Vajradhara ('Ocean Lama, Vajra Bearer') on the head of the Yellow Church; and it subsequently became the most famous of all the titles of the dGe-lugs-pa hierarchs. The old and primitive Mongol religion (akin to the Bon-po) was prohibited together with the cult of the Ongot gods. Blood sacrifices were also forbidden. Those who showed themselves disinclined to fall in with the new ways were threatened with the destruction of their homes. The Lamas were given high rank and placed on a footing of equality with the Mongol nobility. When he left, the Grand Lama appointed a representative, who is regarded as the first Hubilgan (incarnated Lama) of the Mongols.

However, fear that the Mongols might prove inconstant took the Grand Lama back to Mongolia once more, and he actually died there in 1588, before he could accept an invitation to visit the court of the Chinese Emperor. After his death his sagacious followers guided the course of events to their own advantage by finding the child who was the reincarnation of the

Grand Lama in the person of a grandson of the Altan Khan. When this fourth Dalai Lama, the young Yon-tan rgya-mtsho (1589-1616), was taken to Tibet, the saddened Mongols were consoled by the sending of a reincarnated high Lama to them, who, as the embodiment of the future Buddha Maitreya, was called Maidari Hutuhtu, or rJe-btsun dam-pa Hutuhtu, and who established his residence in Urga. The mistrustful Chinese, who feared that this new Prince of the Church might become a source of strength for the much-feared Mongol nationalism, imposed the condition that the Maidari Hutuhtu should be reincarnated only in Tibet. After that the number of reincarnated Lamas steadily increased not only in Tibet and Mongolia, but also in China. The lCang-skya Hutuhtu, resident in Pekin, became the most important Chinese reincarnation.

The reincarnation of the Mongol Dalai Lama, the 'Great Fifth', Ngag-dbang blo-bzang rgya-mtsho (1617-82), probably the most important of all the hierarchs of the Yellow Church, was destined to crown the development of Tibet into a priest State.[1] He came from a family resident in 'Phyongs-rgyas, once the place of origin of the old monarchy. In his sixth year he was brought to 'Bras-spungs, and there the Pan-chen initiated him into the novitiate in his eighth year, ordaining him a full monk in his twenty-second. Like all other young Princes of the Church, he was given a careful education ranging from instruction in the canonical texts to medicine. It is interesting to note that his studies of the Buddhist occult sciences included not only the so-called 'new' Tantras, but also those of the rNying-ma-pa. Later his outstanding ability as a scholar enabled him to write a number of important works on various scholarly subjects, and the collected edition of his works also contains dissertations on grammar, poetry, astrology and history. His important chronicle of the historical development of Tibet, which is of incalculable value today because it is based on the official archives relating to the middle ages in Tibet, has often been quoted in this book. Worthy of note is also his poem on the sacred places in the capital Lhasa, which is provided with a prose commentary.[2] These old holy places, such as the main temple, Ra-mo-che and rMe-ru, were, of course, original centres of the old Red sect

[1] Huth, pp. 265 *et seq*; dPag-bsam ljon-bzang, p. 303; and Schulemann, pp. 127 *et seq*.

[2] A. Grünwedel, 'Die Tempel von Lhasa, Gedicht des ersten Dalai Lama für Pilger bestimmt', in the *Proceedings of the Heidelberg Academy*, 1919.

which had been taken over by the fifth Dalai Lama for his own church. Amongst his many writings on theology and mysticism there are also, astonishingly, a considerable number dealing with the rNying-ma-pa tradition. This previously ignored fact must be specially stressed, and considered in conjuction with the statement of Sum-pa mKhan-po that amongst the teachers of the Dalai Lama there was a Lama who initiated his pupils into the traditions of the 'Master of the Treasures' gLing-pa; that is to say in all probability the discoverer of apocryphal Padmasambhava revelations, Pad-ma gling-pa, who will be referred to again later. The same historian also insists that the Dalai Lama 'penetrated specially into the depths of the rNying-ma teachings'. Laufer has already pointed out, in connection with his attempts to unravel the history of the Padmasambhava biography, that the fifth Dalai Lama turned to the study of these writings and caused a careful edition of the biography itself to be published.[1] And Laufer is justified in asking what was the cause of this interest of the Yellows in the Reds. How did it come about that the head of the Yellow, reformed, church of Tsong-kha-pa, and, incidentally, also the Regent Sangs-rgyas rgya-mtsho he appointed, interested themselves so much in the tradition of unreformed Lamaism, whereas in all other respects they did their best to suppress this sect? We may interpret these facts—to which others will be added later—as an indication that in the seventeenth century there was a circle of high dGe-lugs-pa prelates around the Dalai Lama who for some reason were anxious to create a place in the State church for the traditions which had previously been regarded as heretical, or at least suspect, but who were at the same time not prepared to tolerate the political rivalry of the Red Sect.

In political matters the Dalai Lama proved an energetic and wise ruler. He seems from the beginning to have aimed at securing sole political control of the country in the way the Sa-skya Lamas once held it. In his struggle against the enemies of his church he was able to rely on the support of the orthodox warrior Gu-shri Khan (1582-1654), the Prince of the Oirat Mongols, who acted as his secular arm. For example, the Mongol army overthrew the King of Be-ri in East Tibet, who had attempted to restore the old Bon religion; and Gu-shri also defeated an even more dangerous enemy of the Dalai Lama, the

[1] Laufer, *Roman einer Tibetischen Königin*, pp. 244 and 250.

ruler of the province of Ysang. This prince, Phun-tshogs rnam-rgyal of the dynasty of Rin-spungs, was an inveterate enemy of the Yellow Church, and in his own land he favoured the Red Church, and in particular the Karma-pa and the Jo-nang-pa sects. In consequence the Pan-chen was unable to reside in Tashilhunpo and had to stay in dGal-ldan, whilst the famous monastery of Shigatse fell into desuetude. This dangerous and powerful enemy of the Yellow Church was finally overthrown by Gu-shri Khan in 1642, who thereby brought the whole of Ü and Tsang under his control. However, he handed them over to the Dalai Lama as a gift, and from then on the latter was temporal as well as spiritual ruler of Tibet, so that the theocratic State was now definitely established in the Land of Snows. The victorious Mongols retained certain rights, including the title of King of Tibet, but the personality of the Dalai Lama was so dominant, and the relationship between him and Gu-shri so friendly that during their lives there were no serious differences between them. Some of the tribes of this Mongol ruler were now permanently stationed at Tengri-Nor to the north-east of Lhasa in order to be immediately at the service of the Dalai Lama if required.

The new Prince of the Church was definitely inclined to pomp and the outward signs of power, and he desired that his new position should be clearly demonstrated. In accordance with the changed and much extended authority of the Yellow pontificate, the previous office of sDe-pa, or temporal administrator of church property, was now changed into that of sDe-srid, or Regent. Later on the Dalai Lama, who was a law unto himself, entrusted this important post to his own son, Sangs-rgyas rgya-mtsho (1769). He also ignored the law of celibacy which Tsong-kha-pa had imposed on all the priests of his school. The Red sect was now completely suppressed and robbed of all temporal and economic power, and at the same time many of its monasteries were forcibly annexed by the Yellow Church. The result was that many of the Red faithful preferred to go into banishment in order to escape the power of the Dalai Lama. The stream of Red Lamas into the Himalayan countries now greatly increased, and in Bhutan this led to the foundation of a further theocratic State under the 'Brug-pa sect.

On the basis of an allegedly old and miraculously discovered text called gter-ma, or 'Treasure', in accordance with the yNying-ma-pa tradition, the great hierarch now sanctioned his own claim to pre-eminence and consolidated the hubilganic succession of the Dalai Lamas as the reincarnation of Avalokiteshvara, whilst at the same time the succession of the Pan-chen was pronounced to be the reincarnation of Amitâbha. The Dalai Lama's residences, the monasteries of dGa-ldan and 'Bras-spungs, no longer seemed adequate to him, and he began building a great palace on the 'Red Hill' near Lhasa, a place of symbolic importance because it was where Srong-btsan sgam-po had built his now ruined palace after transferring his residence from Yar-klungs. During the pontificate of bSod-nams rgya-mtsho a special private monastery of the Dalai Lama had already been built on the Red Hill and given the name of rNam-rgyal grva-tshang. The extensive and magnificent buildings of the Potala were now added to it. Named after an Avalokiteshvara temple in India they now became the official residence of the Priest-King, so to speak the Vatican of Lamaism. But the 'Great Fifth' was not destined to see the completion of these building operations, and it was only after his death that his son the Regent (1653-1705) added the White Palace (1694) to the already constructed Red Palace. The residence monastery of the Pan-chen was also restored in this period so that henceforth this Prince of the Church was able to reside permanently in Tashilhunpo.

In China, which had maintained close connections with the Grand Lamas of Tibet since the days of the Mongol dynasty, the Ming dynasty had been replaced by the Manchus (1644), and the first Manchu Emperor Shun-chih was particularly devoted to Buddhism. The Dalai Lama did not fail to take prudent cognisance of the dynastic change in China, and he formally handed back the titles and honours bestowed by the previous dynasty in order to receive them back at the hands of the new rulers. In 1651 a Chinese deputation appeared in Lhasa to invite both the Dalai Lama and the Pan-chen to Pekin. The hierarch of Tashilhunpo asked to be excused on account of his advanced age, but the Dalai Lama accepted and he was received in Pekin in 1652 with all the pomp and circumstance appropriate to a reigning prince. A special Lama monastery (Huang-tze) was built for his occupancy in Pekin, and the honoured guest was given a seal and the same privileges which 'Phags-pa had once received at the hands of Khubilai, thus confirming his position as temporal ruler of Tibet. It is however reported that the Chinese Emperor chose the Pan-chen to be his Guru, perhaps because

14 The sacred mountain Chomo Lhari in the frontier district of Bhutan
Lamas blowing sacred horns on the roof of the medical faculty lCags-po-ri

15 Image of the fifth Dalai Lama

the ambitious Dalai Lama was not really to his liking. On his part the Dalai Lama was not enamoured of the Manchus, and both he and his son and Regent, Sangs-rgyas rgya-mtsho, tended rather towards the inner-asiatic rivals of the Manchus, the West Mongol Dsungaris.

In his later years the Dalai Lama left the affairs of State more and more in the hands of his son the Regent, and withdrew into the interior of his palace. When he appointed his son to the office of Regent he had ordered that in future the Regent should be chosen from the incarnations of the four so-called 'Royal' monasteries in the immediate neighbourhood of Lhasa. The office of Regent was obviously a very important one, because whoever was Regent usually exercised the de facto governmental power, and during the minority of the new Dalai Lama, the de jure power as well. The Fifth Dalai Lama died in 1682, but for political reasons his son, Sangs-rgyas rgya-mtsho, kept the demise secret for some years, explaining the Dalai Lama's non-appearance by saying that he had withdrawn from the world for meditation. With this trick he continued to deceive the Chinese Emperor K'ang-hsi and his representatives for quite a long time. Like his father, Sangs-rgyas rgya-mtsho was a man of some personality, and he also made himself a considerable reputation as a writer. Father Georgi, whose work *Alphabetum Tibetanum* is based on the material collected by the Catholic missionaries in Tibet in those years, describes him with approval as a 'vir ingenii sagacissimi'.[1] Sangs-rgyas wrote a history of the Yellow-Hat sect (zhva-ser chos-'byung, 1698), and he also codified Tibetan law in his book *Mirror of Pure Crystal* (Dvangs-shel me-long), which is an excellent compilation. His voluminous work 'Vaidûrya dkar-po' ('White Beryl') 1683, and its continuation 'Vaidûrya gya-sel', which is an answer to the critics of the previous work, is also quite remarkable. In these works the author provides a thorough compendium of Tibetan astronomical knowledge, and in connection with his astrological matter he also deals with the popular Tibetan gods, the traditional death ceremonies and Tibetan oracular art. At the same time he showed himself to be an upholder of the traditions of his father, particularly in connection with the latter's flirting with the heretical rNying-ma teachings, and his own work reveals a rather more then superficial acquaintance with the Bon religion.

[1] Cf. Schulemann, p. 160.

When circumstances made it impossible to conceal the death of the fifth Dalai Lama any longer, the Regent decided to make it known simultaneously with the discovery of his reincarnation, which had taken place in all secrecy some time previously. This was Tshangs-dbyangs rgya-mtsho (1683-1706).[1] The Regent himself naturally had a decisive part in the finding of the new Prince of the Church,[2] and in view of his own leanings it is hardly a matter for surprise that the new Dalai Lama was discovered in the bosom of a family traditionally attached to the beliefs of the Red sect. This was the house of Pad-ma gling-pa, the rNying-ma 'treasure finder', the line contemptuously referred to by Sum-pa mkhan-po as 'the family of drunkards'.[3]

In accordance with tradition the Pan-chen now undertook the upbringing of the young hierarch and his introduction into the novitiate. The young man proved a bitter disappointment to the spiritual leaders of the dGe-lugs-pa, because he began to lead a dissolute life, and was greatly given to indulgence in drunken orgies in the town of Lhasa with numerous girl friends. He is credited (doubtfully however) with a small collection of engaging love songs which are still alive and popular to this day amongst the Tibetan people. David-Neel has translated some of them for us, including the following:

'Secretly stealing from the house
Whom do I spy on the street
But my lover, sweetly scented and delightful.
And no sooner found, should I abandon
This turquoise of azure blue?
To the wisest Lama of all Lamas I went
Seeking guidance for my soul,
Sitting there in the body at his feet
But alas!—my spirit hurried to the beloved!
Vainly sought I to look only on the master's face,
But unsought and uncalled appeared the face of the beloved,
Victoriously dismissing the face of my Master.'

[1] Cf. dPag-bsam ljon-bzang, p. 304; Schulemann, pp. 167 *et seq.*; Yu Dawchyuan, *Love Songs of the Sixth Dalai Lama Tshangs-dbyangs-rgya-mtsho;* and David-Neel, *Meister und Schüler*, p. 115.

[2] Love Songs, p. 31.

[3] This probably refers to that O-rgyan Pad-ma gling-pa who according to Tucci in his *Tibetan Painted Scrolls*, p. 259, was born in 1490.

This Tshangs-dbyangs rgya-mtsho lives on in the memory of the Tibetan people as the Priest King who was devoted to women, and his sad end only increased the general sympathy which his memory still arouses. But there was obviously more to it than a young man's love of pretty women, and a more critical investigation shows him as a pawn in the game of those circles which were desirous of reviving the old and the new teachings of Padmasambhava in the body of the Yellow Church. Their leader was obviously the Regent himself, who later on gave the young debauchee his own daughter in marriage. The suggestion that the sixth Dalai Lama was nothing but a debauchee is sufficiently discounted by the fact that he was the author of a number of religious works, some of which deal with the cult of the Tantra godhead Hayagrîva, as can be seen from the bibliographical list of the works of the Yellow-Hat Lamas drawn up by kLong-rdol bla-ma.[1] The following theory advanced by Alexandra David-Neel is probably not far from the truth: 'Tsang Yang Gyatso was apparently initiated into practices permitting, and even encouraging, a life which, from our point of view, is one of voluptuousness. It was a life which would mean debauchery for a man not initiated into the wondrous teachings.' A conformation of this theory has since come to hand through the translation of a letter from the Dsungari prince, Tshe-dbang rab-brtan, which was found in a collection of Manchurian State documents.[2] This prince, who was an adherent of the Yellow Church and at loggerheads with the Chinese, addressed his letter to the Chinese Emperor, and it provides us with a valuable insight into the inner history of Lamaism in those days, particularly in view of the fact that the interest of both the Dsungaris and the Chinese in the internal situation of the Tibetan Church was purely political. The letter charges both the Regent and the Dalai Lama with supporting the heretical rNying-ma teachings, and even the second, the false, Padmasambhava. At the time this letter was written, both the Regent and the Dalai Lama were dead. The teachings complained of are identified with those of the 'Treasure Discoverer', Pad-ma gling-pa, and are declared to be influenced by the doctrines of 'the dissident White-Hats'. Up to this time only

[1] Quoted in *Love Songs*, p. 203.

[2] Eva S. Kraft, *Zum Dsungarenkrieg im 18. Jahrhundert. Berichte des Generals Funingga*, Leipzig 1953, pp. 64 *et seq.* I am preparing a detailed editing and interpretation of this difficult letter.

Red, Yellow and Black-Hat (Bon-po) sects were known, and therefore, subject to the finding of still further material bearing on the matter, I think we may assume that this reference to the doctrines of the 'dissident', i.e. heretical, White-Hats is an echo of a later and degenerate form of Manichaeanism, for the Manichaeans are, in fact, represented on Central Asian murals wearing white hats.[1] There is nothing surprising in a connection between Lamaism and Manichaeanism, and the latter religion is expressly mentioned in the literature of the Red-Hat sect; for example in the *History of Buddhism* of gTsug-lag dpa-bo 'phreng-ba. Incidentally, the rites complained of seem to have consisted primarily in those of the sexualized Vajrayâna already very well-known to us from India. The young Dalai Lama is accused of having followed such practices not only in the old Red-Hat centre rMe-ru in Lhasa, but also in his own private monastery rNam-rgyal grva-tshang on the Potala hill. Interesting in this connection is the reference by the Re'u-mig that the rNam-rgyal founded in the year 1574 was later transformed into a rNying-ma institution. The Dalai Lama and his associates in the cult are also charged with the profanation of the famous Jo-bo image in the main temple, and with setting up images in the two previously mentioned holy places for the purpose of desecrating the Buddha Shâkyamuni by stabbing and shooting at it. The emissaries of the Dzungari princes are said, according to this report, to have seen such abominations committed in the monasteries named.

The opposition against the Dalai Lama and the Regent steadily increased, particularly as Lha-bzang Khan, who had inherited the rights of his grandfather Gu-shri, quarrelled with the Regent. In 1702 the young Dalai Lama even formally surrendered to the Pan-chen the spiritual vows he had made in Tashilhunpo—'perhaps because the merits of Tibet had disappeared, or because of some misfortune', as the historian Sum-pa mkhan-po records with dismay. However, the Dalai Lama retained his secular powers. A congregation of priests now decided that the spirit of Avalokiteshvara had abandoned the body of Tshangs-dbyangs and entered that of another Lama named Pad-dkar 'dzin-pa. This candidate enjoyed the support of the Chinese, who were hostile to the Regent. In the ensuing confusion the Mongol Lha-bzang broke into Lhasa with the object of deposing

[1] Cf. A. v. le Coq, *Chotcho*, Berlin 1913, Table 1.

the unworthy Dalai Lama in the interests of and in agreement with the Chinese. The Regent Sangs-rgyas rgya-mtsho was killed in flight, but the Dalai Lama was captured alive. The Tibetans themselves were obviously divided on this question of the authenticity of their Dalai Lama, as can be seen from the fact that the monks of 'Bras-spungs succeeded by a coup in temporarily freeing their hierarch. In the end, however, they were unable to resist the power of the Mongol princes, and Tshangs-dbyangs rgya-mtsho was again seized and carried off to the neighbourhood of Kuku Nor where he died, possibly a violent death, in the year 1706. The pretender put forward by the Chinese, Pad-dkar 'dzin-pa, secured no recognition from the Tibetans. Lhasa was first ruthlessly sacked by the Dzungaris, and the rNying-ma monasteries were also plundered. The town was then taken by a Chinese army. Peace descended again only when the seventh reincarnation took place in Li-thang in Eastern Tibet, and the new Dalai Lama, bsKal-bzang rgya-mtsho (1708-57), was brought with Chinese approval to Lhasa. This Dalai Lama and all his successors were reliable dGe-lugs-pa hierarchs and remained under the strict political tutelage of the Chinese. The attempt at a surreptitious restoration of the heretical rNying-ma had completely failed, and at the same time the independence of the Theocratic State set up by the 'Great Five' was lost.

It is no task of ours to deal any further with the fate of the Tibetan Priest-State under Chinese domination, since the changing events are of no significance for the history of religion, and belong rather in the history of Chinese colonialism under the Manchu dynasty. None of the Dalai Lamas of the ninth to the twelfth reincarnations ever came of age, a circumstance which was in the interests both of the Tibetan Regents and of the two Chinese notables who were stationed in Lhasa to represent their Government. The thirteenth reincarnation, the Dalai Lama Thub-ldan rgya-mtsho (1874-1933) managed to avoid a premature end, and it was under him that the Priest-State first slid into the whirlpool of world politics and became a bone of contention between the British, Russian and Chinese powers. In 1904 the Dalai Lama had to flee into Mongolia before the British military expedition under Sir Francis Younghusband; and in 1910 he had to flee to India to escape the hands of the Chinese. He did not recover his throne until the Chinese Revolution broke out in 1912. After this came a period in which Tibet enjoyed a certain limited independence, and this lasted until the Kuo-min-tang regime in China was overthrown by the Chinese Communists.

The fourteenth reincarnation, the Dalai Lama bsTan-'dzin rgya-mtsho, who was born in 1935 and enthroned in 1950 has no further secular power. It is too early to analyse the effect of the incorporation of this last stronghold of mediaeval religious culture into the sphere of the atheistic-communist Chinese State, but there is already no room for doubt that when the Dalai Lama submitted to the Chinese claim to overlordship in 1951 a Buddhist epoch which had lasted 1,300 years came to an end at last. It is not yet possible to determine the exact features of a highly problematical future.

BIBLIOGRAPHY

Bacot, J., Toussaint, G.-Ch., and Thomas F. W., *Documents de Touenhouang relatifs à l'histoire du Tibet*, Paris 1940-6.

Bacot, J., *Le poète tibétain Milarépa*, Paris 1925.

Bacot, J., *La vie de Marpa le 'traducteur'*, Paris 1937.

Beckh, H., *Buddhismus*, 2 vols, 3rd ed., Berlin and Leipzig 1928.

Bell, Charles, *The Religion of Tibet*, OUP 1931.

Bleichsteiner, R., *Die gelbe Kirche*, Vienna 1935.

David-Neel, Alexandra, *Heilige und Hexer*, Leipzig 1931.

David-Neel, Alexandra, *Meister und Schüler*, Leipzig 1934.

Evans-Wentz, W. Y., *Milarepa, Tibets grosser Yogi*, Munich-Planegg 1937.

Evans-Wentz, W. Y., *Yoga und Geheimlehren Tibets*, Munich-Plannegg 1937.

Filchner-Unkrig, *Kumbum Dschamba Ling. Das Kloster der hundert-tausend Bilder Maitreyas*, Leipzig 1933.

Francke, A. H., *Tibetische Hochzeitslieder*, Hagen und Darmstadt 1923.

Francke, A. H., *gZer-myig, a Book of the Tibetan Bonpos in Asia Major* 1924, 1926, 1927, 1930 and 1939.

Glasenapp, H. von, *Buddhistische Mysterien*, Stuttgart 1940.

Grünwedel, Albert, *Die Geschichten der vierundachtzig Zauberer* in Baessler Archiv 5, Leipzig und Berlin 1916.

Grünwedel, Albert, *Die Legenden des Nâ ro pa*, Leipzig 1933.

Grünwedel, Albert, *Mythologie des Buddhismus in Tibet und der Mongolei*, Leipzig 1900.

Grünwedel, Albert, 'Târanâthas Edelsteinmine' in the *Bibliotheca Buddhica* 18, Petrograd 1914.

Harva, Uno, *Die religiösen Vorstellungen der altaischen Völker*, Helsinki 1938.

Hoffmann, Helmut, 'Geschichte Tibets' in *Oldenbourgs Abriss der Weltgeschichte* II, Part B, Munich 1954.

Hoffmann, Helmut, 'Quellen zur Geschichte der Tibetischen Bon-Religion' in *Proceedings of the Academy of Science and Literature* in Mainz 1950.

Hoffmann, Helmut, *Mi-la Ras-pa, Sieben Legenden*, Munich 1950.

Huth, G., *Geschichte des Buddhismus in der Mongolei* (*hor chos byung*), 2 vols. Strasburg 1893 and 1896.

Laufer, B., *Die Bru-ža Sprache und die historische Stellung des Padmasambhava* (T'oung Pao 1908) pp. 1. *et seq.*

Laufer, B., *Der Roman einer Tibetischen Königin*, Leipzig 1911.

Laufer, B., 'Ein Sühngedicht der Bonpo' in the *Memoranda of the Vienna Academy* 1900.

Laufer, B., *Über ein tibetische Geschichtswerk der Bonpo* (*T'oung pao* 1901) pp. 24 *et seq.*

Obermiller, E., *History of Buddhism* (*Chos-hbyung*) *of Bu-ston*, 2 vols, Heidelberg 1931-2.

Obermiller, E., *Tsong-kha-pa le Pandit. Mélanges chinois et bouddhique*, Vol III, Brussels 1935, p. 319.

Ohlmarks, A., *Studien zum Problem des Schamanismus*, Lund and Copenhagen 1939.

Petech, L., *A Study of the Chronicles of Ladakh*, Calcutta 1939.

Ribbach, S. H., *Drogpa Namgyal. Ein Tibeterleben*, Munich-Planegg 1940.

Ribbach, S. H., 'Vier Bilder des Padmasambhava', in the *Annual of Hamburg Scientific Institutes*, 34, 5th supplement, Hamburg 1917.

Roerich, George N., *The Blue Annals*, 2 vols., Calcutta 1949 and 1953.

Sarat Chandra Das, 'Contributions on the Religion, History . . . of Tibet', in the *Journal of the Asiatic Society of Bengal* 1881, pp. 187 *et seq.*

Sarat Chandra Das, *Pag Sam Jon Zang. History of the Rise, Progress and Downfall of Buddhism by Sumpa Khanpo*, Calcutta 1908. Tibetan Text.

Schiefner, A., *Târanâtha's Geschichte des Buddhismus in Indien*, Petersburg 1869.

Schulemann, G., *Die Geschichte der Dalailamas*, Heidelberg 1912.

Tafel, A., *Meine Tibetreise*, 2 vols., Stuttgart 1914.

Thomas, F. W., *Tibetan Literary Texts and Documents concerning Chinese Turkestan*, Vol .I, London 1935.

Toussaint, G.-Ch., *Le Dict de Padma*, Paris 1933.

Tucci, G., *Il libro tibetano dei morti*, Milan 1949.

Tucci, G., *Rin c'en bzan-po e la rinascità del Buddhismo nel Tibet intorno al mille*, Indo-Tibetica II, Rome 1933.

Tucci, G., *Tibetan Painted Scrolls*, 3 vols., Rome 1949.

Waddell, L. A., *The Buddhism of Tibet or Lamaism*, New Edition, London 1934.

Yu, Dawchyuan, *Love Songs of the Sixth Dalai Lama Tshangs-dbyangs-rgya-mtsho*, in Academia Sinica, Monographs Series A, No. 5, Peiping 1930.

INDEX